DATE DUE

THE DUMBEST GENERATION

THE DUMBEST
GENERATION

HOW THE DIGITAL AGE STUPEFIES YOUNG AMERICANS
AND JEOPARDIZES OUR FUTURE

[*Or, Don't Trust Anyone Under 30*]

MARK BAUERLEIN

JEREMY P. TARCHER/PENGUIN

a member of Penguin Group (USA) Inc.

New York

JEREMY P. TARCHER/PENGUIN
Published by the Penguin Group
Penguin Group (USA) Inc., 375 Hudson Street, New York, New York 10014, USA •
Penguin Group (Canada), 90 Eglinton Avenue East, Suite 700, Toronto,
Ontario M4P 2Y3, Canada (a division of Pearson Canada Inc.) • Penguin Books Ltd,
80 Strand, London WC2R 0RL, England • Penguin Ireland, 25 St Stephen's Green,
Dublin 2, Ireland (a division of Penguin Books Ltd) • Penguin Group
(Australia), 250 Camberwell Road, Camberwell, Victoria 3124, Australia (a division of
Pearson Australia Group Pty Ltd) • Penguin Books India Pvt Ltd, 11 Community Centre,
Panchsheel Park, New Delhi–110 017, India • Penguin Group (NZ),
67 Apollo Drive, Rosedale, North Shore 0632, New Zealand (a division
of Pearson New Zealand Ltd) • Penguin Books (South Africa) (Pty) Ltd,
24 Sturdee Avenue, Rosebank, Johannesburg 2196, South Africa

Penguin Books Ltd, Registered Offices:
80 Strand, London WC2R 0RL, England

Most Tarcher/Penguin books are available at special quantity discounts for
bulk purchase for sales promotions, premiums, fund-raising, and educational needs.
Special books or book excerpts also can be created to fit specific needs.
For details, write Penguin Group (USA) Inc. Special Markets,
375 Hudson Street, New York, NY 10014.

Library of Congress Cataloging-in-Publication Data
Bauerlein, Mark.
The dumbest generation : how the digital age stupefies young Americans and
jeopardizes our future (or, don't trust anyone under 30) / Mark Bauerlein.
p.   cm.
ISBN 978-1-58542-639-3
1. Young adults—Effect of technological innovations on—United States.
2. Technology and youth—United States.   3. Young adults—United States—
Attitudes.   4. Internet—Social aspects—United States.   I. Title.
HQ799.7B38   2008   2008006690
302.23'1—dc22

Printed in the United States of America
3   5   7   9   10   8   6   4

Book design by Amanda Dewey

While the author has made every effort to provide accurate telephone numbers and
Internet addresses at the time of publication, neither the publisher nor the author assumes any responsibility for errors, or for changes that occur after publication. Further,
the publisher does not have any control over and does not assume any responsibility
for author or third-party websites or their content.

CONTENTS

INTRODUCTION

When writer Alexandra Robbins returned to Walt Whitman High School in Bethesda, Maryland, ten years after graduating, she discovered an awful trend. The kids were miserable. She remembers her high school years as a grind of study and homework, but lots more, too, including leisure times that allowed for "well-roundedness." Not for Whitman students circa 2005. The teens in *The Overachievers*, Robbins's chronicle of a year spent among them, have only one thing on their minds, SUCCESS, and one thing in their hearts, ANXIETY. Trapped in a mad "culture of over-achieverism," they run a frantic race to earn an A in every class, score 750 or higher on the SATs, take piano lessons, chalk up AP courses on their transcripts, stay in shape, please their parents, volunteer for outreach programs, and, most of all, win entrance to "HYP" (Harvard-Yale-Princeton).

As graduation approaches, their résumés lengthen and sparkle, but their spirits flag and sicken. One Whitman junior, labeled by Robbins "The Stealth Overachiever," receives a fantastic 2380 (out of 2400) on a PSAT test, but instead of rejoicing, he worries that the company administering the practice run "made the diagnostics easier so students would think the class was working."

Audrey, "The Perfectionist," struggles for weeks to complete her toothpick bridge, which she and her partner expect will win them a spot in the Physics Olympics. She's one of the Young Democrats, too, and she does catering jobs. Her motivation stands out, and she thinks every other student competes with her personally, so whenever she receives a graded test or paper, "she [turns] it over without looking at it and then [puts] it away, resolving not to check the grade until she [gets] home."

"AP Frank" became a Whitman legend when as a junior he managed a "seven-AP course load that had him studying every afternoon, sleeping during class, and going lunchless." When he scored 1570 on the SAT, his domineering mother screamed in dismay, and her shock subsided only when he retook it and got the perfect 1600.

Julie, "The Superstar," has five AP classes and an internship three times a week at a museum, and she runs cross-country as well. Every evening after dinner she descends to the "homework cave" until bedtime and beyond. She got "only" 1410 on the SAT, though, and she wonders where it will land her next fall.

These kids have descended into a "competitive frenzy," Robbins mourns, and the high school that should open their minds and develop their characters has become a torture zone, a "hotbed for Machiavellian strategy." They bargain and bully and suck up for better grades. They pay tutors and coaches enormous sums to raise their scores a few points and help with the admissions process. Parents hover and query, and they schedule their children down to the minute. Grade inflation only makes it worse, an A- average now a stigma, not an accomplishment. They can't relax, they can't play. It's killing them, throwing sensitive and intelligent teenagers into pathologies of guilt and despair. The professional rat race of yore—men in gray flannel suits climbing the business ladder—has filtered down into the pre-college years, and Robbins's tormented subjects reveal the consequences.

The achievement chase displaces other life questions, and the kids can't seem to escape it. When David Brooks toured Princeton and interviewed students back in 2001, he heard of joyless days and nights with no room for newspapers or politics or dating, just "one skill-enhancing activity to the next." He calls them "Organization Kids" (after the old Organization Man figure of the fifties), students who "have to schedule appointment times for chatting." They've been programmed for success, and a preschool-to-college gauntlet of standardized tests, mounting homework, motivational messages, and extracurricular tasks has rewarded or punished them at every stage. The system tabulates learning incessantly and ranks students against one another, and the students soon divine its essence: only results matter. Education writer Alfie Kohn summarizes their logical adjustment:

> Consider a school that constantly emphasizes the importance
> of performance! results! achievement! success! A student
> who has absorbed that message may find it difficult to get
> swept away by the process of creating a poem or trying to
> build a working telescope. He may be so concerned about the
> results that he's not at all that engaged in the activity that
> produces those results.

Just get the grades, they tell themselves, ace the test, study, study, study. Assignments become exercises to complete, like doing the dishes, not knowledge to acquire for the rest of their lives. The inner life fades; only the external credits count. After-school hours used to mean sports and comic books and hanging out. Now, they spell homework. As the president of the American Association of School Librarians told the *Washington Post*, "When kids are in school now, the stakes are so high, and they have so much homework that it's really hard to find time for pleasure reading" (see Strauss). Homework itself has become a plague, as recent titles on the subject show:

The End of Homework: How Homework Disrupts Families, Overbur-dens Children, and Limits Learning (Etta Kralovec and John Buell); *The Homework Myth: Why Our Kids Get Too Much of a Bad Thing* (Alfie Kohn); and *The Case Against Homework: How Homework Is Hurting Our Children and What We Can Do About It* (Sara Bennett and Nancy Kalish).

Parents, teachers, media, and the kids themselves witness the dangers, but the system presses forward. "We believe that reform in homework practices is central to a politics of family and personal liberation," Kralovec and Buell announce, but the momentum is too strong. The overachievement culture, results-obsessed parents, out-comes-based norms . . . they continue to brutalize kids and land concerned observers such as Robbins on the *Today* show. Testing goes on, homework piles up, and competition for spaces in the Ivies was stiffer in 2007 than ever before. A 2006 survey by Pew Research, for instance, found that more than half the adults in the United States (56 percent) think that parents place too little pressure on students, and only 15 percent stated "Too much."

Why?

Because something is wrong with this picture, and most people realize it. They sense what the critics do not, a fundamental error in the vignettes of hyperstudious and overworked kids that we've just seen: they don't tell the truth, not the whole truth about youth in America. For, notwithstanding the poignant tale of suburban D.C. seniors sweating over a calculus quiz, or the image of college students scheduling their friends as if they were CEOs in the middle of a workday, or the lurid complaints about homework, the actual habits of most teenagers and young adults in most schools and colleges in this country display a wholly contrasting problem, but one no less disturbing.

Consider a measure of homework time, this one not taken from a dozen kids on their uneven way to the top, but from 81,499 students in 110 schools in 26 states—the 2006 *High School Survey of Student*

Engagement. When asked how many hours they spent each week "Reading/studying for class," almost all of them, fully 90 percent, came in at a ridiculously low five hours or less, 55 percent at one hour or less. Meanwhile, 31 percent admitted to watching television or playing video games at least six hours per week, 25 percent of them logging six hours minimum surfing and chatting online.

Or check a 2004 report by the University of Michigan Institute for Social Research entitled *Changing Times of American Youth: 1981–2003*, which surveyed more than 2,000 families with children age six to 17 in the home. In 2003, homework time for 15- to 17-year-olds hit only 24 minutes on weekend days, 50 minutes on weekdays. And weekday TV time? More than twice that: one hour, 55 minutes.

Or check a report by the U.S. Department of Education entitled *NAEP 2004 Trends in Academic Progress.* Among other things, the report gathered data on study and reading time for thousands of 17-year-olds in 2004. When asked how many hours they'd spent on homework the day before, the tallies were meager. Fully 26 percent said that they didn't have any homework to do, while 13 percent admitted that they didn't do any of the homework they were supposed to. A little more than one-quarter (28 percent) spent less than an hour, and another 22 percent devoted one to two hours, leaving only 11 percent to pass the two-hour mark.

Or the 2004–05 *State of Our Nation's Youth* report by the Horatio Alger Association, in which 60 percent of teenage students logged five hours of homework per week or less.

The better students don't improve with time, either. In the 2006 *National Survey of Student Engagement,* a college counterpart to the *High School Survey of Student Engagement,* seniors in college logged some astonishingly low commitments to "Preparing for class." Almost one out of five (18 percent) stood at one to five hours per week, and 26 percent at six to ten hours per week. College professors estimate that a successful semester requires about 25 hours of out-of-class study per week, but only 11 percent reached that mark. These young adults have graduated from high school, entered college, declared a major, and lasted seven semesters, but their in-class and out-of-class punch cards amount to fewer hours than a part-time job.

And as for the claim that leisure time is disappearing, the Bureau of Labor Statistics issues an annual *American Time Use Survey* that asks up to 21,000 people to record their activities during the day. The categories include work and school and child care, and also leisure hours. For 2005, 15- to 24-year-olds enjoyed a full five and a half hours of free time per day, more than two hours of which they passed in front of the TV.

The findings of these and many other large surveys refute the frantic and partial renditions of youth habits and achievement that all too often make headlines and fill talk shows. Savvier observers guard against the "we're overworking the kids" alarm, people such as Jay Mathews, education reporter at the *Washington Post*, who called Robbins's book a "spreading delusion," and Tom Loveless of the Brookings Institution, whose 2003 report on homework said of the "homework is destroying childhood" argument, "Almost everything in this story is wrong." One correspondent's encounter with a dozen elite students who hunt success can be vivid and touching, but it doesn't jibe with mountains of data that tell contrary stories. The surveys, studies, tests, and testimonials reveal the opposite, that the vast majority of high school and college kids are far less accomplished and engaged, and the classroom pressures much less cumbersome, than popular versions put forth. These depressing accounts issue from government agencies with no ax to grind, from business leaders who just want competent workers, and from foundations that sympathize with the young. While they lack the human drama, they impart more reliable assessments, providing a better baseline for understanding the realities of the young American mentality and forcing us to stop upgrading the adolescent condition beyond its due.

. . .

THIS BOOK is an attempt to consolidate the best and broadest research into a different profile of the rising American mind. It doesn't
cover behaviors and values, only the intellect of under-30-year-olds.
Their political leanings don't matter, nor do their career ambitions.
The manners, music, clothing, speech, sexuality, faith, diversity, depression, criminality, drug use, moral codes, and celebrities of the
young spark many books, articles, research papers, and marketing
strategies centered on Generation Y (or Generation DotNet, or the
Millennials), but not this one. It sticks to one thing, the intellectual
condition of young Americans, and describes it with empirical evidence, recording something hard to document but nonetheless insidious happening inside their heads. The information is scattered
and underanalyzed, but once collected and compared, it charts a
consistent and perilous momentum downward.

It sounds pessimistic, and many people sympathetic to youth
pressures may class the chapters to follow as yet another curmud-
geonly riff. Older people have complained forever about the derelic-
tions of youth, and the "old fogy" tag puts them on the defensive.
Perhaps, though, it is a healthy process in the life story of humanity
for older generations to berate the younger, for young and old to relate in a vigorous competitive dialectic, with the energy and optimism of youth vying against the wisdom and realism of elders in a
fruitful check of one another's worst tendencies. That's another issue, however. The conclusions here stem from a variety of completed
and ongoing research projects, public and private organizations, and
university professors and media centers, and they represent different
cultural values and varying attitudes toward youth. It is remarkable,
then, that they so often reach the same general conclusions. They
disclose many trends and consequences in youth experience, but
the intellectual one emerges again and again. It's an outcome not as

easily noticed as a carload of teens inching down the boulevard rat-
tling store windows with the boom-boom of a hip-hop beat, and the
effect runs deeper than brand-name clothing and speech patterns. It
touches the core of a young person's mind, the mental storehouse
from which he draws when engaging the world. And what the
sources reveal, one by one, is that a paradoxical and distressing situation is upon us.

The paradox may be put this way. We have entered the Information Age, traveled the Information Superhighway, spawned a Knowledge Economy, undergone the Digital Revolution, converted manual
workers into knowledge workers, and promoted a Creative Class, and
we anticipate a Conceptual Age to be. However overhyped those
grand social metaphors, they signify a rising premium on knowledge
and communications, and everyone from *Wired* magazine to Al Gore
to Thomas Friedman to the Task Force on the Future of American
Innovation echoes the change. When he announced the American
Competitiveness Initiative in February 2006, President Bush directly
linked the fate of the U.S. economy "to generating knowledge and
tools upon which new technologies are developed." In a *Washington
Post* op-ed, Bill Gates asserted, "But if we are to remain competitive,
we need a workforce that consists of the world's brightest minds. . . .
First, we must demand strong schools so that young Americans enter
the workforce with the math, science and problem-solving skills
they need to succeed in the knowledge economy."

And yet, while teens and young adults have absorbed digital tools
into their daily lives like no other age group, while they have grown
up with more knowledge and information readily at hand, taken
more classes, built their own Web sites, enjoyed more libraries, bookstores, and museums in their towns and cities . . . in sum, while the
world has provided them extraordinary chances to gain knowledge
and improve their reading/writing skills, not to mention offering financial incentives to do so, young Americans today are no more

learned or skillful than their predecessors, no more knowledgeable, fluent, up-to-date, or inquisitive, except in the materials of youth culture. They don't know any more history or civics, economics or science, literature or current events. They read less on their own, both books and newspapers, and you would have to canvass a lot of college English instructors and employers before you found one who said that they compose better paragraphs. In fact, their technology skills fall well short of the common claim, too, especially when they must apply them to research and workplace tasks.

The world delivers facts and events and art and ideas as never before, but the young American mind hasn't opened. Young Americans' vices have diminished, one must acknowledge, as teens and young adults harbor fewer stereotypes and social prejudices. Also, they regard their parents more highly than they did 25 years ago. They volunteer in strong numbers, and rates of risky behaviors are dropping. Overall conduct trends are moving upward, leading a hard-edged commentator such as Kay Hymowitz to announce in "It's Morning After in America" (2004) that "pragmatic Americans have seen the damage that their decades-long fling with the sexual revolution and the transvaluation of traditional values wrought. And now, without giving up the real gains, they are earnestly knitting up their unraveled culture. It is a moment of tremendous promise." At *TechCentralStation.com*, James Glassman agreed enough to proclaim, "Good News! The Kids Are Alright!" Youth watchers William Strauss and Neil Howe were confident enough to subtitle their book on young Americans *The Next Great Generation* (2000).

And why shouldn't they? Teenagers and young adults mingle in a society of abundance, intellectual as well as material. American youth in the twenty-first century have benefited from a shower of money and goods, a bath of liberties and pleasing self-images, vibrant civic debates, political blogs, old books and masterpieces available online, traveling exhibitions, the History Channel, news feeds . . . and on and on. Never have opportunities for education, learning, political action, and cultural activity been greater. All the ingredients for making an informed and intelligent citizen are in place.

But it hasn't happened. Yes, young Americans are energetic, ambitious, enterprising, and good, but their talents and interests and money thrust them not into books and ideas and history and civics, but into a whole other realm and other consciousness. A different social life and a different mental life have formed among them. Technology has bred it, but the result doesn't tally with the fulsome descriptions of digital empowerment, global awareness, and virtual communities. Instead of opening young American minds to the stores of civilization and science and politics, technology has contracted their horizon to themselves, to the social scene around them. Young people have never been so intensely mindful of and present to one another, so enabled in adolescent contact. Teen images and songs, hot gossip and games, and youth-to-youth communications no longer limited by time or space wrap them up in a generational cocoon reaching all the way into their bedrooms. The autonomy has a cost: the more they attend to themselves, the less they remember the past and envision a future. They have all the advantages of modernity and democracy, but when the gifts of life lead to social joys, not intellectual labor, the minds of the young plateau at age 18. This is happening all around us. The fonts of knowledge are everywhere, but the rising generation is camped in the desert, passing stories, pictures, tunes, and texts back and forth, living off the thrill of peer attention. Meanwhile, their intellects refuse the cultural and civic inheritance that has made us what we are up to now.

This book explains why and how, and how much, and what it means for the civic health of the United States.

CHAPTER ONE

KNOWLEDGE
DEFICITS

E verybody likes the "Jaywalking" segment on *The Tonight Show*. With mike in hand and camera ready, host Jay Leno leaves the studio and hits the sidewalks of L.A., grabbing pedestrians for a quick test of their factual knowledge. "How many stars are on the American flag?" he asks. "Where was Jesus born? Who is Tony Blair?" Leno plays his role expertly, slipping into game-show patter and lightly mocking the "contestants." Sometimes he allows them to select the grade level of the questions, offering a choice from eighth-grade, sixth-grade, fourth-grade, and second-grade primers. A few of his best guests reappear on a mock quiz show presented on the *Tonight Show* stage.

The respondents tend toward the younger ages, a sign that their elders perform better at recall. It's the 20-year-olds who make the comedy, and keep "Jaywalking" a standard set piece on the air. Here are some snippets:

"Do you remember the last book you read?" Leno queries a young man.

"Do magazines count?" he wonders. Moments later, a long-haired guy replies, "Maybe a comic book."

Another:

"Where does the Pope live?"
"England."
"Where in England?" Leno follows, keeping a straight face.
"Ummm, Paris."

And:

"Who made the first electric lightbulb?"
"Uh," a college student ponders, "Thomas Edison." Leno congratulates the student until he adds, "Yeah, with the kite." Leno corrects him, "That's Ben Franklin."

And:

"Do you ever read any of the classics?" Leno inquires. The guest draws a blank. "Anything by Charles Dickens?" Another blank. "*A Christmas Carol?*"

"I saw the movie," she blurts out. "I liked the one with Scrooge McDuck better."

The ignorance is hard to believe. Before a national audience and beside a celebrity, the camera magnifying their mental labor, interviewees giggle and mumble, throwing out replies with the tentative upward lilt of a question. Stars on the flag: "Fifty-two?" Tenure of a Supreme Court judge: "I'm guessing four years?" They laugh at themselves, and sometimes, more hilariously, they challenge the content. On the mock-game-show set, Leno quizzes, "What's another name for the War Between the States?" "Are we supposed to know this off the top of our heads?" one contestant protests. "What kind of question is this?"

The comedy runs deeper, though, than the bare display of young people embarrassed not to know a common fact. Something unnerving surfaces in the exchanges, something outside the normal course of conversation. Simply put, it is the astonishing lifeworld of someone who can't answer these simple queries. Think of how many things you must do in order *not* to know the year 1776 or the British prime minister or the Fifth Amendment. At the start, you must forget the lessons of school—history class, social studies, government, geography, English, philosophy, and art history. You must care nothing about current events, elections, foreign policy, and war. No newspapers, no political magazines, no NPR or Rush Limbaugh, no CNN, Fox News, network news, or *NewsHour with Jim Lehrer.* No books on the Cold War or the Founding, no biographies, nothing on Bush or Hillary, terrorism or religion, Europe or the Middle East. No political activity and no community activism. And your friends must act the same way, never letting a historical fact or current affair slip into a cell phone exchange.

It isn't enough to say that these young people are uninterested in world realities. They are actively cut off from them. Or a better way to put it is to say that they are encased in more immediate realities that shut out conditions beyond—friends, work, clothes, cars, pop music, sitcoms, *Facebook.* Each day, the information they receive and the interactions they have must be so local or superficial that the facts of government, foreign and domestic affairs, the historical past, and the fine arts never slip through. How do they do it? It sounds hard, especially in an age of so much information, so many screens and streams in private and public places, and we might assume that the guests on "Jaywalking" represent but a tiny portion of the rising generation. No doubt *The Tonight Show* edits the footage and keeps the most humiliating cases, leaving the smart respondents in the cutting room. Leno's out for laughter, not representative data. In truth, we might ask, what does a cherry-picked interview on Santa Monica Boulevard at 9 P.M. on a Saturday night say about the 60 million Americans in their teens and twenties?

A lot, it turns out. That's the conclusion drawn by a host of experts who in the last 10 years have directed large-scale surveys and studies of teen and young adult knowledge, skills, and intellectual habits. Working for government agencies, professional guilds, private foundations, academic centers, testing services, and polling firms, they have designed and implemented assessments, surveys, and interviews of young people to measure their academic progress, determine their intellectual tastes, and detail their understanding of important facts and ideas. They don't despise American youth, nor do they idealize it. Instead, they conduct objective, ongoing research into the young American mind. Their focus extends from a teen or 20-year-old's familiarity with liberal arts learning (history, literature, civics . . .) to calculations of how young adults spend their time (watching TV, surfing the Web, reading . . .). They probe a broad range of attitudes and aptitudes, interests and erudition, college and workplace "readiness." Much of the inquiry centers precisely on the kinds of knowledge (under)represented in the "Jaywalking" segments.

The better-known examples of monitoring include the SAT and ACT tests, whose annual results appear in every newspaper as each state in the Union reckons where it stands in the national rankings. Nielsen ratings for television and radio shows provide a familiar index of youth tastes, while every election season raises doubts about the youth vote—where does it fall, will it turn out . . . ? Added to these measures are dozens of lesser-known projects that chart the intellectual traits of young Americans. Some of them excel in the scope and consistency of their coverage:

National Assessment of Educational Progress (NAEP)—a
regular assessment of student learning in various subjects,

mainly reading and math, conducted by the U.S. Department
of Education. Nicknamed "the Nation's Report Card," NAEP
involves national- and state-level inquiries, with the former
gathering a respondent group of 10,000 to 20,000 students,
the latter around 3,000 students from each participating
jurisdiction (45–55 jurisdictions per assessment). (http://nces
.ed.gov/nationsreportcard/)

National Survey of Student Engagement (NSSE)—Housed at
Indiana University, NSSE (nicknamed "Nessie") is a national
survey administered to college freshmen and seniors each fall
semester, the questions bearing upon their demographic traits,
campus experiences, and intellectual habits. In 2006, nearly
260,000 students participated. (http://nsse.iub.edu/index.cfm)

**Kaiser Family Foundation Program for the Study of
Entertainment Media and Health**—a research project funded
by Kaiser and concentrating on media and children, with an
emphasis on the media's effect on mental and physical
health. Important data collections include surveys of media
consumption by infants and toddlers and by 8- to 18-year-
olds. (www.kff.org/entmedia/index.cfm)

**American Time Use Survey, Bureau of Labor Statistics
(ATUS)**—an annual survey with a nationally representative
sample of more than 13,000 respondents who chart how
they spend their time on weekdays and weekends. ATUS
tallies work and school time, and among leisure activities
measured are reading, watching TV, playing games, using
computers, and socializing. (www.bls.gov/tus/)

**Survey of Public Participation in the Arts, National
Endowment for the Arts (SPPA)**—a survey conducted

approximately every five years that measures the voluntary participation of adults in different art forms. Respondents numbering up to 17,000 record how many novels and poems they read and how often they visit a museum or a gallery, attend a theater performance, listen to jazz on the radio, etc. (www.nea.gov/research/ResearchReports_chrono.html)

There are many more important ongoing investigations of the young American intellect, such as National Geographic's *Geographic Literacy Survey* and the Intercollegiate Studies Institute's civic literacy surveys, along with one-time reports such as *Are They Really Ready to Work?* (2006), a study of workplace skills of recent graduates by the Conference Board. One after another, though, they display the same dismal results and troubling implications.

Most young Americans possess little of the knowledge that makes for an informed citizen, and too few of them master the skills needed to negotiate an information-heavy, communication-based society and economy. Furthermore, they avoid the resources and media that might enlighten them and boost their talents. An anti-intellectual outlook prevails in their leisure lives, squashing the lessons of school, and instead of producing a knowledgeable and querulous young mind, the youth culture of American society yields an adolescent consumer enmeshed in juvenile matters and secluded from adult realities. The meager findings force the issue as researchers form an inescapable judgment, one that will dismay anyone who cares about the health of U.S. democracy and the intelligence of U.S. culture. The insulated mindset of individuals who know precious little history and civics and never read a book or visit a museum is fast becoming a common, shame-free condition. The clueless youths Leno stops on the street aren't so different from a significant and rising portion of teens and young adults, the future of our country.

That sounds like an alarmist claim, and the fact that the average 18-year-old cannot name his mayor, congressman, or senator, or remember the last book he read, or identify Egypt on a map seems impossible. But the results are in, and they keep accumulating. Here are examples, broken down by discipline.

History. Students reaching their senior year in high school have passed through several semesters of social studies and history, but few of them remember the significant events, figures, and texts. On the 2001 NAEP history exam, the majority of high school seniors, 57 percent, scored "below basic," "basic" being defined as partial mastery of prerequisite knowledge and skills that allow for proficient work at a selected grade level. Only 1 percent reached "advanced." (The NAEP has four scores: Advanced, Proficient, Basic, and Below Basic.) Incredibly, 52 percent of them chose Germany, Japan, or Italy over the Soviet Union as a U.S. ally in World War II. The previous time the history exam was administered—in 1994—the exact same numbers came up for seniors, 57 percent at "below basic" and 1 percent at "advanced." Younger test takers performed better, and showed some progress from test to test. In 1994, fourth-graders stood at only 36 percent below basic, and in 2001 they lowered the number to 33 percent. In 2006, NAEP administered the History exam to 29,000 fourth-, eighth-, and twelfth-graders, and a mild improvement emerged. For twelfth-graders, the "below basic" tally dropped four points to 53 percent, and for eighth-graders it dropped from 38 to 35 percent, although both groups remain at 1 percent in "advanced," and only 12 percent of the older students fall into "proficient." More than one-third (37 percent) of twelfth-graders did not know that the 1962 Soviet-U.S. dispute arose over missiles in Cuba. Two-thirds of high school seniors couldn't explain a photo of a theater whose portal reads "COLORED ENTRANCE."

Diane Ravitch, education professor at NYU and former

member of the NAEP governing board, called the 2001
results "truly abysmal" and worried about a voting bloc
coming of age with so little awareness of American history.
Many believe that college can remedy the deficit, but the
findings of another study belie their hope. Commissioned
by the American Council of Trustees and Alumni, *Losing
America's Memory: Historical Illiteracy in the 21st Century*
(2000) reported the findings of a commissioned survey aimed
at measuring the factual historical knowledge of seniors at
the top 55 colleges in the country. Many of the questions
were drawn from the NAEP high school exam, and the
results were astonishing. Only 19 percent of the subjects
scored a grade of C or higher. A mere 29 percent knew
what "Reconstruction" refers to, only one-third recognized
the American general at Yorktown, and less than one-
fourth identified James Madison as the "father of the
Constitution."

The feeble scores on these tests emerge despite the fact
that young people receive more exposure to history in
popular culture than ever before, for instance, best-selling
books such as Laura Hillenbrand's *Seabiscuit: An American
Legend* and *John Adams* by David McCullough, movies such
as *Braveheart* and *Troy* and *Marie Antoinette*, the History
Channel and *Who Wants to Be a Millionaire?* and *Wikipedia*.
Many mass entertainments have historical content, however
much the facts get skewed. And yet, if teens and young adults
consume them, they don't retain them as history. In spite
of ubiquitous injunctions to know the past by George Will,
Alex Trebek, Black History Month, Holocaust survivors,
Smithsonian magazine, and so on, the historical imagination
of most young people extends not much further than the
episodes in their own lives.

Civics. In 1999, according to the U.S. Department of Education, more than two-thirds of ninth-graders studied the Constitution, while fully 88 percent of twelfth-graders took a course that "required them to pay attention to government issues" (see *What Democracy Means to Ninth-Graders*). As they pass through high school and college, too, they volunteer in strong numbers. Despite the schooling and the activism, however, civic learning doesn't stick. In a 1998 survey of teenagers by the National Constitution Center, only 41 percent could name the three branches of government (in the same survey, 59 percent identified the Three Stooges by name). In a 2003 survey on the First Amendment commissioned by the Foundation for Individual Rights in Education, only one in 50 college students named the first right guaranteed in the amendment, and one out of four did not know *any* freedom protected by it. In a 2003 study sponsored by the National Conference of State Legislatures entitled *Citizenship: A Challenge for All Generations,* barely half of the 15- to 26-year-olds queried agreed that "paying attention to government and politics" is important to good citizenship, and only two-thirds considered voting a meaningful act. While 64 percent knew the name of the latest "American Idol," only 10 percent could identify the speaker of the U.S. House of Representatives. Only one-third knew which party controlled the state legislature, and only 40 percent knew which party controlled Congress.

In the 2004 National Election Study, a mere 28 percent of 18- to 24-year-olds correctly identified William H. Rehnquist as the chief justice of the United States, and one-quarter of them could not identify Dick Cheney as vice president. A July 2006 Pew Research Center report on newspaper readership found that only 26 percent of 18- to 29-year-olds could name Condoleezza Rice as Secretary of State, and only 15 percent knew that Vladimir Putin was the president of Russia. On the 2006 NAEP Civics exam, only 27 percent of twelfth-graders reached proficiency, and 34 percent of them scored "below basic." Since 2004, the Knight Foundation has funded "Future of the First Amendment" surveys of high school students, and in the last round nearly three-fourths of them "don't know how they feel about the First Amendment, or take it for granted."

In civics, too, higher education doesn't guarantee any improvement. In September 2006, the Intercollegiate Studies Institute presented a report entitled *The Coming Crisis in Citizenship: Higher Education's Failure to Teach America's History and Institutions.* The project tested more than 14,000 freshmen and seniors at 50 colleges across the country in American history, government, foreign relations, and the market economy, with questions on topics such as separation of church and state, federalism, women's suffrage, the Bill of Rights, and Martin Luther King. Once again, the numbers were discouraging. The respondents came from Harvard, Johns Hopkins, and Stanford as well as lesser-known institutions such as West Georgia College, Eastern Kentucky, and Appalachian State. The average score for a freshman was an F—51.7 percent. And how much did seniors add to the score? A measly 1.5 percentage points—still an F. With both class levels measured, the ISI study also allowed for assessments of how much progress students made at each institution. At Harvard, freshmen scored 67.8 percent, seniors 69.7 percent, a minuscule gain after $200,000 in tuition fees. At Berkeley, the students actually regressed, going from 60.4 percent in their first year to 54.8 in their last year.

Given the dilution of college curricula and the attitudes

expressed in the *Citizenship* study, we shouldn't be surprised
that college students score so feebly and tread water during
their time on campus. A statistic from the *American Freshman
Survey*, an annual project of the Higher Education Research
Institute at UCLA (sample size, approximately 250,000),
echoes the civic apathy. In 1966, the survey tabulated 60
percent of first-year students who considered it "very
important" to keep up with political affairs. In 2005, that
figure plummeted to 36 percent, notwithstanding 9/11, the
Iraq war, and the upcoming election. No wonder the
Executive Summary of the State Legislatures report opened
with a blunt indictment: "This public opinion survey shows
that young people do not understand the ideals of citizenship,
they are disengaged from the political process, they lack the
knowledge necessary for effective self-government, and their
appreciation and support of American democracy is limited."

Math/Science/Technology. "The United States is in a fierce
contest with other nations to remain the world's scientific
leader." That's the opening sentence of *Tapping America's
Potential: The Education for Innovation Initiative*, a 2005 report
by the Business Roundtable. The premise appears regularly in
discussions of the future of U.S. competitiveness in the
international arena, and so does a corollary to it: to preserve
its economic and military superiority in the world, America
must sustain a flowing pipeline of able math, science, and
engineering graduates. Politicians are quick to respond. In his
2006 State of the State address, New York governor George
Pataki called for more magnet schools focused on math and
science, and for free tuition at SUNY and CUNY campuses
for students majoring in those subjects. In May 2006, the U.S.
House Committee on Science introduced three bills designed
to bolster math and science education, with Chairman

Sherwood Boehlert asserting, "As a nation, we must do everything possible to remain competitive, and that starts with ensuring that we have the best scientists and engineers in the world."

Young Americans haven't answered the call, though. According to the National Science Board, engineering degrees awarded in the United States have dropped 20 percent since 1985. Of the more than 1.1 million high school seniors in the class of 2002 who took the ACT test, less than 6 percent planned to study engineering, a steep drop from the nearly 9 percent who declared an engineering major a decade earlier. The 2006 *American Freshman Survey* found that only 0.5 percent of first-year students intended to major in physics, 0.8 percent in math, and 1.2 percent in chemistry, although engineering improved to 8 percent.

Set alongside rival nations, the numbers look worse. While six million Chinese students tried to win a place in the Intel Science and Engineering Fair, only 65,000 U.S. students did, a ratio of 92 to 1. American universities still have the best engineering programs in the world, but more than 50 percent of the doctorates they grant go to foreign students. At the going rate, in a few years 90 percent of all scientists and engineers in the world will reside in Asia.

The low interest students have in math and science is reflected in their knowledge and skills. On the 2005 NAEP science exam for twelfth-graders, the average score was 147, a drop of three points since 1996. Nearly half of the test takers—46 percent—didn't reach the "basic" threshold, and only 2 percent reached "advanced." Math scores were better, but not by much. NAEP results from 2004 showed that fourth-graders improved significantly over the previous decades, but twelfth-graders made no gains at all, even though the number of them taking calculus nearly tripled from 1978 to 2004 and the number taking second-year algebra rose from 37 percent to 53 percent. Indeed, from 1978 to 2004 the percentage of students reporting doing math homework "often" jumped from 59 percent to 73 percent, but still, no improvement happened.

Again, international comparisons darken the picture. Two major ongoing projects provide the data, the *Trends in International Math and Science Study* (TIMSS) and the Programme for International Student Assessment (PISA). The TIMSS exam tests nine- and 13-year-olds on their curricular knowledge (geometry and algebra, for example). In 2003, with 51 countries participating, nine-year-olds did well, ranking eighth among countries tested. Likewise, 13-year-olds beat the international average, but they slid down the rankings six slots to #14, falling behind Lithuania, Latvia, and the Russian Federation. The PISA findings were worse. In 2003, PISA tested 15-year-olds in 42 countries in math and science (sample size: 4,500–10,000 per country), emphasizing the application of concepts to real-life problems. Fully 26 nations scored significantly higher than the United States, including not only the expected ones (Hong Kong, Finland, and Korea topped the list), but Canada, the Slovak Republic, Poland, and Australia, too. Given the general NAEP findings that show twelfth-graders sliding down the achievement scale, we may assume that if TIMSS and PISA tested older teens, the United States would appear even worse in international comparisons.

Fine Arts. It is hard to compile data on how much teens and young adults know about the fine arts, but we can determine their attraction to different art forms. The 2002 *Survey of Public Participation in the Arts* (National Endowment for the Arts) charted several exposures over the preceding

12 months to record the bare presence of the fine arts in individuals' lives. Except for people 75 and older, 18- to 24-year-olds emerged with the lowest rates of all age groups. Only one in 10 attended a jazz performance, and one in 12 attended a classical music performance. Only 2.6 percent of them saw a ballet, 11.4 percent a play. Less than one in four (23.7 percent) stepped inside a museum or gallery during the previous year, one in 40 played a classical music instrument, and one in 20 sang in a choir. Compared with findings from 1982 and 1992, the 2002 results showed performing arts attendance by 18- to 24-year-olds dropping in every art form included. The decline took place, moreover, at the same time that the opportunity to experience the arts rose. According to the Census Bureau, the number of museums in the United States jumped from 3,600 in Year 2000 to 4,700 in 2003, and performance arts companies went from 19,300 to 27,400. Nevertheless, the younger audiences shrank.

It wasn't because young adults didn't have time to enjoy the arts. According to the 2005 *Youth Risk Behavior Surveillance* (Centers for Disease Control), 37 percent of high school students watch three or more hours of television per day. For college students the numbers may be higher. In 2005, Nielsen Media Research reported that the average college student watches 3 hours, 41 minutes of television each day. "It was a little more than I expected," a Nielsen executive stated, and a little more than professors care to see. Clearly, students love entertainment, but not of the fine arts kind. The 2006 *National Survey of Student Engagement* (Indiana University) reported that fully 27 percent of first-year students "never" attended an art exhibit, gallery, play, dance, or other theater performance, and 45 percent only "sometimes." The rate for seniors, who had three extra years on campus to cultivate their tastes: 45 percent "sometimes," the same as the freshmen, but the "never" rate actually rose a dismaying four points.

These figures apply to leisure time, not to the classroom, where many older adults acquired their initial thirst for non-pop music and the arts. In school, however, we find the same flagging interests, this time on the part of the educators. Partly because of the pressure of No Child Left Behind, which tests reading and math, and partly because of an emphasis on job-skills development, the public school curriculum devotes an ever smaller share of class time to music and the other arts. A recent study sponsored by the Fordham Foundation counted average instructional minutes required for different subject areas in five states. In the early grades, while reading garnered around 40 percent and math 18 percent of the school week, music and other arts combined received only 8 percent. Other developed nations in the world averaged 14 percent on the arts in early grades, which means that foreign students in elementary school spend around 55 more hours on the arts than U.S. students do each year (see Benavot).

With voluntary (or parent-ordered) involvement in the fine arts so subdued among teens and young adults, for many of them the classroom is the only place they will ever encounter Michelangelo, Mozart, Grandma Moses, and Thelonious Monk. Little in their homes and among their friends exposes them to artistic works that have stood the test of time and inspired their forbears, and so, if they don't become attuned to the fine arts in school, they probably never will. Consider the chairman of the National Endowment for the Arts in 2007, Dana Gioia, who credits his escape from the high-crime, low-education streets of Hawthorne, California, to two things: the public library and the piano lessons his mother forced him to take. They

quickened his imagination to a fate other than that of his
classmates—aimlessness, odd jobs, and prison. Rarely will
such transformations reach today's youth, and school trends
aren't helping. In effect, the curriculum cedes the aesthetic
field to mass culture. Young adults end up with detailed
awareness of adolescent fare, and draw a blank with the great
traditions of opera, Impressionism, bebop, Restoration
comedy . . . In *Losing America's Memory*, cited on page 18,
while only 22 percent of college seniors recognized a line
from the Gettysburg Address, 99 percent of them identified
Beavis and Butt-Head, and 98 percent Snoop Doggy Dogg.

Year after year, the findings pour in. The 2006 *Geographic Literacy
Survey* (National Geographic Society) opens, "Americans are far
from alone in the world, but from the perspective of many young
Americans, we might as well be." What else could they conclude
when 63 percent of test takers could not identify Iraq on a map, and
30 percent of them selected U.S./Mexico as the most fortified border in the world? We could add knowledge deficits in foreign lan-
guages, world religions, and politics, filling out a portrait of vigorous,
indiscriminate ignorance. Together they justify a label coined by
Philip Roth in his 2000 novel *The Human Stain:* "The Dumbest
Generation." Too large a segment of young Americans enter adulthood and proceed to middle age with other concerns, the contents
of liberal arts learning and civic awareness receding into a dim memory of social studies class or activated fleetingly by a movie about
World War II. Whatever good news these surveys impart—high rates
of volunteering, for instance—is eclipsed by the steady pileup of apathy and incognizance. Each time a grand initiative comes along to
reinvigorate the curriculum—a new math pedagogy, a laptop for every student, etc.—test scores two years later dash the hopes of the
innovators. Every majestic forecast of today's youth as the most
savvy, wired, adept, and informed cohort ever—"They're young,

smart, brash," opens a 2005 *USA Today* story on Generation Y (see Armour)—is exploded by the following week's educational data. The outcomes have become so consistently poor that researchers and educators collect them with diminishing expectations, tempering the scores with sparse notices of promise in one measure or another.

One can understand their motives, and accept the intuition that things couldn't be this bad, that young Americans must possess mental virtues underappreciated by the tests and surveys. Indeed, some academic commentators have gone further, opting to reject or dismiss the findings altogether. While public reactions usually offer blunt dismay over the results—*Washington Post* coverage of *Losing America's Memory* began, "The best and brightest? I think not" (see Morin)—professors sometimes concoct crafty rationales to explain away their significance.

One of them has it that the assessments measure rote memory, asking respondents merely to cull from a storage of "decontextualized facts," not to execute more sophisticated kinds of understanding. In truth, many of the history and civics tests do broach more than facts, including concepts such as separation of powers and dominant themes in important texts, and they ask for short-answer interpretations of historical and civic materials. Still, however, the complaint is a forceful one. Harvard education professor Howard Gardner expressed it well in a 2002 article in *Daedalus* when he regretted the fact-oriented, multiple-choice test approach to history teaching: "More often than not, history consists of lists and names and dates rather than the more challenging but more generative capacity to 'do history' and to 'think historically.'" And in 2004, the president of the Organization of American Historians, Jacquelyn Dowd Hall, repeated the point. "Using such surveys as a starting point for debate," she said, "diverts us from the challenge at hand: how to use what students do know—the ideas and identities they glean from family stories, museums, historic sites, films, television, and the like—to engage them in the life process of learning to think historically."

"Thinking historically" is one of those higher-order cognitive operations that educators favor. Here, it means the framing and narrating of factual content in historical ways. But the very "high"-ness of the task discounts it. Perhaps at Harvard the notion of students "thinking historically" without first studying the concrete facts of time and circumstance makes some sense, but step outside that tiny haven and enter classrooms in the rest of America, and you find so many barriers to historical understanding that blithe expressions of "the life process of learning to think historically" signify nothing. To speak of teenagers "gleaning" ideas from museums and historic sites may flatter curators and historians, but it overlooks the fact that most young Americans never enter those places at all.

Moreover, this division of basic facts from higher-order thinking runs against common sense. How middle schoolers may apprehend "historical thinking" without learning about Napoleon, the Renaissance, slavery . . . in a word, without delving into the factual details of another time and place far from their own, is a mystery. Newspaper reporters realize better than professors the simple truth. If you don't know which rights are enumerated in the First Amendment, you can't do very much "critical thinking" about rights in the United States. If you don't know which countries border Israel, you can't ascertain the grounds of the Middle East conflict. Such facts are not an end in themselves, to be sure, but they are an indispensable starting point for deeper insight, and the ignorance of them is a fair gauge of deeper deficiencies.

Another response to the knowledge surveys by academics is more a deflection than a denial. It says that young Americans have always been ignorant of civics and history, and to downplay contemporary reports, it cites earlier surveys in the twentieth century that produced similar findings of ignorance among the kids and outcries among the intelligentsia. Responding to the ISI study of civic literacy,

Stanford education professor Sam Wineburg grumbled in the *Chronicle of Higher Education*, "If anything, test results across the last century point to a peculiar American neurosis: each generation's obsession with testing its young only to discover—and rediscover—their 'shameful' ignorance" (see Gravois). The response shifts the judgment from the test takers to the test givers, from the ignorance of the students to the "neurosis" of the researchers. The older crowd, Wineburg and others imply, gangs up on the juniors, berating them for the same deficits that the elders suffered when they were young. These periodic surveys, the argument goes, merely rehearse an enduring generational conflict, and we shouldn't take particular renditions too seriously.

It's a strange reaction for an educator to have, and a quibbling one. In truth, several reports demonstrate signs of decline. In 2002, when the National Association of Scholars administered a test to college seniors whose questions came from a Gallup survey of high school students in 1955, it found that the former scored no better than the latter. The 2003 National Assessment of Adult Literacy found that the literacy of college graduates fell significantly during the 1990s. While 40 percent of grads reached "proficiency" in 1992, only 31 percent did so in 2003. And according to the 2005 NAEP reading report, the percentage of twelfth-graders performing at "below basic" jumped from 20 percent in 1992 to 27 percent in 2005. Furthermore, cultural habits that build knowledge and skills, too, have tapered off, as we saw in the Fine Arts section on pages 23–26, and as I show in the next chapter. Another distressing trend emerges from the age groupings, the fact that on national tests younger students show modest improvement, but middle and high school kids barely budge. In the NAEP 2006 civics report, one header summarized: "**Civics knowledge increasing for fourth-graders, but not for older students**." Why didn't the higher grades sustain the same improvement? Why is it that the older American students get, the worse they perform?

Even if we grant the point that on some measures today's teenagers and 20-year-olds perform no worse than yesterday's, the implication critics make seems like a concession to inferiority. Just because sophomores 50 years ago couldn't explain the Monroe Doctrine or identify a play by Sophocles any more than today's sophomores doesn't mean that today's shouldn't do better, far better. Past performances do provide one standard of comparison, but with such drastic changes in U.S. culture and education in the last half-century, a simple ideal provides a firmer standard—"What must individuals know in order to act as responsible citizens and discerning consumers?" No matter what former results show, that a nation as prosperous and powerful as the United States allows young citizens to understand so little about its past and present conditions, to regard its operative laws and values so carelessly, and to patronize the best of its culture so rarely is a sad and ominous condition. To compile data on the problem isn't an "obsession." It's a duty, and we need more data, not less. The knowledge bar is low enough in the leisure worlds of students, and for educators to minimize findings of ignorance is to betray their charge as the stewards of learning.

It is also to let stand a strange and critical situation. For the comparison of present to past under-30-year-olds does sway how we interpret recent results, but the comparison is cause for worry, not calm. On one crucial measure, the current generation has a distinct advantage. It enjoys access to first-rate culture and vital facts that earlier cohorts couldn't even imagine. Consider how many more opportunities youth today have for compiling knowledge, elevating taste, and cultivating skills.

First of all, they spend more time in school. According to the U.S. Department of Education, college enrollment rose 17 percent from 1984 to 1994, and in the following 10 years it jumped 21 percent (14.3 million to 17.3 million). In 1994, 20 percent of adults had earned a bachelor's degree or higher, and in 2005 the number increased to 27.6 percent (see Department of Education, *Digest of Education Statistics, 2005*).

Second, in terms of the number of cultural institutions available to young Americans, the milieu has flourished. The American Library Association counts 117,341 libraries in the United States, 9,200 of them public libraries. Eight years earlier, there were 300 fewer public libraries. More museums are open now, too, and more galleries and bookstores with the spread of Borders and Barnes & Noble. More community arts programs are available as well, with, for example, the National Guild of Community Schools of the Arts leaping from 60 members in 1979 to 307 in 2004. To follow the news, young adults in every city can find free papers with a clear under-30-year-old appeal (*LA Weekly*, etc.), or they can turn their eyes to screens perched in restaurants, airport gates, gyms, waiting rooms, and lobbies, all of them broadcasting the latest updates on CNN. And this is not to mention the Internet, which provides anyone with a user password, library card, or student ID a gateway to out-of-copyright books, periodicals, public documents, art images, maps, and the rising generation's favorite info source, *Wikipedia*.

Added to that, young Americans have more money to make use of it all. Not many 20-year-olds in 1965 had a credit card, but according to Nellie Mae, by 2002 83 percent of college students carried at least one, and for 18- to 24-year-olds in general, the balances owed on them jumped from $1,461 in 1992 to $2,985 in 2001 (see Draut). According to a 2003 Harris Interactive poll, Generation Y spends $172 billion per year and saves $39 billion. Several years ago, in 1999, a cover story in *BusinessWeek* appraised it as "the biggest thing to hit the American scene since the 72 million baby boomers," and warned that marketers had better be ready for it. This time, it forecast, the young will set their own standards: "As the leading edge of this huge new group elbows its way into the marketplace, its members are making it clear that companies hoping to win their hearts and wallets will have to learn to think like they do." And if some of them work long hours to pay for their consumption, most of them still maintain long hours of freedom. The 2005 *American Time Use Survey* put the leisure time of 15- to 24-year-olds at five and a half hours per day.

By contrast, what did the average teen in the 1950s have? A World Almanac at home, a radio or TV set in the living room (with parents picking the channel), a daily newspaper, an encyclopedia in the school library, and a rare field trip to a downtown museum.

This is the paradox of the Dumbest Generation. For the young American, life has never been so yielding, goods so plentiful, schooling so accessible, diversion so easy, and liberties so copious. The material gains are clear, and each year the traits of worldliness and autonomy seem to trickle down into ever-younger age groups. But it's a shallow advent. As the survey research shows, knowledge and skills haven't kept pace, and the intellectual habits that complement them are slipping. The advantages of twenty-first-century teen life keep expanding, the eighties and nineties economy and the digital revolution providing miraculously quick and effortless contact with information, wares, amusements, and friends. The mind should profit alongside the youthful ego, the thirst for knowledge satisfied as much as the craving for fun and status. But the enlightenment hasn't happened. Young Americans have much more access and education than their parents did, but in the 2007 Pew survey on "What Americans Know: 1989–2007," 56 percent of 18- to 29-year-olds possessed low knowledge levels, while only 22 percent of 50- to 64-year-olds did. In other words, the advantages don't show up in intellectual outcomes. The mental equipment of the young falls short of their media, money, e-gadgets, and career plans. The 18-year-old may have a Visa card, cell phone, *MySpace* page, part-time job, PlayStation 2, and an admissions letter from State U., but ask this wired and on-the-go high school senior a few intellectual questions and the façade of in-the-know-ness crumbles.

I don't mean to judge the social deportment, moral outlook, religious beliefs, or overall health of members of the Dumbest Generation. Nor should we question their native intelligence. I'm speaking of intellectual habits and repositories of knowledge, not anything else. Other factors such as illegitimacy, church attendance, and IQ display different rates and trends, and some of them correlate to knowledge measures, some don't. Intellectual outcomes are distinct, and the *trends* they show don't always follow the same pattern as other features such as race and income. To take an example: students from low-income households perform worse on reading tests than do middle- and upper-income students, and one might assume that as the economy has benefited upper and middle tiers more than the lower ones the reading gap would have increased. In fact, though, the test gap has remained constant. In 1998, the spread between eighth-graders eligible for free/reduced-price school lunch and those not eligible was 24 points. In 2005, it was 23 points—an insignificant change. The pattern suggests that something besides money, race and ethnicity, region, gender, religion, and education is at work, and as we interpret intellectual outcomes we need to invoke other variables, in particular, we shall see, youth leisure choices such as video game playing and television time.

Observe how often test scores and survey results are converted into the standard demographics of race, gender, and income, however, and you realize how hard this is to do. The contrary patterns we see in intellectual areas (income and access going up, knowledge staying down), along with the isolated and specialized sites in which they unfold (the classroom, the survey result) make the problem easy to overlook. With so much intellectual matter circulating in the media and on the Internet, teachers, writers, journalists, and other "knowledge workers" don't realize how thoroughly young adults and teens tune it out. Most knowledge workers reside in one domain, in a single discipline, field, school, laboratory, or organization, and the young people who enter their domain already care about the subject (or pretend to). A biology professor doesn't notice the benighted attitude. Her students want to apply to med school, and they work extra hard to outdo each other. An eighth-grade social studies teacher might register the civic ignorance of the kids, but he won't generalize about it. He gets too close to them as the weeks pass, and as a professional duty he envisions greater possibilities for them, not the knowledge deficits that will never go away. A newspaper editor knows that circulation is dropping in part because 20-year-olds don't subscribe at nearly the rate of Baby Boomers, but what can he do about it? He has to prepare tomorrow's page, and he worries more about Internet competition than age groups.

Knowledge has become so specialized and niche-oriented that knowledge purveyors don't notice a decline of general knowledge among large population segments. Besides, who wants to chastise the young? People who do notice a spreading dumbness and proclaim it run the risk of being labeled a curmudgeon and a reactionary. Ever since the ancients, writers have made sport of men and women who resent their juniors as stupid or calculating, and in the wake of the 1960s youth movements the casting has only become more rigid and farcical. For every knowledge person who rebukes the young and is admired for it—such as Jaime Escalante, hero of the 1988 film *Stand and Deliver*—there are two dozen caricatured portraits such as the outwitted principal in *Ferris Bueller's Day Off* and the bullying monitor in *The Breakfast Club*. In a 2004 article in *The Weekly Standard*, Joseph Epstein regretted what he called the "perpetual adolescent"— the extension of adolescent demeanors and interests well into adulthood. For every lament like Epstein's, though, we have countless efforts to understand, to reach out, to explore without judgment the adolescent temper.

The knowledge problem remains, however, in spite of the forbearance of middle-aged folk, and the material blessings of adolescent life haven't helped at all. The trappings of prosperity are plainly in view, and they eclipse the intellectual shortfalls all too well, but when poor learning and feeble skills surface, they are resolute. If a young clerk has a hard time counting change, her cool photos on the Web won't save her from the disrespect of fellow workers. A freshman might best his dorm buddies in a dozen video games, but when a teacher asks him to name the three branches of government and he goes mute, the aura of his expertise dims. If a student interviews for an internship at a local museum and shows up wearing the hippest garments but can't name a single eighteenth-century artist, the curators will pass. The clothes, merchandise, and e-aptitudes officiate in the social world of teens and young adults, whose currency is pop styles and techno-skills. Outside that heated habitat, however, in the workplace, grad school, and politics, what glorifies youth among their peers is, at best, a distraction and, at worst, a disqualification.

The situation marks an important contrast: material possessions vs. intellectual possessions, adolescent skills vs. adult skills. Young Americans excel in the first and fail in the second. They seem so adept with technology, multitasking to the amazement of their parents. They care so much about the trappings of cool, and are so conversant with pop culture. But they blink uncomprehendingly at the mention of the Reformation, the Second Amendment, Fellow Travelers, and Fellini. For all their technological adroitness, they don't read or write or add or divide very well. A 2005 Harvard poll of college students announces, "The 27 million Americans between the ages of 18 and 24 are poised to make their presence known in community and civic life," and a 2004 U.S. Department of Education report says that 47 percent of high school seniors believe it is "very important" to be an active and informed citizen. And yet in the 1998 NAEP civics exam, only 26 percent of high school seniors scored "proficient" or "advanced," and eight years later, the next NAEP civics test of twelfth-graders produced a gain of only 1 percentage point.

Fully 45 percent could not understand basic information on a sample ballot.

The contrasts are stark, and they suggest a troubling conclusion: the abundant material progress in an adolescent's life hasn't merely bypassed or disengaged him or her from intellectual progress, but has, perhaps, hindered it. Greater spending power for teens and 20-year-olds has steered them away from books, museums, and science shows, not toward them. The Internet doesn't impart adult information; it crowds it out. Video games, cell phones, and blogs don't foster rightful citizenship. They hamper it. Maybe it is true, as the Ad Council declares in a report on youth volunteering, that "young adults today are fiercely individualistic, and are media-savvy to a degree never seen before." And maybe it is true that teenagers relate better to their parents—*Time* magazine found in 2005 that more than half of them termed the relationship "excellent." Those positives, though, only underscore the intellectual negatives, and pose a worrisome contrary connection between areas of youth progress and liberal arts learning. The enhancements and prosperities claimed to turn young Americans into astute global citizens and liberated consumers sometimes actually conspire against intellectual growth.

Hence the middle-class teenager may attend a decent high school and keep a B+ average, pack an iPod and a handheld, volunteer through his church, save for a car, and aim for college, and still not know what the Soviet Union was or how to compute a percentage. None of the customary obstacles to knowledge interfere—poverty, bad schools, late-night jobs—but they might as well, given the knowledge outcomes. All the occasions and equipment for learning are in place, but he uses them for other purposes. Adolescents have always wasted their time and chances, of course, but the Dumbest Generation has raised the habit into a brash and insistent practice. No cohort in human history has opened such a fissure between its material conditions and its intellectual attainments. None has experienced so many technological enhancements and yielded so little mental progress.

It remains to us to uncover how they do it. We must identify and describe the particular routines of the members of the Dumbest Generation that freeze their likings in adolescence despite more occasions for high culture, that harden their minds to historical and civic facts despite more coursework, that shut out current events and political matters despite all the information streams. To do that, however, we mustn't follow the standard approach of delving into schools and curricula, as noted education leader Chester E. Finn explained why back in 1992.

> To put this in perspective, a child reaching her 18th birthday has been alive for about 158,000 hours. If she has attended school without miss—no absences for 6 hours a day, 180 days a year, for 12 years—she will have spent almost 13,000 hours in school. If we add kindergarten, the number increases to 14,000 hours. But that is only 9 percent of her time on Earth. Consider what this means in terms of the leverage of formal education, if much of what goes on during the other 91 percent is at cross purposes to the values and lessons of school.

Even Finn's generous calculation—he assumes no absences at all—plus five or six hours a week of homework (which exceeds the high school seniors' average) allow the schools a meager portion of the kids' time. The unique failings of the Dumbest Generation don't originate in the classroom, then, which amounts to only one-eleventh of their daily lives. They stem from the home, social, and leisure lives of young Americans, and if changes in their out-of-school habits entail a progressive disengagement from intellectual matters, then we should expect their minds to exhibit some consequences in spite of what goes on in school. If leisure diversions complement academic performance, then the enhancement of them will show up in education scores and surveys. If the numbers remain low and flat while leisure improves, as is the case today, then teen and young adult customs and mores must have an anti-intellectual effect.

Here lies the etiology of the Dumbest Generation—not in school or at work, but in their games, their socializing, and their spending. It begins with a strange and spreading phobia.

CHAPTER TWO

THE NEW
BIBLIOPHOBES

B ack in 2004, I went on the air with an NPR affiliate in the Midwest to talk about leisure reading habits in the United States. I was with the National Endowment for the Arts at the time, and we had just issued a report showing that adults then read literature at significantly lower rates than adults had in previous decades, and that the biggest drop was in the 18- to 24-year-old age group. The report was titled *Reading at Risk: A Survey of Literary Reading in America*, and after its release in July 2004 it sparked a national discussion of the decline of reading, with more than 600 newspaper stories and commentaries appearing by the end of the summer. The radio interview was one of many of my appearances during those weeks, and aside from simply recounting the findings, I was startled again and again at the reactions of the audience. In this case, after 15 minutes spent reviewing the study, the host opened the phone lines and a bright young voice came through. I tried to capture the exchange word for word just after the show concluded.

CALLER: I'm a high school student, and yeah, I don't read and my friends don't read.

HOST: Why not?

CALLER: Because of all the boring stuff the teachers assign.

HOST: Such as?

CALLER: Uh . . . that book about the guy. [Pause] You know, that guy who was great.

HOST: Huh?

CALLER: The great guy.

HOST: You mean *The Great Gatsby*?

CALLER: Yeah. Who wants to read about him?

The call ended there, and I regret not asking another question in reply: "What do you like to read?" She objected to *Gatsby*, a novel about Jazz Age figures who interested her not a whit, but she didn't offer anything in its place. A social drama of the rich and notorious in 1920s New York bored her, but she never mentioned anything else in print that amused her. No Austen and no Faulkner, certainly, but no Harry Potter, Mitch Albom, or Sophie Kinsella either. She didn't like to read, period, and she wanted to tell us just that, throwing our assumption that every young person should read books right back in our faces.

I didn't laugh at the "that guy who was great" remark, though it made for lively radio. I was too busy pondering a young woman's eagerness to broadcast the disdain for reading across southern Ohio. She suffered no shame for her anti-literary taste, and no cognizance of its poverty. The refusal to read seemed to her a legitimate response to a wearisome syllabus, and if the turnoff extended to her leisure time, well, that, too, was the adults' fault.

It's a new attitude, this brazen disregard of books and reading. Earlier generations resented homework assignments, of course, and only a small segment of each dove into the intellectual currents of the time, but no generation trumpeted *a-literacy* (knowing how to read, but choosing not to) as a valid behavior of their peers. The 1960s youth movements had enough intellectuals of their own to avoid it, and their gurus (Herbert Marcuse, Paul Goodman, the Beats . . .) wrote many books. Generation X delivered grunge music and slacker attitude, and its primary voice, Douglas Coupland, highlighted X-ers' exile from 1980s commercial lifestyles, but they didn't make their disaffection into so much of a boast. Today's rising generation thinks more highly of its lesser traits. It wears anti-intellectualism on its sleeve, pronouncing book-reading an old-fashioned custom, and it snaps at people who rebuke them for it.

As I write, this week's issue of the *Chronicle of Higher Education* (January 2007) just hit my mailbox, and it contains a revealing section on technology and Millennials. One article entitled "How the New Generation of Well-Wired Multitaskers Is Changing Campus Culture" records a symposium in Nevada at which local college students related their interests and habits. The opening paragraphs note that Millennials "think it's cool to be smart," but discloses also that "They rarely read newspapers—or, for that matter, books." In answer to the question "How often do you go to a library, and what do you do there?" one panelist replied:

> My dad is still into the whole book thing. He has not realized that the Internet kind of took the place of that. So we go to the library almost every Sunday. I actually have a library card, but I have not rented a book for a long time, but I go to our school's library a lot because they have most of the course books.

How serenely this undergrad announces the transfer from "the whole book thing" to the Internet, as if the desertion of civilization's principal storehouse merits little more than a shrug. And note the scale of awareness. The father just doesn't "realize" how things have changed, that his world is over. The inversion is settled. It's the bookish elders who know so little, and the young ones countenance them as they would a doddering grandpa on the brink of senility.

The student speaks for herself, but behind her verdict lies the insight of a new generation. The consignment of books to the past wouldn't be so blithely assumed if it weren't backed by a poised peer consciousness. We may smile at the compliment the hubris pays to adolescence, but the rejection of books by young adults is a common feature, and it isn't always so condescendingly benign. In fall 2004, I joined a panel of faculty members at the University of Maryland to discuss, once again, reading trends for young adults and their implications for American culture. Facing about 250 students, I told them the truth, reciting the findings of several knowledge surveys as the inevitable outcome of not reading. Their interests lead them in polar directions, their knowledge running to zero in areas of civics, history, etc., while rising to a panoramic grasp of the lives of celebrities, the lyrics of pop music, and *MySpace* profiling. They wrinkle their brows if offered a book about Congress, but can't wait for the next version of *Halo*. "Let's get specific," I goaded. "You are six times more likely to know who the latest American Idol is than you are to know who the Speaker of the U.S. House is." At that point, a voice in the crowd jeered, "*American Idol* is more important!"

She was right. In her world, stars count more than the most powerful world leaders. Knowing the names and ranks of politicians gets her nowhere in her social set, and reading a book about the Roman Empire earns nothing but teasing. More than just dull and nerdish, reading is counterproductive. Time spent reading books takes away from time keeping up with youth vogues, which change every month. To prosper in the hard-and-fast cliques in the schoolyard, the fraternities, and the food court, teens and 20-year-olds must track the latest films, fads, gadgets, *YouTube* videos, and television shows. They judge one another relentlessly on how they wear clothes, recite rap lyrics, and flirt. Having career goals may not draw their mockery, but a high school guy found by his buddies reading *The Age of Innocence* on a summer afternoon never regains his verve, and a girl with *Bowling Alone* in hand is downright inscrutable. The middle school hallways can be as competitive and pitiless as a Wall Street trading floor or an episode of *Survivor.* To know a little more about popular music and malls, to sport the right fashions and host a teen blog, is a matter of survival.

The momentum of the social scene crushes the budding literary scruples of teens. Anti-book feelings are emboldened, and heavy readers miss out on activities that unify their friends. Even the foremost youth reading phenomenon in recent years, the sole book event, qualifies more as a social happening than a reading trend. I mean, of course, Harry Potter. The publisher, Scholastic, claims that in the first 48 hours of its availability *Harry Potter and the Half-Blood Prince* sold 6.9 million copies, making it the fastest-selling book ever. In the first hour after its release at 12:01 A.M. on July 16, 2005, Barnes & Noble tendered 105 copies per second at its outlets. Kids lined up a thousand deep in wizard hats to buy it as Toys "R" Us in Times Square ran a countdown clock and the Boston Public Library ordered almost 300 copies to be placed on reserve. In Edinburgh, author J. K. Rowling prepared for a reading with 70 "cub reporters" from around the world who'd won contests sponsored by English-speaking newspapers.

It sounds like a blockbuster salute to reading, with a book, for once, garnering the same nationwide buzz that a *Star Wars* film did. But the hoopla itself suggests something else. Kids read Harry Potter not because they like reading, but because other kids read it. Yes, the plots move fast, the showdown scenes are dramatic, and a boarding school with adults in the background forms a compelling setting, but to reach the numbers that the series does requires that it accrue a special social meaning, that it become a youth identity good. Like *Pokémon* a few years ago, Harry Potter has grown into a collective marvel. We usually think of reading as a solitary activity, a child alone in an easy chair at home, but Harry Potter reveals another side of the experience, and another motivation to do it. Reading *Harry Potter and the Sorcerer's Stone, Harry Potter and the Chamber of Secrets,* and the rest is to bond with your peers. It opens you to a fun milieu of after-school games, Web sites, and clubs. Not to know the characters and actions is to fall out of your classmates' conversation.

If only we could spread that enthusiasm to other books. Unfortunately, once most young readers finished *Harry Potter and the Goblet of Fire*, they didn't read a book with the same zeal until the next Potter volume appeared three years later. No other books come close, and the consumer data prove it. Harry Potter has reached astronomical revenues, but take it out of the mix and juvenile book sales struggle. The Book Industry Study Group (BISG) monitors the book business, and its 2006 report explicitly tagged growth in the market to Potter publications. Here is what the researchers predicted:

> Since no new *Potter* hardcover book is scheduled for release in 2006, but the paperback *Potter* VI will appear, we are projecting a 2.3 percent increase in hardcover revenues and a 10 percent surge in paperback revenues. Because *Potter* VII is not likely to be published in 2007, the projected growth rate for that year is a lackluster 1.8 percent.

In fact, another Potter book did come out in July 2007, one year ahead of the BISG's forecast, but that only pushes up the schedule. Keep in mind that growth here is measured in revenue, which keeps the trend in the plus column. For unit sales, not dollar amounts, the numbers look bleak. In a year with no Potter, BISG estimated that total unit sales of juvenile books would fall 13 million, from 919 to 906 million. Sales would jump again when cloth and paper editions of the next Potter arrive, but after that, unit sales would tumble a stunning 42 million copies. If Harry Potter did spark a reinvigoration of reading, young adult sales would rise across the board, but while the Harry Potter fandom continues, the reading habit hasn't expanded.

The headlong rush for Harry Potter, then, has a vexing counterpart: a steady withdrawal from other books. The results of *Reading at Risk* supply stark testimony to the definitive swing in youth leisure and interests. The report derives from the latest *Survey of Public Participation in the Arts*, which the National Endowment for the Arts designed and the U.S. Bureau of the Census executed in 2002. More than 17,000 adults answered questions about their enjoyment of the arts and literature (an impressive 70 percent response rate), and the sample gave proportionate representation to the U.S. population in terms of age, race, gender, region, income, and education.

When the SPPA numbers first arrived and researchers compared them to results from 1982 and 1992, we found that most participations—for example, visiting a museum—had declined a few percentage points or so, not an insignificant change in art forms whose participation rates already hovered in the single digits. The existing percentage of people reading literature stood much higher, but the trend in reading literature, it turned out, was much worse than trends in the other arts. From 1982 to 2002, reading rates fell through the floor. The youngest cohort suffered the biggest drop, indicating something unusual happening to young adults and their relationship to books. The numbers deserved more scrutiny, and Dana Gioia, chairman of the Endowment, ordered us to draft a separate report complete with tables and analyses.

The survey asked about voluntary reading, not reading required for work or school. We aimed to determine how people pass their leisure hours—what they want to do, not what they have to do—and we understood leisure choices as a key index of the state of the culture. The literature assigned in college courses divulges a lot about the aesthetics and ideology of the curriculum, but it doesn't reveal the dispositions of the students, preferences that they'll carry forward long after they've forgotten English 201. Young people have read literature on their own for a variety of reasons—diversion, escape, fantasy, moral instruction, peer pressure—and their likings have reflected their values and ambitions, as well as their prospects.

A 14-year-old girl reading Nancy Drew in bed at night may not appear so significant a routine, but the accumulation of individual choices, the reading patterns of 60 million teens and young adults, steer the course of U.S. culture, even though they transpire outside the classroom and the workplace. A drastic shift in them is critical.

Here are the literary reader rates broken down by age:

	1982	1992	2002
• 18–24-year-olds	59.8	53.3	42.8
• 25–34-year-olds	62.1	54.6	47.7
• 35–44-year-olds	59.7	58.9	46.6
• 45–54-year-olds	54.9	56.9	51.6
• 55–64-year-olds	52.8	52.9	48.9
• 65–74-year-olds	47.2	50.8	45.3

A 17-point drop among the first group in such a basic and long-standing behavior isn't just a youth trend. It's an upheaval. The slide equals a 28 percent rate of decline, which cannot be interpreted as a temporary shift or as a typical drift in the ebb and flow of the leisure habits of youth. If all adults in the United States followed the same pattern, literary culture would collapse. If young adults abandoned a product in another consumer realm at the same rate, say, cell phone usage, the marketing departments at Sprint and Nokia would shudder. The youngest adults, 18- to 24-year-olds, formed the second-strongest reading group in 1982. Now they form the weakest, and the decline is accelerating: a 6.5 fall in the first decade and a 10.5 plummet in '92–'02.

It isn't because the contexts for reading have eroded. Some 172,000 titles were published in 2005, putting to rest the opinion that boys and girls don't read because they can't find any appealing contemporary literature. Young Americans have the time and money to read, and books are plentiful, free on the Internet and in the library, and 50 cents apiece for Romance and Adventure paperbacks at used bookstores. School programs and "Get Caught Reading"–type campaigns urge teens to read all the time, and students know that reading skills determine their high-stakes test scores. But the retreat from books proceeds, and for more and more teens and 20-year-olds, fiction, poetry, and drama have absolutely no existence in their lives.

None at all. To qualify as a literary reader, all a respondent had to do was scan a single poem, play, short story, or novel in the previous 12 months outside of work or school. If a young woman read a fashion magazine and it contained a three-page story about a romantic adventure, and that was the only literary encounter she had all year, she fell into the literary reading column. A young man cruising the Internet who came across some hip-hop lyrics could answer the survey question "In the last 12 months, did you read any poetry?" with a "Yes." We accepted any work of any quality and any length in any medium—book, newspaper, magazine, blog, Web page, or music CD insert. If respondents liked graphic novels and considered them "novels," they could respond accordingly. James Patterson qualified just as much as Henry James, Sue Grafton as much as Sylvia Plath. No high/low exclusions here, and no minimum requirements. The bar stood an inch off the ground.

And they didn't turn off literature alone. Some commentators on *Reading at Risk* complained that the survey overemphasized fiction, poetry, and drama. Charles McGrath of the *New York Times*, for instance, regretted the "perplexing methodological error" that led us to "a definition of literature that appears both extremely elastic and, by eliminating nonfiction entirely, confoundingly narrow." *The Atlantic Monthly* grumbled that the survey defined literature "somewhat snobbishly as fiction, plays, and poetry," a strange complaint given that the questions accepted Stephen King and nursery rhymes as literature. Most important, though, the survey included general reading as well, the query asking, "With the exception of books required for work or school, did you read any books during the last 12 months?" Cookbooks, self-help, celebrity bios, sports, history . . . any book could do. Here, too, the drop was severe, with 18- to 24-year-olds leading the way.

	1992	2002
• 18–24-year-olds	59.3	51.0
• 25–34-year-olds	64.4	58.4
• 35–44-year-olds	65.9	58.1
• 45–54-year-olds	63.9	60.3
• 55–64-year-olds	58.7	57.2
• 65–74-year-olds	55.0	53.5

The general book decline for young adults matches the decline in literary reading for the same period, 8.3 points to 10.5 points. The comparison with older age groups holds as well, with young adults nearly doubling the book-reading change for the entire population, which fell from 60.9 percent in 1992 to 56.6 percent in 2002. *The Atlantic Monthly* found the lower figure promising: "The picture seems less dire, however, when one considers that the reading of all books, nonfiction included, dropped by only four points over the past decade—suggesting that readers' tastes are increasingly turning toward nonfiction." In fact, the survey suggests no such thing. That book reading fell less than literary reading doesn't mean that readers dropped *The Joy Luck Club* and picked up Howard Stern's *Private Parts*. It means that they dropped both genres, one at a slower pace than the other. And in both, young adults far outpaced their elders. The 8.3-point slide in book reading by 18- to 24-year-olds averages out to a loss of 60,000 book readers per year.

The same reading discrepancy between young adults and older Americans shows up in the latest *American Time Use Surveys* (ATUS), sponsored by the Bureau of Labor Statistics and conducted by the U.S. Census Bureau. ATUS asks respondents to keep a diary of their leisure, work, home, and school activities during a particular day of the week, and "oversamples" weekend tallies to ensure accurate averages. In the first ATUS, whose results were collected in 2003, the total population of 15-year-olds and older averaged about 22 minutes a day in a reading activity of any kind. The youngest group, though, 15- to 24-year-olds, came up at barely one-third the rate, around eight minutes per day (.14 hours). They enjoyed more than five hours per day of free time, and they logged more than two hours of television. The boys put in 48 minutes playing games and computers for fun—they had almost an hour more leisure time than girls, mainly because girls have greater sibling and child-care duties—and both sexes passed an hour in socializing. Of all the sports and leisure activities measured, reading came in last. Moreover, in the Bureau of Labor Statistics design, "reading" signified just about any pursuit with a text: Harry Potter on the bus, a story on last night's basketball game on *www.si.com*, or the back of the cereal box during breakfast. We should consider, too, that reading is easier to carry out than all the other leisure activities included in ATUS except "Relaxing/thinking." It costs less than cable television and video games, it doesn't require a membership fee (like the gym), and you can still read in places where cell phones are restricted and friends don't congregate. Nevertheless, it can't compete with the others. The meager reading rate held up in the next two ATUS surveys. In 2005, 15- to 24-year-olds came in at around eight minutes on weekdays, nine minutes on weekends, while the overall average was 20 minutes on weekdays and 27 minutes on weekends.

The youngest age group in ATUS, 15- to 24-year-olds, covers people in high school and high school dropouts, college students and college graduates, those who never enrolled in college and those who dropped out. The category thereby mixes individuals of wholly different circumstances. To a 24-year-old, a 16-year-old lives in another universe entirely, whereas a 43-year-old regards a 36-year-old's world as pretty much the same as his own. Fortunately, other surveys provide more tailored reading numbers for the younger ages, and in

recent years they have revealed deeper and darker intellectual profiles of the rising generation.

One report compiled National Assessment of Educational Progress (NAEP) data on reading for the last few decades to chart long-
term trends in academic performance and contexts. Entitled *NAEP
2004 Trends in Academic Progress: Three Decades of Performance in
Reading and Mathematics*, the study reviewed 36 years of the existence of NAEP to measure academic scores and track them through
various demographic groupings and out-of-school experiences.
NAEP is best known for the annual test scores it publishes, and those
results have assumed crucial significance for schools and teachers in
the wake of the No Child Left Behind Act of 2001, whose legislation
ties funding to what is termed Adequate Yearly Progress, which is
measured by test scores. But another aspect of NAEP included in the
report examines "Contextual Factors Associated with Reading," one
of them being "reading for fun." At each extreme, an astonishing shift
took place. The percentage of 17-year-olds who "Never or hardly
ever" read for fun more than doubled from 1984 to 2004, 9 percent
to 19 percent. Over the same period, the percentage of 17-year-olds
who read for fun "Almost every day" dropped by 9 points. Nearly
half of high school seniors (48 percent) read for fun "once or twice a
month or less."

The numbers mark an elemental turn in youth literacy, and it
can't be accounted for by more reading in class. A few pages earlier,
the report charted homework by pages assigned. The percentage of
students who had to complete more than 20 pages per day went
from 21 percent to 23 percent from 1984 to 2004, and those assigned 16 to 20 pages jumped only one point (14 to 15 percent).
Neither figure comes close to matching the leisure reading slump.

While leisure reading doesn't reflect in-class reading trends, it
may bear directly upon reading comprehension scores. Despite all
the attention showered upon reading skills ever since the landmark
report *A Nation at Risk* and the rise of the standards movement in

the 1980s, reading comprehension scores for high school seniors haven't budged. Fourth-graders show significant improvement and eighth-graders display some progress as well, but through middle school the gains taper off, and by the end of high school the trend flattens. This is an unfortunate pattern, and it calls out for investigation. Indeed, another large longitudinal survey, the University of Michigan Institute for Social Research's *Changing Times of American Youth: 1981–2003*, unveils the same pattern. The questionnaire asked about leisure reading for 6- to 17-year-olds, and a disappointing number came up for 2002–03: only 1 hour and 17 minutes per week. There was an optimistic sign, we should note, because that total beat the 1981–82 total by eight minutes. The optimism disappears, however, when the group is broken down by age. On an average weekend day, while six- to eight-year-olds jumped from 9 to 14 minutes, 9- to 11-year-olds from 10 to 15 minutes, and 12- to 14-year-olds from 10 to 13 minutes, 15- to 17-year-olds reversed the gains entirely, dropping from 18 to 7 minutes.

The *NAEP Trends 2004* includes other data comparisons that echo the implication that leisure reading is a significant factor in academic progress. The report relates reading for school and reading for fun to test scores, and a consistent pattern appears.

- 17-year-olds who read for fun almost every day scored 305
- 17-year-olds who read for fun once or twice a week scored 288
- 17-year-olds who read more than 20 pages per day for class scored 297
- 17-year-olds who read 16–20 pages per day for class scored 293

The more kids read out of school *and* in school, the higher their scores. Observe, too, that the test score differences between heavy and light out-of-class readers exceed the differences between heavy and light in-class readers. The gap between the highest and next-highest out-of-class readers is 17 points, while the gap between the highest and next-highest in-class readers is only four points. The results also set the gap between the highest and lowest out-of-class readers at 37 points, and between the highest and lowest in-class readers at 29 points. Because the measurements of reading for school and reading for fun don't use precisely the same scale (pages read vs. frequency of reading), we can't draw hard-and-fast conclusions about their respective effects on reading scores. But these discrepancies indicate that leisure reading does have substantial influence on school performance, much more than one would assume after listening to public and professional discourse about reading scores, which tend to focus on the classroom and the curriculum, not on the leisure lives of teens.

Yet another high school project providing reading data is the annual *High School Survey of Student Engagement* (HSSSE), housed at Indiana University. With a sample size of 80,000 high school students in all four grades, HSSSE boasts one of the largest national databases gauging school experiences and academic habits. It asks students about sports, clubs, homework, coursework, and leisure activities including reading. In 2005 one question asked, "About how much reading do you do in a typical 7-day week?" Fully 77 percent said that they spend three hours or less per week on "personal reading." In 2006, the question changed slightly, but showed equally abysmal results. About one in six students logged zero hours of "Reading for self" per week, while 40 percent scored less than an hour. Only 5 percent surpassed 10 hours. When it came to "Reading/studying for class," only 2 percent exceeded 10 hours, and 55 percent came in at one hour or less. More than half the high school student body, then, spend few moments reading because they have to or because they want to.

Another segment of the survey, one querying attitudes, helps explain why. Once again, time and money play no part in the with-drawal. Fully 45 percent of the students just don't think leisure reading is important ("a little" or "not at all"). Unconvinced of what adult readers feel deep in their hearts and know from long experi-ence, nearly half of the student body disregards books by choice and disposition, and they don't expect to suffer for it. In their minds, a-literacy and anti-intellectualism pose no career obstacles, and they have no shame attached. Uninterested in reading and unworried about the consequences, kids reject books as they do their vegetables, and the exhortations of their teachers fall flat. A quick glance at a newspaper once a day would augment their courses in government, a subscription to *Popular Science* magazine might enliven their chem-istry homework, and an afternoon browsing in the public library might expose them to books they find more compelling than those discussed in class. But those complements don't happen.

We might assume that the weaker and alienated high school kids pull down the average, and that seniors and juniors headed for col-lege display better attitudes and higher reading rates. But three large national surveys of college freshmen say otherwise, drawing the bib-liophobia up into the more ambitious ranks. In January 2007, higher education consulting firm Noel-Levitz released its *National Fresh-man Attitudes Report*, a 100-question survey of students who'd just entered college. The 97,000 freshmen who completed the question-naire expressed the optimism and determination one would expect from young adults in a new phase of life. Nearly all of them (93.6 percent) pledged to finish college "no matter what obstacles get in my way," and 88.8 percent intended to "make the effort and sacrifice that will be needed" to attain their goals. Their enthusiasm, however, doesn't correspond to the reality that only 46.9 percent of entering students graduate within five years. Another portion of the survey shows why. It includes measures of their reading interest—or recoil. To the statement "I get a great deal of satisfaction from reading," 53.3 percent disagree. And to "Over the years, books have broadened my horizons and stimulated my imagination," 42.9 percent disagree. Fully 40.4 percent concur with "I don't enjoy reading serious books and articles, and I only do it when I have to," while 39.6 percent admit that "Books have never gotten me very excited."

Significantly, the questions don't distinguish between in-class reading and personal reading, which means that two-fifths of the entering class can't recollect a single book assigned by others or chosen by themselves that inspired them. Furthermore, the survey showed that students in four-year private institutions profess book interests not much more than those of students in community colleges. Wealthier students enroll in the former, but higher-income households don't produce proportionately higher reading rates. Even though the bulk of their undergraduate training will involve "serious books and articles," a sizable portion of both student populations detests them and reads them only under command. The connection between general intellectual interest and academic performance doesn't register. Students aim high, but the attitudes undercut them and they don't seem to realize it.

The annual *American Freshman Survey* duplicates the findings for leisure reading rates, and because it dates back to 1966 it allows for longitudinal comparisons. To the question "During your last year in high school, how much time did you spend during a typical week reading for pleasure?" freshmen in 2005 answered as follows: "None" at 24.8 percent; "Less than one hour" at 26.1 percent; and "1–2 hours" at 23.8 percent. Add these three lowest times, covering 0–2 hours per week, and you get three-quarters of the entering class (74.7 percent) that reads outside of school for less than 17 minutes per day. Unbelievably, one-quarter of high school graduates who've gone on to college never read a word of literature, sports, travel, politics or anything else for their own enjoyment or illumination. But the percentage of students answering "None" has held steady for several years. In 2001, the figure was roughly the same. The big change happened in the seven years before 2001, when the trend shifted sharply downward. The "None" category rose from 19.6 percent in 1994 to 24.8 percent in 2001, a jump of 26 percent. The "Less than one" category went from 25.4 percent to 27.4 percent. In fact, every group slid downward. At the same time, during the 1990s, enrollments in higher education jumped 9 percent, with more high schoolers following loftier ambitions, but the intellectual habits that would sustain them on campus went the other way.

With high school doing less and less to inspire off-campus reading, we can still hope that higher education sparks young people's curiosity once they've departed the stultifying social climate of senior year. The *National Survey of Student Engagement* asks dozens of questions about in- and out-of-class habits and goals, and one of them queries students about their book reading "for personal enjoyment or academic enrichment." Here are the results for number of books read for 2003 and 2005.

	2003		2005	
	Freshmen	*Seniors*	*Freshmen*	*Seniors*
• None	26%	21%	24%	19%
• Between 1–4	55%	53%	56%	54%
• Between 5–10	12%	16%	13%	16%

The low rates suggest that for a majority of college students intellectual life belongs mainly to the classroom. Perhaps freshmen spend too much of their leisure time adapting to campus life, searching for ways to fit in and find themselves, choose a major and envision a career, not create a bedtime reading list. But the reading rates don't get much better as they approach graduation. For young Americans who've passed through six semesters of coursework to receive a liberal arts education at a cost of up to $200,000, the gains here seem a disappointing improvement. If 81 percent of freshmen in '03 read four books or fewer in a full year's time and seniors lowered that dreary figure to only 74 percent, one wonders why college courses didn't inspire them to pick up books at a faster rate. Does campus social life dampen their inquisitiveness, dividing what they do in class and what they do at night cleanly into the pro-studious and anti-studious? Has the undergraduate plan become so pre-professionalized that the curriculum functions as a high-level vocational training that dulls the intellectual curiosity that encourages outside book reading? Perhaps the rise of business as the most popular major signals a new careerism among undergraduates, a loss of interest in general education. Maybe many of the best and brightest students aim for medical and law school, not the humanities, and the competition for graduate admissions leaves them little energy to read on their own.

Whatever the reason, the upturn looks feeble, for all a larger increase in the NSSE numbers requires is that students add another book or two every 12 months. The school year lasts only 30 weeks, leaving 22 weeks to plow through some trashy novels at the beach or pick up a popular text or two related to their studies, *Freakonomics* for econ majors, for instance. Coursework should inspire more intellectual probing. It won't hurt their chemistry grades, and outside books might even raise their scores on the GMAT and the LSAT, which have reading-comprehension sections. Young Americans have everything to gain from reading, more civic and historical knowledge, familiarity with current events and government actions, a larger vocabulary, better writing skills, eloquence, inexpensive recreation, and contact with great thoughts and expressions of the past. And yet even in the intellectual havens of our universities, too many of them shield themselves from the very activity that best draws them out of the high school mindset.

Compare their attitude with that of young Frederick Douglass, a slave in Baltimore whose mistress started to teach him the ABCs until her husband found out and forbade it. Years later, Douglass remembered his master's words as brutal truth: "Learning would spoil the best nigger in the world," he overhears him say. "Now if you teach that nigger (speaking of myself) how to read, there would be no keeping him. It would forever unfit him to be a slave." Douglass listened closely and realized well the liberating power of written words (and why Southern states made teaching slaves to read illegal). "Though conscious of the difficulty of learning without a teacher," he pledged in his autobiography, "I set out with high hope, and a fixed purpose, at whatever cost of trouble, to learn how to read."

Or that of John Stuart Mill, the great Victorian liberal intellectual. Born in 1806, Mill was a prodigy, learning Greek starting at age three and algebra at age eight, and by his late teens he'd acquired expert knowledge of logic, economics, and history. But a crushing depression hit him soon after, "the dry heavy dejection of the melancholy winter of 1826," he called it in his *Autobiography* (1873). Life seemed vapid and pointless, and the promise of renown failed to cheer him. As months passed and despondency deepened, one unexpected encounter rescued him: "my reading of Wordsworth for the first time (in the autumn of 1828)." The poems presented scenes of rural beauty and moments of pious sympathy, bringing Mill into "the common feelings and common destiny of human beings." His depression lifted, and forever after Mill honored the *Lyrical Ballads* as "a medicine for my state of mind."

Or that of Walt Whitman, for years a journeyman printer and hack writer in Brooklyn until Ralph Waldo Emerson's speeches and essays set him on a pioneering ascent toward *Leaves of Grass* in 1855. "I was simmering, simmering, simmering," he divulged a few years later. "Emerson brought me to a boil."

Or W. E. B. Du Bois, born in 1868, who found solace from living in a Jim Crow nightmare in the imaginary worlds of books. "I sit with Shakespeare and he winces not," he wrote in 1902. "Across the color line I move arm in arm with Balzac and Dumas, where smiling men and welcoming women glide in gilded halls. From out the caves of Evening that swing between the strong-limbed earth and the tracery of the stars, I summon Aristotle and Aurelius and what soul I will, and they come all graciously with no scorn nor condescension."

Their testimony sets the bibliophobia of today's youth into mer-
ciless relief. Books carried them out of torment and torpor, and the
readings transformed them into something more and better than
they were before. Adolescents today have the same feelings and
experiences—depression, abuse, uncertainty—and they don't have
to be geniuses like Mill and Du Bois to profit from books. And the
books don't have to be classics, either. Given the turn of his peers
away from reading, and the power of peer pressure, a 17-year-old
boy in suburbia who likes the mall, plays b-ball every afternoon, and
carts an iPod at all times, but reserves an hour at night for a number
in the Conan series deserves praise. Douglass and other greats who
attributed their growth to reading don't shame the current generation because of their personal brilliance or their literary choices, but
simply because of their acute appreciation of the written word.

An average teenager with the same devotion will receive the same
benefits, if to lesser degrees. His ego is shaky, and the ordinary stuff
of youth culture plays on his doubts with puerile dramas, verbal cli-
chés, and screen psychodelia. With *MySpace*, *YouTube*, teen blogs,
and Xbox added to Tupac and Britney, *Titanic* and *Idol*, the Internet
doubles the deluge of images and sounds from movies, TV, and radio.
Lengthy exposure to finer things is the best education in taste, and
it's hard to sustain it when the stuff of pop culture descends so per-
sistently on leisure time. There is no better reprieve from the bom-
bardment than reading a book, popular literature as well as the
classics. Books afford young readers a place to slow down and reflect,
to find role models, to observe their own turbulent feelings well expressed, or to discover moral convictions missing from their real situations. Habitual readers acquire a better sense of plot and character,
an eye for the structure of arguments, and an ear for style, over time
recognizing the aesthetic vision of adolescent fare as, precisely,
adolescent.

The survey data show that young Americans increasingly go the
other way, far from books and into the maelstrom of youth amuse-

ments. In the Pew Research Center's 2006 report on newspaper readership, only 39 percent of 18- to 29-year-olds said they "enjoy reading a lot," far less than the national average of 53 percent, and a harbinger of worse numbers to come. A small core of teens and young adults still read avidly, but the number who read now and then is dwindling. The biggest loss in the *Reading at Risk* study took place in the "light" reader category (one to five works per year), which fell at a faster rate than did the rates of people who read numerous books per year. The consequences of the shift extend much further than they appear to at first glance. This is because of the cumulative, developmental nature of reading, a cognitive benefit that says that the more you read, the more you can read. Reading researchers call it the "Matthew Effect," in which those who acquire reading skills in childhood read and learn later in life at a faster pace than those who do not. They have a larger vocabulary, which means that they don't stumble with more difficult texts, and they recognize better the pacing of stories and the form of arguments, an aptitude that doesn't develop as effectively through other media. It's like exercising. Go to the gym three times a week and the sessions are invigorating. Go to the gym three times a month and they're painful. As the occasions of reading diminish, reading becomes a harder task. A sinister corollary to the cognitive benefit applies: the more you don't read, the more you can't read.

SO WHAT? "Who Cares If Johnny Can't Read? The value of books is overstated." That's the title and subtitle of an essay in *Slate* by Larissa MacFarquhar, now a "profiles" writer with *The New Yorker*. It appeared 11 years ago, in 1997, but the sentiment pops up often, strangely enough in literary and education circles. The surveys I've invoked usually produce a chorus of newspaper stories and public commentary on the descent of popular culture into ever coarser and more idiotic enjoyments, and they identify a-literacy as a signal trait of heedless youth. Just as predictably, however, comes a small counterresponse as academics and the more hip, youngish intellectuals pooh-pooh the alarm and yield to, or even embrace, the very advents that worriers decry. I witnessed one example at a meeting of literary scholars in Boulder in 2004 after I presented the findings of *Reading at Risk*. With my dozen PowerPoint charts lined up and commentary completed, a distinguished professor of Renaissance literature on the panel had heard enough. "Look, I don't care if everybody stops reading literature," she blurted. "Yeah, it's my bread and butter, but cultures change. People do different things." What to say about a hypereducated, highly paid teacher, a steward of literary tradition entrusted to impart the value of literature to students, who shows so little regard for her field? I can't imagine a mathematician saying the same thing about math, or a biologist about biology, yet, sad to say, scholars, journalists, and other guardians of culture accept the deterioration of their province without much regret.

A 2005 editorial I spotted a while back in the *Los Angeles Times* was merrily blatant. It first asserted how much kids learn from video games, which unite play with information. Books and classrooms, on the other hand, divide learning and joy in two. Hence, the *Times* went on, no wonder boys who play Microsoft's "Age of Empires II" know more about the Crusades than do kids in history class. The title of the editorial offered a new rule for parents to pass to their children—"Put That Book Down!"—as if it were a twenty-first-century counterpart to Ben Franklin's lessons ("Early to bed and early to rise . . ."). It concluded: "Tell our children to stop fooling around and go play their Xbox for a couple of hours? It affronts our cherished notions of academic excellence. Get over it." What to say about a flagship daily that resorts to smug demotions of bookishness?

MacFarquhar adopts the same impatient, dismissive tone. The essay says nothing insightful about the issue, but it illustrates well this curious tendency of educators and intellectuals to downplay evidence of mental stagnation in America. "Among the truisms that make up the eschatology of American cultural decline," she begins, "one of the most banal is the assumption that Americans don't read." She proceeds to mock "fears of cultural apocalypse," and observes, "The sentimentalization of books gets especially ripe when reading is compared with its supposed rivals: television and cyberspace." The characterization is plain. People who worry about reading declines and book culture are just overwrought handwringers, alarmists disposed to neurotic visions of the end. MacFarquhar supports the send-up with data from Gallup polls in the 1950s showing lower reading rates than today, along with the fact that five times as many titles were published in 1981 as were published in 1950. In assessing the state of our culture, she concludes, "Reading *per se* is not the issue."

The evidence supposedly puts to rest a cultural panic, shifting the issue from the facts of the matter to the ideology of the alarmists. In truth, however, the Gallup reading polls MacFarquhar cites produced erratic results from year to year, indicating flaws in the design, and the number of titles published each year means a lot less than the number of units sold. From 2003 to 2004, for instance, the number of book titles published rose 14 percent, but according to the Book Industry Study Group, the number of books sold dropped by nearly 44 million. A better survey than the Gallup polls appeared in 1946, commissioned by the Book Manufacturers' Institute and drawing from a sample of 4,000 respondents. Published as *People and Books: A Study of Reading and Book-Buying Habits* by Henry C. Clink and Harry Arthur Hopf, it reported fully 71 percent of adults reading a book in the preceding year, the Bible being the most popular (*A Tree Grows in Brooklyn,* by Betty Smith, ranked third, Richard Wright's *Black Boy* twelfth). Broken down by age, reading rates followed a consistent pattern, this time with the youngest ages tallying the highest percentage. Remarkably, 15- to 19-year-olds came in at 92 percent reading a book in the previous year, and 20- to 29-year-olds at 81 percent. The rates progressively fell among each older group, with 60 and over bottoming out at 56 percent. The survey transpired, of course, just before the dawn of television.

But MacFarquhar cares too much about tweaking the bibliophiles for their "maudlin paeans to books" to ponder objectively the extent and implications of reading declines. She and other anti-alarmists cite a statistic mainly to discredit the other side, not to clarify the issue. The central question—"Have reading rates really declined, and if so does the trend portend a decline in intelligence or just a normal shift of popular habits?"—acquires in their hands a culture wars angle. Conservatives and reactionaries fear the disappearance of books as a harbinger of more vulgarity and corruption, while progressives and libertarians let such changes slide and recast the fears as moralistic blather. That's the setup, and beneath it lie other, familiar tensions over family values, public schooling, and childrearing.

A polemical edge in a *Slate* column can be diverting, of course, but the antagonistic spirit stretches to the central powers in education as well. One typical example appeared in a 2005 column in the *Council Chronicle* by President Randy Bomer of the National Council of Teachers of English (membership: 60,000+). The springboard for Bomer's commentary was a curricular reform called the American Diploma Project, a public-private initiative geared to improving the college- and workplace-readiness of high school graduates. In 2004, the Project developed a new set of benchmarks for English language arts, guidelines that included injunctions such as, "The high school graduate can synthesize information from multiple informational and technical sources," and "The high school graduate can analyze the setting, plot, theme, characterization, and narration of classic and contemporary short stories and novels." The designers strove for range and rigor, including grammar, oral presentation, literature, "informational text," mixed media, technical writing, and a host of other language skills and genres in their vision of high school instruction.

Flatly unimpressed, Bomer denounces the results straight off: "I was struck by their narrowness and smallness." The drafters of the benchmarks responded to two current problems—one, the excessive number of high school graduates entering the workplace with atrocious reading and writing skills, and two, the excessive number of entering freshmen who end up in remedial courses. I participated in the discussions, and we observed then, and could gather still more now, voluminous complaints from professors and employers about poor literacy levels in the young adults entering their classrooms and workplaces. For example, a 2006 survey of college professors by the *Chronicle of Higher Education* found that only 6 percent of them believe that entering students are "very well prepared in writing," and in 2005 only 51 percent of high school graduates who took the ACT test met the college-readiness benchmark in reading, and only 21 percent in all four subjects (math, science, English, reading). Even in the manufacturing sector, employers say that literacy skills are critical, and in short supply. In 2001, members of the National Association of Manufacturers ranked "poor reading/writing skills" the #2 deficiency among current employees, and in 2005 38 percent of them agreed that high school produces workers with inadequate "reading and comprehension" skills.

As for remedial classes in college, the National Center for Education Statistics estimated that in 2004, 20 percent of freshmen students end up in remedial reading courses and 23 percent in remedial writing courses. In August 2006, the Alliance for Excellent Education estimated that two-year colleges spend $1.4 billion a year improving skills that should have been acquired in high school. The economy as a whole suffers, and the Alliance calculated, "Because too many students are not learning the basic skills needed to succeed in college or work while they are in high school, the nation loses more than $3.7 billion a year." The numbers are staggering. An April 2007 story in the *Miami Herald*, for instance, reported that at Miami Dade College and Broward Community College, four out of five entering students need remedial coursework and advising before they can even start college-level instruction. The cost to taxpayers tops $35 million annually. Less than 25 percent of enrollees earn a degree or certificate within three years (see Bierman).

But Bomer finds the benchmarks we prepared in light of those reports hopelessly out-of-date: "They describe an academic subject of English from 50 years ago, not the one that is practiced in most universities today." He belittles the "quaintly archaic" benchmarks for sticking to work and school, rather than engaging larger "life" literacies, and that's all he says about them. From there, in predictable steps, he turns his censure to the character of the people behind them. Absorbed in "the policing of correctness in employee prose," he alleges, they damage the very children they claim to help: "I am struck by how mean and weak their hopes are for our students and our future society."

Literary traditionalists might agree that the benchmarks overemphasize verbal skills suitable for the workplace and downplay humanistic learning, which includes immersion in the best literary traditions. But more Chaucer, Blake, and Woolf isn't what Bomer has in mind. Instead, he contends that adolescents already possess an advanced and creative literacy, just not the kind that we retrograde folks at the Diploma Project acknowledge.

> An ample and growing body of research shows us that adolescents are expert users of many and varied forms and technologies of literacy. Their practices are purposeful and sophisticated, and they use literacy to do the kinds of things people have always done with literacy. As most parents of adolescents know very well, kids are more likely to be expert at emerging information and communications technologies than their parents or their teachers are. They have sophisticated viewer literacies—understandings about how video, TV, and film work and vast reserves of knowledge

about how what they are watching now exists in dialogue with older stories, characters, and forms.

This is an extraordinary statement by the head of English teachers across the country, people delegated to tutor children and adolescents in verbal literacy and literary aptitude, not "viewer literacy." It recalls the student in the *Chronicle of Higher Education* symposium who cast her father as a dinosaur stuck in the library stacks, and her own generation as the digital avant-garde. To applaud young people for harboring "vast reserves of knowledge," to judge them "sophisticated" and "expert" with information, to claim that "They are inventing new forms of literature," as Bomer does later, is to slip into precisely the callow hubris that prompts teens to reject the certainties of their parents, and their books, too. Bomer wants to treat traditionalists as "archaic" and pessimistic scolds, and teens who love the Web and eschew books will agree. But the evidence from the knowledge and skill surveys isn't so easy to dismiss, nor are complaints from employers and the college remediation rates. In truth, the teens Bomer exalts are drowning in their own ignorance and a-literacy, and to aggrandize the minds and skills of the kids isn't just a rhetorical weapon to use against the alarmists. It feeds the generational consciousness that keeps kids from growing up.

BOMER'S DISCOURSE isn't unusual, to be sure, and for decades teachers have grown weary of hearing how many students pass through their classes without acquiring the rudiments of liberal education. The recourse to "viewer literacy," however, modifies the terms of the debate. It says that the import of books and the practice of literacy themselves have changed. No longer should we worry whether kids read enough books or not. Instead, we should recognize a new order of reading and text in the world, a newfangled cognition and knowledge. They don't read books? Well, they read other things.

They don't know any history? Well, maybe not history recorded in books, but they know other kinds.

That's the contention, and it echoes throughout the discussion of literacy today. Former Deputy Secretary of Education Eugene Hickok proclaims of the MTV generation, "They think differently, they act differently, they want to be engaged, they're more engaged than ever before, their attention span is quicker, they are not inclined to sit down and spend hours quietly reading a book. They're more inclined to be reading three or four books at one time while they multi-task on their Palm Pilots" (see Federation of American Scientists—we'll skip over the absurdity of their reading three or four books at once). Such assertions accept digital literacy as a full-fledged intellectual practice, a mode of reading and learning a lot more exciting and promising than the old kinds. In spite of the confidence, though, there is no "ample and growing body of research" on the digital facility of adolescents, only the commonplace assertion of their techno-aptitudes. The unmistakable sign of its spread comes from the young practitioners themselves, who evoke digital catchphrases with the coolness of veteran users. Here a 20-something contributor to a *USA Today* blog on "Generation Next" pronounces one as neatly as the professionals:

> Today's young people don't suffer from illiteracy; they just
> suffer from e-literacy. We can't spell and we don't know
> synonyms because there's less need to know. What smart
> person would devote hours to learning words that can be
> accessed at the click of a button? Spell-check can spell.
> Shift+F7 produces synonyms. What is wrong with relying on
> something that is perfectly reliable? (Andrukonis)

E-literacy—that's the new virtue, the intellectual feat of the rising generation. Alarmists and traditionalists interpret it as ignorance and a-literacy, but, the e-literacy fans retort, they only thus display their antiquarianism. In a June 2007 op-ed in the *Philadelphia Inquirer* entitled "With Prodigious Leaps, Children Move to the Technological Forefront," President Jonathan Fanton of the MacArthur Foundation claims that "today's digital youth are in the process of creating a new kind of literacy, which extends beyond the traditions of reading and writing into an evolving community of expression and problem-solving that is changing not only their world, but ours, as well." Young people shirk books, maybe so, but not because they're lazy and stupid. The twenty-first-century economy requires rapid communications, faster transfers of info, the reasoning goes, and ambitious teens don't have time to deliberate over a volume of Robert Frost or learn five new words a day. E-literacy derives not from bibliophobia, then, but from the miraculous and evolving advent of digital technology, the Information Age and the Electronic Word. The more young adults master the practices of digital life, the better they succeed. With the *American Freshman Survey* reporting in 2005 that 71 percent of students attend college "to be able to make more money" (up from 44.6 percent in 1971), e-literacy makes a lot more sense than book learning.

The e-literacy argument proceeds everywhere, and with so many benefits from technology shoring it up, bibliophiles have lost their primary rationale. Book reading doesn't seem to improve young people's money and prospects, so why do it? If the national leader of English teachers commends them for their viewer know-how, why spend four hours on a Sunday afternoon digging through *Middlemarch* or *Up from Slavery*? When science writer Steven Johnson appears on *The Colbert Report* and asserts that 12-year-olds who play *Civilization IV*, the second most popular game in 2005, "re-create the entire course of human economic and technological history," the screen rises into a better and faster teacher than the textbook. Bibliophiles end up in the rearguard, bereft of cultural capital, forced to reargue the case for books.

Most of the time, they lose. To argue against screen diversions is to take on an economic and cultural juggernaut, and an even stronger force, too: the penchants of adolescents. An April 2007 *Education Week* article whose header runs "Young people typically plug in to new technology far more often on their own time than in school," neatly illustrates the attitude. "When I step out of school, I have a pretty high tech life," a Providence, Rhode Island, high school senior tells the reporter. "When I step in school, I feel like I'm not me anymore. I have to jump into this old-fashioned thing where everything is restricted" (see Gewertz). Digital technology reflects his identity, books alienate him, teachers restrict him, and hundreds of peers echo his disquiet. Furthermore, they have a host of experts to reinforce the self-centered view, as educator and futurist Marc Prensky does just a few paragraphs later in the article. "School represents the past," he says. "After-school is where they are training themselves for the future. The danger is that as school becomes less and less relevant, it becomes more and more of a prison."

But however much the apologists proclaim the digital revolution and hail teens and 20-year-olds for forging ahead, they haven't explained a critical paradox. If the young have acquired so much digital proficiency, and if digital technology exercises their intellectual faculties so well, then why haven't knowledge and skill levels increased accordingly? As we've seen, wealth, cultural access, and education levels have climbed, but not intellectual outcomes. If the Information Age solicits quicker and savvier literacies, why do so many new entrants into college and work end up in remediation? Why do one-third of students who go straight to college out of high school drop out after one year (according to the National Center for Public Policy and Higher Education)? If their digital talents bring the universe of knowledge into their bedrooms, why don't they handle knowledge questions better? A 2004 study from the National Commission on Writing surveyed business leaders and found that a significant portion of them complain of serious reading and writing problems among new employees, forcing corporate America to spend approximately $3.1 billion annually on in-house literacy tutoring. "The skills of new college graduates are deplorable—across the board," one replied. Another grumbled, "Recent graduates aren't even aware when things are wrong." The American Political Science Association declared in 1998 that "current levels of political knowledge, political engagement, and political enthusiasm are so low as to threaten the vitality and stability of democratic politics in the United States," and few people would argue that the maturation of the wired generation, the "digital natives," has improved the climate. Digital habits have mushroomed, but reading scores for teens remain flat, and measures of scientific, cultural, and civic knowledge linger at abysmal levels. Why?

CHAPTER THREE

SCREEN TIME

The Apple Store at Lenox Square is clean and bright. The portal doesn't contain any words, just two white Apple logos set in black panels flanking the entry. In the display window to the right sit two hand-size iPods on a small stand with poster-size reproductions hanging behind them, one showing on its screen Bono singing in the spotlights, another with the cast of *The Office* seated glumly around a meeting table.

Step inside and the white walls, white lights, and ash floors rouse you from the dreary escalators, potted plants, and dull metal railings in the mall promenade. Laptop and desktop screens line the sides of the room and flash pictures of canny urban youths until someone touches the mouse and icons appear bidding customers to check email and browse the Web. Halfway back, iPods, photo printers, digital cameras, and video take over, with salespersons hovering eager to demonstrate. Two modest shelves run up the middle exhibiting games and books such as *GarageBand 3: Create and Record Music on a Mac, Final Draft* (a scriptwriting program for TV and film), *The Sims 2*, and various "Brainbuilding Games for Kids." A bright red rug marks the youngsters' section, where four screens rest on a low table with chairs that look like fuzzy black basketballs. Behind it rises the

Genius Bar, where three clerks in black T-shirts guide clients through digital snags as others wait on benches arranged in front of a large screen on the rear wall with a video streaming nonstop.

It's eleven o'clock on Friday morning and only 20 customers, all adults, have entered. By tomorrow afternoon, though, the Atlanta mall will overflow with teenagers, and packs of 16-year-olds and resolute young stragglers will pile into the Apple Store for an hour of sampling, surfing, and (sometimes) buying. An affable clerk with three-inch spikes in a Mohawk from forehead to nape responds with a smile when I ask him how many kids will arrive. "Oh, it'll be crazy," he chortles. On a weekday morning you can wander freely, but on Saturday afternoon with the kids in force, he says, "It takes a little bit of 'intentionality' to get around."

No other spot in the mall, at school, or at home provides so much concentrated and inviting fun and experimentation. Three doors away, Abercrombie & Fitch lures young shoppers with a 10-by-12-foot black-and-white photo of a shirtless male seen from the rear, his jeans sliding down his hips as he peers into a turbulent sky. Two floors below, the music/video shop f.y.e. stocks compact discs and movies in the standard layout, and a single bored employee nods behind the cash register. Farther down, the theaters have closed, but in the food court diners gobble pizza and cashew chicken while watching *Entertainment Tonight* on eight plasma screens hanging from the ceiling.

They sound like tepid fare set beside the joys and wonders of Apple offerings. And not only is the machinery ever-improving, ever more prosthetic. It has a special relationship to teens and 20-year-olds. More and more, it seems, the technology itself is their possession, their expression. The press release for a 2005 report by the Pew Internet & American Life Project on online usage has the grand subtitle "Youth are leading the transition to a fully wired and mobile nation." The report marvels that half the teenagers in the United States are not merely passive consumers. They are "content creators," making their own Web pages or posting their artwork, photos, stories, or videos online. People at Pew's Research Center call them the "Dot-Nets," director Scott Keeter says, "because of their technological savvy." They form the first generation reared on Google, never knowing a time when television meant ABC, NBC, CBS, PBS, and a local station showing reruns. They blink at the terms "LP," "station wagon," "Betamax," "IBM Selectric," "rabbit ears," and a thousand other apparatuses from their parents' time, and if they encountered them now they would hoot at the primitivism. A world with only land lines impresses them as ridiculously inconvenient. No cohort has witnessed such enabling advances in personal gadgetry. What perplexes their elders they act out as the natural thing to do, passing days and nights rapping comments into a blog, role-playing in a chat room, surfing paparazzi photos, logging onto *Facebook*, running *Madden NFL*, checking for voice messages, and uploading pictures of themselves while watching TV shows at the same rate they did before the other diversions appeared.

Keeter calls them savvy, and countless commentators recite their tech virtues with majestic phrases, as does *Get Ready: The Millennials Are Coming!*, a 2005 Forrester Research report whose Web summary announces: "The 'Millennials'—those born between 1980 and 2000—have an innate ability to use technology, are comfortable multitasking while using a diverse range of digital media, and literally demand interactivity as they construct knowledge." Young users don't just possess good skills—they have "innate ability." They don't just tinker online; they "construct knowledge." In his *Philadelphia Inquirer* op-ed, Jonathan Fanton effuses about digital kids who've "created communities the size of nations . . . mastered digital tools to create new techniques for personal expression . . . redefined the notion of 'play'"—all through games, message boards, and social networking. As we shall see, some research questions the Millennials' digital wisdom, but nobody doubts the connectedness of their lives. Indeed, the degree of their immersion in digital technology and screen media itself sets them apart.

Political commentators often observe that blogs have altered the way campaigns and elections work, but in 2004 a little more than half of the 4.1 million blogs counted by Perseus Development Corporation were kept by 13- to 19-year-olds. A July 2007 report sponsored by the National School Boards Association ("Creating and Connecting: Research and Guidelines on Online Social—and Educational—Networking") found that 30 percent of students with online access run their own blogs, and "More than one in 10 (12 percent) say they upload music or podcasts of their own creation at least weekly." Many of them, the study affirms, "are adventurous nonconformists who set the pace for their peers." Indeed, Glenn Reynolds, pioneering host of *InstaPundit.com*, believes that blogs have produced an "army of Davids," young and inquisitive Net users who free knowledge and information from the control of mainstream media and Big Government, although in truth, few of the under-30-year-olds' blogs have much political content (Pew found in 2005 that only 7 percent of 18- to 29-year-olds go online for "political news"). And in the cell phone field, an August 2006 *Wall Street Journal* article headed "Dialing into the Youth Market: Cellphone Services and Products Become Increasingly Tailored to Teenager Users" explains that teens provide most of the growth for the industry. Furthermore, they bring new demands that steer innovations in the market: "Phone executives say a high priority is making it possible for teens to access, from their cellphones, blogs, online photo galleries and social-networking sites" (see Ricketts). Indeed, a *Wall Street Journal* story seven months later predicted that cell phones will soon be the primary medium for streaming news clips, sports, network television shows, video and photo sharing, and advertising ("What's New in Wireless"; see Sharma), and we may expect youths to be the earliest adopters.

The daunting size of Generation DotNet energizes the digital trades, and the intensity of its digital thirst never seems to wane. The Kaiser Family Foundation's ongoing research project demonstrates how steadily screen activities saturate the younger populations. As noted earlier, Kaiser's Study of Entertainment Media and Health conducts surveys of the home and leisure lives of children and families, highlighting media types and exposure. In 2003, it released *Zero-to-Six: Electronic Media in the Lives of Infants, Toddlers, and Preschoolers*, a study of children's media exposure in the first six years of life. The American Academy of Pediatrics advises parents to keep two-year-olds and under away from the television screen altogether, and to restrict older children to one to two hours of educational programming per day. But the 1,000+ subjects in the Kaiser study, ranging from six months to six years old, went well beyond that. They averaged fully one hour and 58 minutes per day on screen media. That's three times the amount they devoted to reading or being read to (39 minutes per day). Children pass as many moments in front of a screen as they do playing outside (two hours and one minute), and the number of kids who let a day pass without enjoying screen images is less than the number of those who spend a day without opening a book.

The home environment supports the behaviors. One-third of the subjects (36 percent) reside in homes in which the television is on "always" or "most of the time." Half of the children occupy homes with three or more television sets in use, and 36 percent of them have one in their bedroom. Half the households have a video game player, and 49 percent of them have Internet access (since 2003, of course, that figure has climbed steadily), while only 34 percent subscribe to a newspaper.

We might assume that with children at such tender ages the screen activities follow a parent's directive. While father fights the traffic, mother must prepare dinner, and so she sets their two-year-old on the living room carpet and starts a *Sesame Street* video that the child soaks up agreeably for 30 minutes. In truth, however, most of the children have acquired enough knowledge of the screen to form preferences of their own, and they act on them. Fully 77 percent of them, the study found, turn the TV on by themselves, and two-thirds request particular shows, 71 percent a preferred video or DVD. Sixty-two percent change channels with the remote control, 36 percent install their own music CDs or tapes, 23 percent insert CD-ROMs into the computer, and 12 percent surf the Net in search of favorite Web sites. The media selection habits don't quite parallel the selection of a book from the shelf, either. Book browsing is sometimes an exploratory thing, with children finding stories and pictures they hadn't seen before. Each book is a new world, and the object itself is unique. Parents see the process unfold every time they take their four-year-olds to the public library and have to narrow down the checkouts to five books. The screen, however, is always the same, a generic object. There is nothing magical about it except its function as gateway to something else. Kids usually know exactly what they want and where they want to go, and they get there with a few mouse clicks or channel changes.

In the Kaiser study, television tops the list, but other screen habits fill ample daily minutes as well. In fact, while 73 percent of infants to six-year-olds watch TV every day, an equal percentage watches videos and DVDs. Eighteen percent use a computer and 9 percent play video games. For the four- to six-year-old group alone, the digital side of screen media jumps. One-quarter of them (27 percent) use a computer in a "typical day," and 64 percent know how to use a mouse.

For the *Zero-to-Six* report, surveyors collected data in spring 2003, and certainly the numbers have risen since then. The preschoolers in the study have almost finished elementary school by now, and they've refined their screen acumen at every grade level. Another study from Kaiser, released in March 2005, picked up the older age group and asked similar questions. Aiming to provide "reliable and objective data documenting the patterns and trends of media use among young people," *Generation M: Media in the Lives of 8–18-Year-Olds* collected information on recreational consumption—not school or work—from 2,032 third- to twelfth-graders through question-naires and week-long diaries. The foremost conclusion: the total amount of leisure time kids spend with media "is the equivalent of a full-time job." On average, the subjects in the study log six hours and 21 minutes a day. And because they spend many of those min-utes multitasking, playing a video game while listening to the radio, for instance, eight- to 18-year-olds actually take in eight and one-half hours of media content. Here's a breakdown of the percentage of kids who consume different media in an average day and for how long:

- watch television: 84 percent (3:04 hours)
- use a computer: 54 percent (48 minutes in online usage alone)
- read a magazine: 47 percent (14 minutes)
- read a book: 46 percent (23 minutes)
- play video games: 41 percent (32 minutes at console, 17 minutes with handheld)
- watch videos/DVDs: 39 percent (32 minutes)
- watch prerecorded TV: 21 percent (14 minutes)
- go to a movie: 13 percent

Add up the television times and they reach three hours and 18 minutes, and coupled with 49 minutes with a video game and 48 minutes online, they yield a daunting screen time of 295 minutes a day, 2,065 minutes per week. Book reading came in higher than the results from studies of late teens cited in the previous chapter, sug-gesting, perhaps, that the lower ages, eight- to 14-year-olds, pull the average up, or that many responses included homework reading with leisure reading. If reading included class assignments, the voluntary rate looks positively negligible alongside the screen options.

Once again, the home environment supports the pattern. Here's a tally of media access in the homes and in the bedrooms of eight- to 18-year-olds.

- television: in the home (99 percent), children's bedroom (68 percent)
- VCR/DVD player: home (97 percent), bedroom (54 percent)
- computer: home (86 percent), bedroom (31 percent)
- video game console: home (83 percent), bedroom (49 percent)

The 10-year-old's bedroom has become, as Kaiser puts it, a "multi-media center." Children leave the dinner table, which is often accompanied by network news, reruns of *Seinfeld*, and other 6 P.M. fare, and head off to their rooms to turn on their own shows or crank up iTunes while poring over some homework. Bored with that, they can check a *MySpace* forum, or play *Mortal Kombat*, or look at school pictures. The long division exercises await while the computer dings a new email coming through, the cell phone buzzes with a new message, and *Toonami* comes on in a half hour. They never need exit their bedroom doors, and in most households, parents won't interrupt them. For 55 percent of the eight- to 10-year-olds, parents don't lay down any rules for TV. For older teens, only 5 percent have parents who set limits on the video games they can play. The private access continues outside the home, too, with 55 percent of eight- to 18-year-olds taking a handheld video game player with them, and 65 percent carrying a portable music player.

Cell phones provide the mobility, and they encourage more initiative on the part of the kids. In a 2004 survey by NetDay, an initiative of Project Tomorrow, a nonprofit education group, more than half (58 percent) of the students in sixth through twelfth grade carried a cell phone, and 68 percent of those students took them to school. On campus, one-fifth of them had text and video/photo capabilities, no doubt producing thousands of funny and embarrassing snapshots that got passed around the cafeteria. A year later another NetDay survey came out, the findings published as *Our Voices, Our Future: Student and Teacher Views on Science, Technology, and Education* (sponsored by Bell South and Dell). Using the Internet to collect data from 185,000 students and 15,000 teachers, NetDay concluded that "Younger students are continuing to adopt more sophisticated technologies in the footsteps of their older siblings." Researchers asked students if they use various tools in a typical week, and while computers and cell phones came up at the expected high rates, other gadgets scored big as well.

- digital camera: 25 percent of third- through sixth-graders, 43 percent of sixth- through twelfth-graders
- video camera: 16 percent of third- through twelfth-graders, 22 percent of sixth- through twelfth-graders
- DVD or CD burner: 31 percent and 59 percent
- video game player: 55 percent and 61 percent

The way children and teens use this equipment grows more individualized by the year, too, NetDay found. Thirty percent of K–3 students have their own email accounts, and one-fifth of them say they prefer email to any other medium of communication. For sixth- through twelfth-graders, though, email already appears clunky. Overwhelmingly, they prefer Instant Messaging. They like variety, too. Thirty percent report using a computer, cell phone, DVD or CD burner, *and* a video game player on a weekly basis, a 10 percent jump from a year earlier. One-third admit that they update their personal Web sites "on a regular basis."

The expansion of media options and access never stops, and one wonders how sixth-graders juggle them all. But, to return to *Generation M*, a counterintuitive drift holds steady. With leisure time finite,

one would think that increased Internet and video game minutes
would cut into TV and radio time, but the Kaiser study found a contrary trend. Youngsters who spend more time with computers and
games also watch more television and listen to more radio. Multitasking enables it. As *Generation M* concludes, "media use begets
media use," and as more connections and feeds and streams and
channels enter their private space, kids assimilate them with accelerating ease, adding one without dropping another.

Forty-year-olds don't get it, the cluttered airspace, the joy in multiple input. Growing up in what appears to their offspring a sluggish
and elementary sensory ambiance, they welcome the latest invention as an add-on, something else to do besides reading the newspaper or watching a movie. Kids regard it differently. They mature in
and with the flashing, evolving multimedia environment, integrating
each development into a new whole, a larger Gestalt. They don't experience the next technology as a distraction or as a competition
with other diversions. It's an extra comfort, and it joins nicely with
the rest. As one of my students just declared last week in class, "I
can't concentrate on my homework without the TV on. The silence
drives me crazy."

The craving for input begins in the home, and as a follow-up to
Generation M revealed, parents understand it well from the earliest
ages. In May 2006, Kaiser released *The Media Family: Electronic Media in the Lives of Infants, Toddlers, Preschoolers, and Their Parents*.
The study produced similar findings of media immersion for six-
month- to six-year-olds, but added observations by parents about
their children's habits. Kaiser assembled fathers and mothers into focus groups that reflected rates of media consumption found in the
national survey, and then posed questions about reasons and outcomes. The predictable answer quickly followed: setting kids in front
of the screen frees up time for cooking, cleaning, or just plain rest. A
single mother coming home from work needs a few moments to re-
group, and a beloved DVD keeps the children docile and preoccu-

pied. A mother from Columbus, Ohio, reports, "He's a good little boy. He won't bother anything. He won't get into stuff. He's glued to the TV." A Denver mother who'd recently lost her job recalls that when she arrived home that day she could say, "Let's watch *Finding Nemo*, kids. Here are some chicken strips, here are sippy cups—I'll see you in about an hour and a half." Half the parents agreed that television calms their children, while only one in six noted that it pumps them up. Three in ten installed TV sets in the kids' bedrooms because it helps them fall asleep (and lets parents watch their own shows in the living room). With DVDs, video games, and computers added to television, the division of tastes between younger and older family members is handled smoothly, parents have more ways to pacify their kids, and screen minutes climb accordingly.

Some parents feel guilty about the virtual babysitting, but not as much as they would if they let the children play with blocks on the kitchen floor while mother stepped around them while washing dishes. The screen, they contend, has educational benefits. Kids learn from what they watch. One mother from Irvine, California, insisted, "Anything they are doing on the computer I think is learning." And another parent: "Out of the blue one day my son counted to five in Spanish. I knew immediately that he got that from *Dora*." And another: "My daughter knows . . . her letters from *Sesame Street*. I haven't had to work with her on them at all." One parent highlighted the social lessons imparted through the screen: "I think they are exposed to a little bit more diversity. I think that it's good for them to be comfortable with that . . . to know that it's okay for everyone to be different." Yes, the children play alone, but they learn, too, so that as the new technologies relieve harried parents, they also improve impressionable little minds.

Left to themselves nightly with three screen options, wired for music and podcast as they hit the treadmill, reaching in their pocket for an email between classes, stocked with 600 cell phone minutes a month, a DVD collection by age 12 . . . young Americans tune in and turn on as routinely and avidly as they eat lunch. They "live" technology the way high school garage bands in the seventies lived rock 'n' roll, sporting long hair and fraying jeans, idolizing Page and Richards, and blasting *Houses of the Holy, Get Your Wings,* and *Ted Nugent* all weekend. Except that what was then a short-term fad for a sub-sub-group of juniors and seniors whom the rest of us thought were a set of cool outsiders is now a thoroughgoing lifestyle for the majority of students from kindergarten upward. "Without question," *Generation M* ends, "this generation truly *is* the media generation," and new and old media practices have settled into essential youth rituals. It starts early, with researchers finding in one study that by three months of age around 40 percent of children are regular watchers of television, DVDs, or videos, and by 24 months the rate reaches 90 percent (Zimmerman et al., "Television and DVD/Video Viewing in Children Younger than 2 Years"). In 2002, in *Media Unlimited: How the Torrent of Images and Sounds Overwhelms Our Lives,* Todd Gitlin phrased it in a simple existential axiom: *"being with media."*

In Pew Research's 2006 survey of cell phone use, 32 percent of 18- to 29-year-olds acknowledge that "they couldn't live without their cell." A January 2007 study by Pew, *How Young People View Their Lives, Futures, and Politics: A Portrait of "Generation Next,"* found that about half the 18- to 25-year-olds interviewed had sent or received a text message over the phone the previous day, and more than four in 10 "Nexters" have created a personal profile on a social networking site such as *MySpace.* In a parallel study of younger ages, Pew discovered that fully 55 percent of all 12- to 17-year-olds have created a personal profile page, and 48 percent of them visit social networking Web sites at least once a day (*Social Networking and Teens: An Overview,* 2007). A follow-up Pew study, *Teens, Privacy & Online Social Networks* (April 2007), reported that one in four online teens make friends through the Web, and their virtual social life is a genuinely multimedia exchange. Three-quarters of social networking teens post photos online, and one in five posts videos. In early 2007, Harris Interactive surveyed teens and tweens (eight- to 12-year-olds) for their video game usage and found that the average tween plays 13 hours per week, the average teen 14 hours per week. About one in 12 of them counted as clinically addicted. Their social/ visual habits have so proliferated that Nielsen//NetRatings could report in a July 2006 press release, "YouTube U.S. Web Traffic Grows 75 Percent Week over Week," ranking it the fastest-growing Web brand for the year. And a press release two months earlier from Nielsen//NetRatings declared, "Social Networking Sites Grow 47 Percent, Year over Year, Reaching 45 Percent of Web Users." The growth rate of *MySpace* reached an astronomical 367 percent.

No wonder they associate technology with their leisure, with their distinguishing youthfulness. The newer screens become a generational hinge, allowing 68 percent of 18- to 25-year-olds (according to Pew's *Generation Next* report) to "see their generation as unique and distinct from other generations." The writers of *Generation Next* echo the opinion: "This generation's relation with technology is truly unique." And while 18- to 25-year-olds claim uniqueness for themselves, they grant it much less so (44 percent) to the previous generation. After all, their elders may have had the Sexual Revolution and Civil Rights, *The Breakfast Club* and *Less Than Zero*, but Generation Next grasps its predecessors' ideals and icons while experiencing something no youth group has before: the Digital Revolution. They play rock 'n' roll and hook up at parties just like Boomers and X-ers did, but their parents never loaded a thousand songs into a palm-size gadget when they were 18, or sent a message to 50 friends at once with a double-click, or kept a blog. And it is the youngsters themselves discovering novel practices. "They are innovative users of technology," NetDay's 2005 report gushes, "adopting new technologies to support their learning and their lifestyles."

The digital accoutrements signify much more than a lifestyle, too, more than yet another youth cohort's rebellious social mores and personal tastes. Digital habits reach down into their brains. As kids

fixate on the twenty-first-century screen, they learn to count and
spell, cut and paste, manage information, relate to others, and "construct knowledge." New technologies induce new aptitudes, and
bundled together in the bedroom they push consciousness to diver-
sify its attention and multiply its communications. Through blogs
and Listservs, young Americans join virtual communities, cultivating
interests and voicing opinions. Video games quicken their spatial intelligence. Group endeavors such as *Wikipedia* and reality gaming
nurture collaborative problem-solving skills. Individuals who've
grown up surrounded by technology develop different hard-wiring,
their minds adapted to information and entertainment practices and
speeds that minds maturing in pre-digital habitats can barely comprehend, much less assimilate.

That's the claim. Screen time is cerebral, and it generates a breakthrough intelligence. E-literacy isn't just knowing how to download
music, program an iPod, create a virtual profile, and comment on a
blog. It's a general deployment capacity, a particular mental flexibil-
ity. E-literacy accommodates hypermedia because e-literates possess
hyperalertness. Multitasking entails a special cognitive attitude toward the world, not the orientation that enables slow concentration
on one thing—a sonnet, a theorem—but a lightsome, itinerant awareness of numerous and dissimilar inputs. In a white paper entitled
"Confronting the Challenges of Participatory Culture: Media Education for the 21st Century," MIT professor Henry Jenkins sketches the
new media literacies in precisely such big, brainy terms: *distributed
cognition*—the "ability to interact meaningfully with tools that expand mental capacities" (search engines, etc.); *collective intelligence*—
the "ability to pool knowledge and compare notes with others toward
a common goal" (Listservs, etc.); *transmedia navigation*—the "ability
to follow the flow of stories and information across multiple modali-
ties"; and so on. A report from EDUCAUSE affirms, "We take it to be
self-evident that college-bound digital natives are in fact *digital co-*

gnoscenti, sophisticates, and perhaps even *digital connoisseurs*" (*ECAR Study of Undergraduate Students and Information Technology,* 2006).

Over and over, commentators stress the mental advance, the learning side over the fun and fantasy side. In describing *Second Life,* the virtual universe in which people log on as themselves or as make-believe identities, become "residents," and manufacture their own settings, the *Wikipedia* entry claims that users "learn new skills and mature socially." When reading expert Professor James Gee, author of *What Video Games Have to Teach Us about Learning and Literacy,* started to play a video game for the first time, he discovered a whole new consciousness. "Suddenly," he avows, "all my baby-boomer ways of learning and thinking, for which I had heretofore received ample rewards, did not work." At a panel on "Technology and Community" at the 2006 Aspen Institute, humanitarian activist and architect Cameron Sinclair announced, "there is a real problem with education in the U.S., and, you know what, the students know it more than the teachers do, and they're beginning to mobilize [through the Web], and they're forming their own ways of learning." In February 2007, Jonathan Fanton, president of the MacArthur Foundation, announced a new digital youth initiative by wondering, "Might it be that, for many, the richest environment for learning is no longer in the classroom, it is outside the classroom—online and after school?" The MacArthur project is called Digital Media and Learning, a five-year $50 million initiative to study how digital technologies affect young people's lives. At the same event, University of Wisconsin Professor David Williamson Shaffer, a "Game Scientist," asserted that computers alter "the way people think in the digital age," and that the invention of computers ranks with "the development of language itself" in the advancement of human intelligence. Consider that analogy: the caveman stands to the average 1950s person as the average 1950s person stands to us.

With so much money supporting digital research, and so many

students going online hourly, the faith in young people's digital intelligence reaches well into the academic sphere, and the academic
press has made the students' digital mentality into a topic of the day.
Here's a paragraph from "The Net Generation in the Classroom," a
2005 story in the *Chronicle of Higher Education* that explores the
prospect of aligning college teaching with the entering classes'
e-mindset.

> Born between roughly 1980 and 1994, the Millennials have
> already been pegged and defined by academics, trend spotters,
> and futurists: They are smart but impatient. They expect
> results immediately. They carry an arsenal of electronic
> devices—the more portable the better. Raised amid a barrage
> of information, they are able to juggle a conversation on
> Instant Messenger, a Web-surfing session, and an iTunes
> playlist while reading *Twelfth Night* for homework.

The author, Scott Carlson, adds a skeptical note at the end—
"Whether or not they are absorbing the fine points of the play is a
matter of debate"—but the main voice in the article, librarian and
higher-ed consultant Richard T. Sweeney, has no doubts. Millennials
"want to learn," he observes, "but they want to learn only what they
have to learn, and they want to learn it in a different style that is best
for them." The approach grants remarkable discretion to the kids, assuming that they know what "is best," and that their preferences
mark a distinct "learning style." Another voice in the article, educator
and futurist Marc Prensky, likewise insists that young people have
turned learning itself into a whole different process. In 2004, Prensky stated in a paper entitled "The Death of Command and Control"
that "The unprecedented changes in technology . . . have led to **new
patterns of thinking**, especially in young people" (emphasis in original). Here in the *Chronicle* piece, in casual tones that belie the grave

transformation at work, he wonders, "The things that have tradition-
ally been done—you know, reflection and thinking and all that
stuff—are in some ways too slow for the future. . . . Is there a way to
do those things faster?"

The fervor spills freely in public discourse as well. When Steven
Johnson published *Everything Bad Is Good for You: How Today's Popular Culture Is Actually Making Us Smarter* in early 2005, it sparked
across-the-country newspaper reviews, radio spots, and television
appearances, including one on *The Daily Show.* The appeal was overt,
and as Johnson observes on his Web site, "The title says it all." As a
specimen of contrary mischievousness, an anti-anti-pop culture polemic, the book offered a crisp and witty argument for the good of
the mouse and the console, and also for the helpful tutelage of
twenty-first-century sitcoms and next-version video games. Everyone with a stake in the rise of screen diversions or who treasured the
virtual universe seized upon the thesis, and Johnson unveiled it with
élan. To turn a commonsense notion on its head—"TV is good, not
bad"—was a winning tactic, and Johnson added an image of himself
as defender of a pop culture world disdained by widespread powers
as vulgar, violent, and infantile. While Joe Lieberman railed against
the "amoral pop-culture threat to public values," as *Time* magazine
put it in 2000 (see Poniewozik), and as Hillary Clinton fretted "about
the content [of video games] and what that's doing to my child's
emotional psychological development," as she stated at the Kaiser
Foundation's release of the report *Generation M, Everything Bad Is
Good for You* turned it all around. In the last 30 years, Johnson insisted, popular culture has become "more complex and intellectually
challenging . . . demanding more cognitive engagement . . . making
our minds sharper." Often the content of popular culture is coarse
and inane, he conceded, but the formal elements—rules, plotlines,
feedback, levels, interactivity—have grown more sophisticated, making today's games and reality shows into "a kind of cognitive work-

out" that hones mental gifts. Screen diversions provide something more lasting and effectual than "healthy messages." They inculcate "intellectual or cognitive virtues," aptitudes for spatialization, pattern recognition, and problem solving, virtues that reflect twenty-first-century demands better, in fact, than do traditional knowledge and reading skills.

Once again, the thinking element prevails, and screens are praised for the way they shape the consciousness of users, not pass along to them ideas and values. The case for cognitive benefits begins with a fundamental feature of games: "far more than books or movies or music," Johnson asserts, "games force you to make decisions." True, books involve judgment, but they don't allow readers to determine the next chapter or decide a character's fate. Game realities, by contrast, let them steer the car, invest money, and grab weapons. The content is juvenile, yes, but "because learning how to think is ultimately about learning how to make the right decisions," game activity evokes a collateral learning that carries over to users' real lives. As Malcolm Gladwell noted in his fawning review in *The New Yorker*, "When you play a video game, the value is in how it makes you think." The images may be flashy and jumbled, the action silly and inconsequential, but when you play the game, Johnson explains, "It's not about tolerating or aestheticizing chaos; it's about finding order and meaning in the world, and making decisions that help create that order."

The advantages continue with the progressive complexity of television shows. *Hill Street Blues* introduced multiple plotlines and character tensions, Johnson recalls. *The Simpsons* and *Seinfeld* abound with allusions and double entendres, forcing viewers to work harder to "fill in" the context in which they make sense. The pace of their delivery makes the old comedies, *Andy Griffith* et al., seem like slow motion. Reality shows are crass, but they enact "elaborately staged group psychology experiments." Johnson alludes to *The Apprentice* and says that, compared with *The Price Is Right*, it's "an intellectual masterpiece."

All of them signal an evolution in programming from the linear plots and dull patter of *Good Times* and *Starsky and Hutch*, and the more clever and modish shows activate the minds of those who watch them. When young viewers catch reruns of shows from the sixties, they chuckle at the low-tech action and fidget at the understimulating imagery and camera work. Pop culture hasn't plunged downward into puerile deviancy and artificial violence and general stupidity, Johnson concludes. It has fostered "a race to the top," and the moralists and doomsayers and elitists with their sky-is-falling pronouncements should cease. Audiences are smarter.

The claim is bold, and it ultimately rests not upon the structural elements of screen materials, but upon the cognitive outcomes for those who consume them. If we stick to the latter, several objections to Johnson's breezy applause stand out. For instance, buried in the depths of the Kaiser report *Generation M* is a startling finding about different media use and student achievement. It shows that leisure reading of any kind correlates more closely with a student's grades than any other media. While eight- to 18-year-olds with high and low grades differed by only one minute in TV time (186 to 187 minutes), they differed in reading time by 17 minutes, 46 to 29— a huge discrepancy in relative terms (a 36 percent drop in leisure reading for kids with low grades), one that suggests that TV doesn't have nearly the intellectual consequences that reading does. Furthermore, on Johnson's "multiple plotlines are more sophisticated" criterion, dramas that fail include not only *Dragnet* and *Kung Fu* but also *Oedipus* (Sophocles), *Medea* (Seneca), and *Phédre* (Racine). The complexity he approves lies wholly on the surface—plotlines and verbal play—while other complexities (moral, psychological, and philosophical) go unremarked. Finally, while Johnson neatly divides form from content, the act of decision-making isn't so distinct from the things decided upon. The content of screen substance—at its worst, juvenile loves and lusts, blood and guts, distortions of historical fact, petty clashes of reality contestants—is more important than he thinks.

In May 2007, another study appeared showing long-term outcomes for television viewing, and it relied on long-term observations by trained researchers. Published as "Extensive Television Viewing and the Development of Attention and Learning Difficulties During Adolescence" in *Archives of Pediatrics & Adolescent Medicine*, the research tracked children in 678 families in upstate New York at ages 14, 16, and 22 years. The article abstract summarizes:

> Frequent television viewing during adolescence was
> associated with elevated risk for subsequent attention and
> learning difficulties after family characteristics and prior
> cognitive difficulties were controlled. Youths who watched 1
> or more hours of television per day at mean age 14 years
> were at elevated risk for poor homework completion,
> negative attitudes toward school, poor grades, and long-term
> academic failure. Youths who watched 3 or more hours of
> television per day were the most likely to experience these
> outcomes. In addition, youths who watched 3 or more hours
> of television per day were at elevated risk for subsequent
> attention problems and were the least likely to receive
> postsecondary education. (Johnson et al.)

Contrast that bleak assessment derived over several years with the evidence-lite enthusiasm of Johnson and other pop culture fans.

But while Johnson cites few of the knowledge/skill/habit surveys we've seen so far, he does point to one significant intellectual trend: average intelligence. In the general fund of mental talent, something remarkable has happened. IQ scores have risen markedly over the century, about three points per decade since before World War II, doing so, Johnson observes, at the same time that popular culture has expanded and evolved. It's the so-called Flynn Effect, named after New Zealand political scientist James Flynn, who noted the rise (which is masked by the fact that the test is re-normed every few years). In the early 1980s, Flynn surveyed studies in which subjects took IQ tests dating from different years and disclosed the rising pattern. For instance, one experiment recorded a group scoring 103.8 on a 1978 test leaping to 111.3 on a 1953 version of the same test. Successive tests aimed to keep the average at 100 points, but to do so they had to become harder.

The question is, Why has intelligence jumped? Cognitive psychologists explain the gain variously, noting improved nutrition, better early schooling, smaller families, and wider acquaintance with tests themselves. With the largest increases occurring in the area of "spatial reasoning," however, some researchers attribute them to escalating cognitive demands of an increasingly visual environment. Johnson agrees, and gives screen diversions most of the credit. With the proliferation of screens, people have grown up in a more visually challenging habitat. Brains have developed with more complex spatial stimuli than before, and teens experienced with screen technology now handle those IQ questions showing a chart of numbers with one vacant space—fill in the space with the correct number or shape—more adroitly than teens who are not.

IQ tests are controversial, of course, and questions of cultural bias, test-taking situations, and the fuzzy definition of intelligence have made them easy targets. Furthermore, research indicates that the bulk of the Flynn Effect has taken place in the lower percentiles, which have raised the average but not touched the upper tiers. Geniuses yesterday are just as smart as geniuses today. Still, the overall advances in IQ scores signify too sweeping and consistent a change to downplay, and the idea that more visual stimuli in children's lives should yield higher visual aptitudes makes intuitive sense. With IQ scores complementing it, and so many voices in academia, foundations, popular journalism, and the entertainment industries pushing the point, the connection of screen time to new learning styles, visual intelligence, media literacy, and other cognitive progressions seems sure. It is reasonable to think that media-wise youths have minds more attuned to visual information, that multitasking hours grant them a more mobile consciousness.

Maybe that's the case, but if so, then Johnson and other votaries of the screen have something else to explain. It's the question we ended with in the previous chapter. Why haven't knowledge and skill levels followed the same path? If cognitive talents rise correspondingly with the proliferation of screens and the sophistication of shows and games, why hasn't a generation of historically informed, civically active, verbally able, and mathematically talented young adults come forth and proven the cultural pessimists and aged curmudgeons wrong?

Surprisingly, the IQ issue suggests an answer, and it works against those who invoke it to promote the benefits of the screen. For, while incontestable in its data, the Flynn Effect has an extraordinary generational implication. Assuming that scores have indeed risen three points per decade, psychologist Ulric Neisser laid out the repercussions in a 1997 article in *American Scientist:*

> If a representative sample of the American children of
> 1997 were to take that 1932 test, their average IQ would
> come out to be around 120. This would put about one-
> quarter of the 1997 population above the 130 cutoff for
> "very superior"—10 times as many as in 1932. Does that
> seem plausible?
>   If we go by more recent norms instead, we arrive at an
> equally bizarre conclusion. Judging the American children of
> 1932 by today's standards—considering the scores they
> would have obtained if they had somehow taken a test
> normalized this year—we find that their average IQ would

have been only about 80! Hardly any of them would have scored "very superior," but nearly one-quarter would have appeared to be "deficient." Taking the tests at face value, we face one of two possible conclusions: Either America is now a nation of shining intellects, or it was then a nation of dolts.

Two possibilities, both extreme, yet both in accord with the notion that pop culture makes us smarter, that better tools make better minds, that more wiring and more channels yield more intelligence. Either way, we should notice momentous signs and wonders of intellect all around us.

Flynn himself recognized in 1987 that the Effect should have thrown us into an era of genius, and that we should be enjoying "a cultural renaissance too great to be overlooked." Needless to say, the 1980s fell far short, and Flynn found no evidence in Europe that mathematical or scientific discovery had increased in the preceding decades, adding as well that "no one has remarked on the superiority of contemporary schoolchildren." So, he concluded, IQ scores must measure something less than general intelligence. Observing that results for verbal and mathematical tests hadn't increased at nearly the rate that those for spatial-reasoning tests did, he characterized the intelligence measured by IQ tests as an "abstract problem-solving ability." The more tests emphasize "learned content" such as vocabulary, math techniques, and cultural knowledge, the less the Flynn Effect shows up. The more they involve "culturally reduced" material, puzzles and pictures that require no historical or verbal context, the more the gains surface. Moreover, the significance of those gains apart from the test itself diminishes. "We know people solve problems on IQ tests; we suspect those problems are so detached, or so abstracted from reality," Flynn remarked, "that the ability to solve them can diverge over time from the real-world problem-solving ability called intelligence."

Flynn's analysis explains the curious bifurcation in the intellectual lives of young adults. On one hand, they navigate the multimedia environment like pros, wielding four email accounts and two virtual identities, jumping from screen to keypad to iPod without pause, creating "content" and expressing themselves to the world. On the other hand, they know remarkably little about the wider world, about civics, history, math, science, and foreign affairs, and their reading and writing skills remain at 1970s levels. If Johnson, Richard Sweeney, Randy Bomer, and, more important, some serious cognitive researchers are right to link screen activities to higher intelligence, we may agree with them partway, but, with Flynn, limit the intelligence that screen activities produce. The screen doesn't involve learning per se, but, as Sweeney says, a particular "learning style," not literacy in general, but "viewer literacy" (Bomer's term). It promotes multitasking and discourages single-tasking, hampering the deliberate focus on a single text, a discrete problem. "Screen-mindedness" prizes using search engines and clicking 20 Web sites, not the plodding, 10-hour passage through a 300-page novel. It searches for information, fast, too impatient for the long-term acquisition of facts and stories and principles. As an elementary school principal told me last year, when the fifth-grade teachers assign a topic, the kids proceed like this: go to Google, type keywords, download three relevant sites, cut and paste passages into a new document, add transitions of their own, print it up, and turn it in. The model is information retrieval, not knowledge formation, and the material passes from Web to homework paper without lodging in the minds of the students.

Technophiles celebrate the ease and access, and teens and young adults derive a lesson from them. If you can call up a name, a date, an event, a text, a definition, a calculation, or a law in five seconds of key-punching, why fill your mind with them? With media feeds so solicitous, the slow and steady methods of learning seem like a bunch of outmoded and counterproductive exercises. In this circumstance, young people admit the next connection, the new gadget, smoothly into their waking hours, but the older "learning styles," the parents' study habits, are crowded out. Years of exposure to screens prime young Americans at a deep cognitive level to multitasking and inter-activity. Perhaps we should call this a certain kind of intelligence, a novel screen literacy. It improves their visual acuity, their mental readiness for rushing images and updated information. At the same time, however, screen intelligence doesn't transfer well to non-screen experiences, especially the kinds that build knowledge and verbal skills. It conditions minds against quiet, concerted study, against imagination unassisted by visuals, against linear, sequential analysis of texts, against an idle afternoon with a detective story and nothing else.

This explains why teenagers and 20-year-olds appear at the same time so mentally agile and culturally ignorant. Visual culture im-proves the abstract spatialization and problem solving, but it doesn't complement other intelligence-building activities. Smartness there parallels dumbness elsewhere. The relationship between screens and books isn't benign. As "digital natives" dive daily into three visual media and two sound sources as a matter of disposition, of deep mental compatibility, not just taste, ordinary reading, slow and uni-form, strikes them as incompatible, alien. It isn't just boring and ob-solete. It's irritating. A Raymond Chandler novel takes too long, an Emily Dickinson poem wears them down. A history book requires too much contextual knowledge, and science facts come quicker through the Web than through *A Brief History of Time.* Bibliophobia is the syndrome. Technophiles cast the young media-savvy sensibility as open and flexible, and it is, as long as the media come through a screen or a speaker. But faced with 100 paper pages, the digital mind turns away. The bearers of e-literacy reject books the way eBay ad-dicts reject bricks-and-mortar stores.

Or rather, they throw them into the dustbin of history. In the video "Are Kids Different Because of Digital Media?" sponsored by the MacArthur Foundation as part of its 2006 Digital Learning proj-

ect, one young person declares as a truism that "books are not the
standard thing for learning anymore." Another divulges, "My parents
question me why I don't have my books. . . . The books are online
now, so you don't really need the books." They back their dismissal
up with their purchases. In 1990, according to the *Consumer Expenditure Survey* (Bureau of Labor Statistics), the average person under
25 spent $75 on reading and $344 on television, radio, and sound
equipment. In 2004, reading spending dropped to a measly $51,
while TV, radio, and sound climbed to $500. Imagine the propor-
tions if computers were added to the mix.

The rejection of books might be brushed aside as just another
youthful gripe, today's version of the longstanding resistance by kids
to homework. But the kids aren't the only ones opposing books to
screens and choosing the latter. In 2005, Steven Johnson stated in a
Canadian Broadcasting interview that "reading books and playing
video games are equally beneficial, roughly and in distinct ways."
Around the same time, however, he wrote an article in *Wired* magazine with a provocative either/or subtitle: "Pop Quiz: Why Are IQ
Test Scores Rising Around the Globe? (Hint: Stop reading the great
authors and start playing *Grand Theft Auto.*)" A 16-year-old boy who
hates reading could hardly concoct a better rationale for his C grades
in English class. In the article, Johnson rehearses the Flynn Effect,
then highlights the test questions that produce the largest gains,
those involving spatial problem solving and pattern recognition.
"This is not the kind of thinking that happens when you read a book
or have a conversation with someone or take a history exam," he observes, and for this kind of aptitude, "the best example of brain-
boosting media may be video games." Johnson inserts a few cautionary
remarks, noting that the real test of media-inspired intelligence will
come when the generation of kids who "learned to puzzle through
the visual patterns of graphic interfaces before they learned to read"
reaches adulthood and provides a new round of IQ scores. But his
enthusiasm is clear, and it's all on the side of games. Kids may look

no further than the subtitle to justify their multitasking, nonreading lives. Forget your books, even the "great" ones, and grab the joystick. When your parents bother you about it, tell them you do it for your own brain development.

With a thousand marketers and stores to entice them, and popular commentators backing them up, teens and 20-year-olds hear the book-pushing voices of teachers and librarians as pesky whispers. They vote with their feet. One day after I entered the Apple Store at Lenox, as young customers flooded the floor on a Saturday afternoon, I went to the Buckhead library five minutes away. Only eight teens and 20-year-olds were there in the entire building, half of them at a computer station. Clusters of small children climbed around the kiddie section, a half-dozen elderly folks sat quietly in the periodicals room, and middle-aged women browsed the fiction stacks. The very young and the middle and elder ages might make the library a weekend destination, but the 13- to 29-year-old group had other plans.

On those days when teens and twenty-somethings do visit the library, they don't give up their interests, the technology-over-books disposition. Fortunately for them, the library now offers both, and the kids make their choice clear. At every university library I've entered in recent years, a cheery or intent sophomore sits at each computer station tapping out emails in a machine-gun rhythm. Upstairs, the stacks stand deserted and silent. Audiovisuals at the library draw more attention every year, and books are losing out as the center of attraction for younger patrons. From 1994 to 2004 at the St. Louis Public Library, for instance, the percentage of total item circulation made up of books fell from 82 to 64 percent, while audiovisuals doubled from 18 to 36 percent. In New Orleans from 1999 to 2003, book circulation dropped by 130,000 while audiovisuals rose 8,000. As a result, for libraries to survive in the digital future, many librarians and administrators have determined that they must transform themselves from book-lending institutions to multimedia information centers. In just one year, 2000 to 2001, the number of public-use Internet terminals in public libraries jumped from 99,453 to 122,798, a 23 percent increase (National Center for Education Statistics, *Public Libraries in the United States, 1993–2001*). The title of the New York Public Library's 2005 annual report declaims the shift: *The Digital Age of Enlightenment*. A story in the *Wall Street Journal* titled "Libraries Beckon, But Stacks of Books Aren't Part of the Pitch" (see Conkey) found that even academic libraries join the trend: "Threatened with irrelevance, the college library is being reinvented—and books are being de-emphasized. The goal: Entice today's technology-savvy students back into the library with buildings that blur the lines between library, computer lab, shopping mall and living room" (see Conkey).

The Apple Store couldn't be happier. Apple favors the screens-over-books setup, and the message came through loud and clear in summer 2005 when I first spotted one of its outlets. It was in Arlington, Virginia, two blocks from the Clarendon Metro station, where a bunch of trademark shops had opened (Whole Foods, Ann Taylor, Crate & Barrel) and energized a suburban village, drawing hundreds of loungers and promenaders for the day. My wife and I sauntered along the street on a Sunday afternoon, pushing our son in a stroller, enjoying an ice cream, and hearing a Janet Jackson song pumping through speakers hidden in the planters lining the sidewalk. We paused outside the glistening façade, eyeing the sleek design and bustling atmosphere of the place. It had the same layout of goods as the Lenox Square location, and store personnel drifted throughout demonstrating the latest gadgets to curious customers as if they, too, marveled at the wizardry. No need to make a hard sell here. The machines marketed themselves.

Except for the entry. Apple had arranged a display inside the plate-glass window in front that posed a decisive lifestyle choice to anyone who passed by. It had three parts, top, middle, and bottom. At the top was a 15-foot-wide and three-foot-tall photograph hanging from the ceiling and mounted on posterboard showing three shelves of books, mostly classics of literature and social science. Along the bottom was a parallel photograph of serious books, two shelves running from the side wall to the store entrance. In the break between them was propped a real shelf, smooth and white and long, with five lustrous ivory laptops set upon it, their screens open to the street.

The shelf had a caption: "The only books you'll need." It didn't say, "Here's the new Apple model, the best ever!" No announcements about speed or weight or price. Nothing on compatibility or wireless features. Usually, advertisers present a good as preferable to other brands of the same good—say, auto insurers promising the best rates—but in this case, Apple offered the laptop as preferable to something entirely different: books. In fact, it proclaimed, the laptop has rendered all those books pictured in the display window obsolete. Who needs them? The computer is now the **only** book you need. Many books and journals you can find online, especially now that the Google project is well under way. And soon enough, e-publishers predict, all books will appear in digital format, making hardcover and paperback books something of a curiosity, like card catalogs and eight-track tapes. Already, with the Internet, we have enough handy information to dispense with encyclopedias, almanacs, textbooks, government record books, and other informational texts.

That was the argument behind the declaration, and with so many techno-marvels inside, one could understand a 15-year-old absorbing the slogan as patently true. While everything else inside the store looked positive and pluralistic, with books in the picture the marketing turned aggressive and territorial. Apple set up an explicit antagonism, not books and computers, but books vs. computers, and it backed it up with a blooming, buzzing profusion of electronic gifts on sale inside. It even provided pictures of the very books that the e-book eclipsed. When I showed my wife the display (and had her snap a photograph of it), she proposed, "Maybe when they say 'the only books' they mean to include the books in the picture, too."

"C'mon," I replied. "Maybe the people inside are just kidding," she suggested. In fact, though, Apple had erected similar displays all across the country as part of a national marketing campaign to reach college students during back-to-school time. Culture critic Virginia Postrel termed it "The Apple Store's Campaign Against Books," and provided a picture of another store window just like this one. "Just in case there are any students who still read books," she commented, "the Apple Store wants them to know that paper technology is obsolete. After all, if it's not online, it's not important. Right?" Indeed, Apple didn't have any of those books for sale inside, and it certainly wasn't telling customers to leave Apple once they made a purchase and head 100 feet away to Barnes & Noble. For the average teenager looking for the latest in iTunes, the titles in the pictures meant nothing, and the display assured them that they do, indeed, mean nothing.

We should recognize the consumer reality at work here. In our varied and prosperous society, we assume that more choices mean more freedom and pleasure, and that newer, better technology provides more leisure time and spending money. Wealth generates wealth, and the advent of one consumer pleasure doesn't necessitate the loss of another. In this case, though, the things sought—young people's time and money—are finite. It's a zero-sum game. The dollars they spend on books are not spent on *QuickTime7*. The minutes they spend reading books are not spent playing *Vortex*. The more digital matter fills young people's bedrooms and hours, the less will books touch their lives, for you can't multitask with *The Sound and the Fury* or with *King Lear*. Most of the time, the marketing of one commodity doesn't include the denigration of another, unrelated commodity. A commercial for one car rental firm might dramatize the disastrous things that happen if you choose another rental firm, but it won't contrast car rentals to hiking in the park. The Apple display does just that, promoting one activity and negating another.

This is to say that the Apple strategy amounts to more than just a marketing ploy, chasing market share in a limited environment. It advocates. To replace the book with the screen is to remove a 2,500-year-old cornerstone of civilization and insert an altogether dissimilar building block. The enthusiasts of digital learning maintain that screen-influenced brains possess qualitatively different mentalities than book-influenced brains, and so we must conclude that the e-book and all the rest will spawn other knowledges and altered communications. In 50 years, as Boomers and X-ers pass away, digital natives grow up, and technology proceeds apace, civilization will look different. Knowledge will reside less in the minds of people and more on the pages of Web sites. The past will come alive on the screen, not in the imagination. The factual inventory that makes for a good *Jeopardy!* contestant will belong to individuals who tap quickly into the right information sources, not to individuals with the best memories and discipline. Texts will be more visual, reading more "browsy" and skimming.

These are suppositions about an all-digital world, and I don't know whether they will pan out or not. Most of the discourse about digital learning doesn't make book reading sound so obsolete. An October 2006 report by the Federation of American Scientists urges the integration of video games into the classroom specifically as a way to improve workplace readiness. "When individuals play modern video and computer games," it observes, "they experience environments in which they often must master the kinds of higher-order thinking and decision-making skills employers seek today." Such credulous tributes to the benefits of video games pop up throughout the document, but the only charges against books emerge in comments about state bureaucracies and their habits of textbook adoption. A November 2006 story in the *Miami Herald* covers a fifth-grade Florida classroom for one reason: it's "paperless." There, "Web sites are used in lieu of textbooks, PowerPoint Presentations substitute for written essays and students get homework help from their teacher over e-mail." But the worst thing it says about books is that they don't excite the kids as much as screens do. Added to that, without this classroom, the teacher maintains, many students have no access to a computer, and hence "don't have a chance at the American Dream." Such versions envision digital learning more as an augmentation of the old-fashioned way, not a termination of it (see Deluzuriaga).

Still, the predictions for digital behavior sometimes reach apocalyptic tones, and with books spoken of in the customary "reading is fundamental" terms, they appear to the 15-year-old, already recalcitrant and overstimulated, as ever more inferior and unnecessary. The inventor of the computer mouse, Douglas Englebart, once declared that "the digital revolution is far more significant than the invention of writing or even of printing," and the Associations of Elementary and of Secondary School Principals thought enough of his opinion to lead with it in a large ad in *Education Week* proclaiming, "We Can't Leave Our Students Behind in the Digital Revolution." Jon Katz of *Wired* magazine heralded in a celebrated article from 1997 that "the digital young are revolutionaries. Unlike the clucking boomers, they are not talking revolution; they're making one." The article had a momentous title, "Birth of a Digital Nation," and with fulminations about how the digital young are "bright," "challenge authority," and "take no one's word for anything," it played straight to the adolescent hubris that links youth to technology to genius to the future. Teens and 20-year-olds love their blogs and games, they carry the iPod around like a security blanket, and now they have a discourse to justify shirking the books and playing/watching longer. The youngsters' either/or actions explode the sanguine visions of hypersmart 18-year-olds reading books while they multitask with other diversions. More and more, they don't read books or newspapers, and their choices ensure the screen society to come. It's a self-fulfilling prophecy. Digital visionaries foresee a future of screens everywhere and books as collector's items, and digital natives act on the vision in the present, dropping books and going online, making the prediction come true.

To anyone who regrets the trend, digital enthusiasts have a ready rejoinder. The screen, they say, incorporates all the things book reading entails, and supplies so much more. Interactive screen practices may differ qualitatively from book reading, but users can always gear down to reading page by page in PDF format. Thousands of books and old essays go online every day, and e-books will soon match the old reading experience when they grow as light and sturdy and vision-friendly as a dog-eared, four-ounce paperback that slides into a back pocket.

More important, they argue, the screen actually encourages more reading and writing, more inquiry and activism, more decision-making, as Johnson would say. The interactivity of the digital screen solicits opinions and judgments, and follows with feedback. You read and you write, listen and speak out, plan and predict, watch a video and share one of your own. Will Richardson, author of *Blogs, Wikis, Podcasts, and Other Powerful Web Tools for Classrooms*, calls it the "Read/Write Web," and maintains that it "is changing our relationship to technology and rewriting the age old paradigms of how things work." A half century ago, Ray Bradbury envisioned screen entertainment as an enervating drug, portraying Montag's wife in *Fahrenheit 451* (1953) as a reality/interactive TV junkie who's lost her social consciousness and her capacity to love. She spends her days in her room, which has television screens covering three walls. Her favorite show, *The Family*, includes her in the plot, and the characters sometimes turn to address her directly—a hypnotically meaningful thing for her. Thirty years later, in *Amusing Ourselves to Death* (1985), Neil Postman claimed that television's omnivorous eye turned every event and experience into entertainment, the moral meaning of joy, pain, defeat, and justice subordinated to their showtime potential. Postman contrasted George Orwell's *1984* nightmare, in which totalitarian power is imposed from without, to Aldous Huxley's *Brave New World*, in which people enjoy so many mechanisms of pleasure that they "adore the technologies that undo their capacities to think." Bradbury and Postman form high points in a tradition of media commentary that claims the screen "atomizes" individuals, isolating and pacifying them while purveying illusions of worldly contact.

Richardson finds the opposite process at work, users ascending from couch-potato quietude to community and collaboration. "We are no longer limited to being independent readers or consumers of information; as we'll see," he announces, "we can be collaborators in the creation of large storehouses of information. In the process, we can learn much about ourselves and our world." Knowledge flows in both directions, from scattered but connected users to a central, evolving site/forum, and then back again to users, with comments and corrections attached. The process gives birth every month to thousands of junior reporters and editors, amateur filmmakers and photographers, local muckrakers, consumer advocates, and social trendsetters. They post comments, reveal secrets, criticize news stories (the Dan Rather affair), record historic events as they unfold (the 2004 tsunami), and initiate colloquies on school, music, bullying, elections, and games. A January 2006 BBC News story on "The Year of the Digital Citizen" reviewed the new gadgets and practices of the preceding year and pronounced, "what 2005 proved was that far from these techno tools being purely dumb funnels for the same paid-for content from mainstream media, they had the chance to become powerful tools for political expression and reportage" (see Twist). The old system of politics, journalism, and entertainment kept entry passes to a minimum, allowing only a precious few musicians into the recording studio, only certified reporters into the room. Technology has broken the grip of Big Media, producing an army of watchdog citizens and opening the gates to creative expression to individuals far from Hollywood and Manhattan. And amid all the tasteless images, bad grammar, and puerile showmanship appear marginalized voices and important testimonials. Out of the mass of content creators will come the next Mamet, the next Soderbergh.

This is why *Time* magazine named "You" the Person of the Year for 2006. Lev Grossman explained the choice:

> But look at 2006 through a different lens and you'll see another story, one that isn't about conflict or great men. It's a story about community and collaboration on a scale never seen before. It's about the cosmic compendium of knowledge Wikipedia and the million-channel people's network YouTube and the online metropolis MySpace. It's about the many wresting power from the few and helping one another for nothing and how that will not only change the world, but also change the way the world changes.
>
> The tool that makes this possible is the World Wide Web. Not the Web that Tim Berners-Lee hacked together (15 years ago, according to Wikipedia) as a way for scientists to share research. It's not even the overhyped dotcom Web of the late 1990s. The new Web is a very different thing. It's a tool for bringing together the small contributions of millions of people and making them matter. Silicon Valley consultants call it Web 2.0, as if it were a new version of some old software. But it's really a revolution.

Again, a "revolution." A related *Time* piece calls it "the New Digital Democracy," and even though a few other articles worry about, for instance, the dangers of Web collectivism and how cell phones have encouraged a dispersed surveillance system, overall *Time*'s year-end summary depicts a positive historical transformation under way. The most intense and seasoned actors in the drama, the rising digital generation, experience it as a personal change—a new game to play, screen to watch, message to send—but their choices in sum alter the general social habitation in America. A democratic empowerment spreads, and more and more commentators and journalists far from hi-tech circles commend it.

Young people absorb the fervor inside their classrooms and at home alone. Not only does it license them to tinker with e-tools as a proper mode of study, solidifying the so-called "*Sesame Street* effect" (if learning isn't fun, it isn't any good). It also provides an aggrandized sense of their own activity, their own voice. Here's a fifth-grade student quoted in an article on blogs in the classroom in *EDUCAUSE Review* (2004):

> The blogs give us a chance to communicate between us and
> motivate us to write more. When we publish on our blog,
> people from the entire world can respond by using the
> comments link. This way, they can ask questions or simply
> tell us what they like. We can then know if people like what
> we write and this indicate[s to] us what to do better. By
> reading these comments, we can know our weaknesses and
> our talents. Blogging is an opportunity to exchange our point
> of view with the rest of the world not just people in our
> immediate environment. (See Downes.)

The remarks sound scripted, as if a bright 11-year-old had hearkened to the blog hype and learned to talk the talk. But the vision is so compelling, the expectations so upbeat, that we can hardly blame her. To an eager eighth-grader just discovering the vastness of the planet, developing an ego, and hoping to make a mark, the blog offers what so many other things in her fresh preteen life hinder: freedom and reach. People 3,000 miles away may be watching and listening, and the students' receptivity to feedback grants it an air of conscience and progress. Even if we contend that the vision stands on a set of callow and self-centered illusions—for instance, teenagers aiming to become the next lonelygirl15—it still compels students to read and write, reflect and criticize. The nineties Web, "Web 1.0," kept users in passive mode, simply delivering content in faster, easier ways. The twenty-first-century Web, Web 2.0, makes users partici-

pants in critical, intellectual, artistic enterprises, and their own actions direct the growth of the virtual sphere in the way, say, links in
blogs groove further usage patterns. Nielsen//NetRatings found in
August 2006 that "User-Generated Content Drives Half of U.S. Top
10 Fastest Growing Web Brands," indicating the living and breathing
nature of interactive usage. As tech guru Tim O'Reilly put it in 2005,
"Much as synapses form in the brain, with associations becoming
stronger through repetition or intensity, the web of connections
grows organically as an output of the collective activity of all web
users." The brain metaphor is telling. Blogs, wikis, and the rest swell
the public intelligence. Adolescents adept at them advance the collective mind and expand the storehouse of knowledge. They engage in creativity and criticism, dialogue and competition, kindling
thought, not deadening it. Why, then, should bibliophiles and traditionalists carp so much?

BECAUSE THAT GLORIOUS creation of youth intelligence hasn't
materialized. The Web expands nonstop, absorbing everything it can,
and more knowledge and beauty settle there by the hour. But no
such enhancement has touched its most creative and frequent users,
the digital natives. There is no reciprocal effect. Digital enthusiasts
witness faithfully the miraculous evolution of the digital sphere, but
they also assume a parallel ascent by its consumers, an assumption
with no evidence behind it. In 2007, Pew Research compared current affairs knowledge with information and news technology and
concluded:

> Since the late 1980s, the emergence of 24-hour cable news as
> a dominant news source and the explosive growth of the
> internet have led to major changes in the American public's
> news habits. But a new nationwide survey finds that the
> coaxial and digital revolutions and attendant changes in news

audience behaviors have had little impact on how much
Americans know about national and international affairs.
("Public Knowledge of Current Affairs Little Changed by
News and Information Revolutions, What Americans Know:
1989–2007")

The youngest age group in the survey, 18- to 29-year-olds, scored
the lowest, with only 15 percent reaching "high knowledge." By
2005, high school students had inhabited a Web world for most of
their lives, and the participatory capabilities of the screen (the "Read/
Write Web") had existed for years. Nonetheless, when the 2005
NAEP test in reading was administered to twelfth-graders, the outcomes marked a significant decrease from 1992, before cell phones
came along and back when few classrooms had a computer.

The latest NAEP figures are but another entry in the ongoing cat-
alogue of knowledge and skill deficits among the Web's most dedicated partakers. When we look at the front end of digital usage,
at the materials and transactions available online, we discover a
mega-world of great books, beautiful artworks, historical information, statistical data, intelligent magazines, informative conversations,
challenging games, and civic deeds. But when we go to the back end
of digital usage, to the minds of those who've spent their formative
years online, we draw a contrary conclusion. Whatever their other
virtues, these minds know far too little, and they read and write and
calculate and reflect way too poorly. However many hours they pass
at the screen from age 11 to 25, however many blog comments they
compose, intricate games they play, videos they create, personal profiles they craft, and gadgets they master, the transfer doesn't happen.
The Web grows, and the young adult mind stalls.

As we've seen, it isn't for lack of surfing and playing time, and the
materials for sturdy mental growth are all there to be downloaded
and experienced. Enough years have passed for us to expect the intellectual payoff promised by digital enthusiasts to have happened.

Blogs aren't new anymore, and neither is *MySpace*, *The Sims*, or text messaging. Students consult *Wikipedia* all the time. If the Web did constitute such a rich learning encounter, we would have seen its effects by now. An article on *Wikipedia* in *Reason* magazine by Katherine Mangu-Ward announces, "as with Amazon, Google, and eBay, it is almost impossible to remember how much more circumscribed our world was before it existed" (June 2007). But what evidence do we have that the world has dilated, that the human mind reaches so much further than it did just a decade or two ago? The visionary rhetoric goes on, but with knowledge surveys producing one embarrassing finding after another, with reading scores flat, employers complaining about the writing skills of new hires as loudly as ever, college students majoring in math a rarity, remedial course attendance on the rise, and young people worrying less and less about *not* knowing the basics of history, civics, science, and the arts, the evidence against it can no longer be ignored. We should heed informed skeptics such as Bill Joy, described by *Wired* magazine as "software god, hero programmer, cofounder of Sun Microsystems," who listened to fellow panelists at Aspen Institute's 2006 festival gushing over the learning potential of blogging and games, and finally exclaimed, "I'm skeptical that any of this has anything to do with learning. It sounds like it's a lot of encapsulated entertainment. . . . This all, for me, for high school students sounds like a gigantic waste of time. If I was competing with the United States, I would love to have the students I'm competing with spending their time on this kind of crap."

In the education and hi-tech worlds, Joy is a countercultural, minority voice, but the outcomes support his contention. In an average young person's online experience, the senses may be stimulated and the ego touched, but vocabulary doesn't expand, memory doesn't improve, analytic talents don't develop, and erudition doesn't ensue. Some young users excel, of course, and the Web does spark their intellects with fresh challenges, but that's the most we can say right

now about digital technology's intellectual consequences. Digital enthusiasts and reporters looking for a neat story can always spotlight
a bright young sophomore here and there doing dazzling, ingenious
acts online, but they rarely ask whether this clever intellect would do
equally inventive things with pencil and paper, paint and canvas, or
needle-nose pliers and soldering iron if the Web weren't routinely at
hand. Game researcher James Gee tells *pc.gamezone.com*, "We have
interviewed kids who have redesigned the family computer, designed
new maps and even made mods, designed Web sites, written guides,
and contracted relationships with people across the world," but he
doesn't state how representative such extraordinary cases are. Large-
scale surveys and test scores do, and the portrait they draw gainsays
the bouncy profiles of young Web genius. For most young users, it is
clear, the Web hasn't made them better writers and readers, sharper
interpreters and more discerning critics, more knowledgeable citizens and tasteful consumers. In ACT's National Curriculum Survey,
released in April 2007, 35 percent of college teachers agreed that the
college readiness of entering students has declined in the last several
years, and only 13 percent stated that it had improved. Furthermore,
college teachers found that the most important prerequisites for
success lay not in higher-order talents such as critical thinking, which
enthusiasts of technology often underscore, but in lower-order thinking skills, that is, the basic mechanics of spelling, punctuation, and
arithmetic. One month later, in May 2007, ACT reported in *Rigor at
Risk: Reaffirming Quality in the High School Core Curriculum* that
"three out of four ACT-tested 2006 high school graduates who take
a core curriculum are not prepared to take credit-bearing entry-level
college courses with a reasonable chance of succeeding in those
courses." Furthermore, their momentum toward college readiness
remains stable from eighth to tenth grade, and slips only in the last
two years of high school, when those higher-order thinking skills
supposedly blossom in their schoolwork and online hours.

In light of the outcomes, the energetic, mind-expanding communitarian/individualist dynamic of Web participation described by digital enthusiasts sounds like rosy oratory and false prophesy. A foundation hosts symposia on digital learning, a science group affirms the benefits of video games, humanities leaders insist that we respect the resourceful new literacies of the young, reading researchers insist that Web reading extends standard literacy skills to hypermedia comprehension, school districts unveil renovated hi-tech classrooms, and popular writers hail the artistry of today's TV shows. All of them foretell a more intelligent and empowered generation on the rise. The years have passed, though, and we're still waiting.

CHAPTER FOUR

ONLINE LEARNING AND NON-LEARNING

In November 2006, Educational Testing Service (developer of the SAT) released the findings of a survey of high school and college students and their digital research skills. The impetus for the study came from librarians and teachers who noticed that, for all their adroitness with technology, students don't seek, find, and manage information very well. They play complex games and hit the social networking sites for hours, the educators said, but they don't always cite pertinent sources and compose organized responses to complete class assignments. They're comfortable with the tools, but indiscriminate in their applications. ETS terms the missing aptitude Information and Communications Technology (ICT) literacy, and it includes the ability to conduct research, evaluate sources, communicate data, and understand ethical/legal issues of access and use. To measure ICT literacy, ETS gathered 6,300 students and administered a 75-minute test containing 15 tasks. They included determining a Web site's objectivity, ranking Web pages on given criteria, and categorizing emails and files into folders.

The first conclusion of the report: "Few test takers demonstrated key ICT literacy skills" (www.ets.org/ictliteracy.org). Academic and workplace performance increasingly depends on the ability to identify trustworthy sources, select relevant information, and render it in clear, useful form to others, tasks that exceeded the talents of most students. While the majority of them knew that .edu and .gov sites are less biased than .com sites, only 35 percent of them performed the correct revision when asked to "narrow an overly broad search." When searching the Web on an assigned task, only 40 percent of the test takers entered several terms in order to tailor the ensuing listing of sources. Only 52 percent correctly judged the objectivity of certain Web sites, and when "selecting a research statement for a class assignment," less than half of them (44 percent) found an adequate one. Asked to construct a persuasive slide for a presentation, 8 percent of them "used entirely irrelevant points" and 80 percent of them mixed relevant with irrelevant points, leaving only 12 percent who stuck to the argument.

A story on the report in *InsideHigherEd.com* brandished the headline "Are College Students Techno Idiots?" (see Thacker). An official at the American Library Association remarked of the report, "It doesn't surprise me," and Susan Metros, a design technology professor at Ohio State, thought that it reflected a worrisome habit of online research: less than 1 percent of Google searches ever extend to the second page of search results. Because the sample wasn't gathered in a consistent manner from school to school, ETS warned against generalizing too firmly from the results, but even with that caution its drift against the flow of what digital enthusiasts maintain is arresting. This was not—to use the idiom of anti-testing groups—another standardized, multiple-choice exam focused on decontextualized facts and rewarding simple memorization. The exam solicited precisely the decision-making power and new literacies that techno-enthusiasts claim will follow from long hours at the game console. The major finding: "More than half the students failed to sort the information to clarify related material." It graded the very communications skills Web 2.0, the Read/Write Web, supposedly instills, and "only a few test takers could accurately adapt material for a new audience."

The ETS results were anticipated a year earlier in another report, the *ECAR Study of Students and Information Technology, 2005: Convenience, Control, and Learning.* ECAR reports come out every year (the 2006 version was quoted earlier), and its sponsor, EDUCAUSE, is "a nonprofit association whose mission is to advance higher education by promoting the intelligent use of information technology" (http://www.educause.edu/). EDUCAUSE researchers approached the project assuming that students want more technology in the classroom, possess strong information technology skills, and need little further training, and that their teachers need to bolster their own techno-knowledge to "appeal to the attention and learning styles of this generation of students." To their surprise, the outcomes showed the opposite. "Ironically," the Executive Summary ran, "we found that many of the students most skilled in the use of technology had mixed feelings about technology in their courses." Furthermore, many students entering college lacked information-technology skills necessary to perform academic work, and the skills that they did have stemmed from school curricula, not from their leisure digital habits. As for the importance of learning, students ranked it fourth on the list of benefits provided by technology, behind convenience, connectedness, and course management.

The ETS and EDUCAUSE results, purveyed by organizations that favor technology in classrooms, belie the high-flying forecasts of digitally inspired dexterity and intelligence. Students can image and browse and post and play, but they can't judge the materials they process, at least not in the intellectual or professional terms of college classes and the workplace. Irvin Katz, senior scientist at ETS, sharpens the discrepancy: "While college-age students can use technology, they don't necessarily know what to do with the content the technology provides." Fans of digital youth behaviors believe in a carry-over effect, that gaming, blogging, IM, and wikis yield cognitive habits and critical-thinking skills that make for an intelligent, informed citizen. The energetic forms of thought inspired by those practices produce more discerning minds, they say, and while the content of games and blogs slips into adolescent trivia, when young Americans do encounter serious content, they'll possess the acumen to digest it. On the first large tests of the aptitude, however, they failed. It seems that the judgment of Web content involves mental faculties different from the faculties cultivated by standard Web consumptions by young Americans.

These surveys aren't the only empirical data casting doubt on the technological savvy of young users. In the newly wired public school classroom we have a gigantic, heterogeneous laboratory of digital learning, and one of the most expensive experiments in education reform in our history. Ever since President Clinton signed the Telecommunications Act of 1996, which included annual subsidies for schools to develop technology programs (funded through taxes on phone bills), school officials, technology providers, and excited politicians have conspired to carry screens into classrooms and integrate Web activities into curricula with suitable optimism and zeal. In 1995, the President's Panel on Educational Technology recommended that at least 5 percent of all public K–12 educational spending go to technology, and in his 1996 State of the Union Address, President Clinton avowed, "In our schools, every classroom in America must be connected to the information superhighway, with computers and good software, and well-trained teachers." Seven years later, in *The Flickering Mind: The False Promise of Technology in the Classroom and How Learning Can Be Saved* (2003), education journalist Todd Oppenheimer summarizes the investment: "In the decade that ran from the early 1990s to the first years of the twenty-first century, technovangels in city after city have been creating new schools and restructuring old ones, spending approximately $70 billion on new programs that revolve around the computer."

Each year a new digital initiative begins, with the promise of engaging wayward middle schoolers, updating textbooks, closing the "digital racial gap," easing the teachers' burden, and raising test scores. In his lengthy appraisal of the enterprise, Oppenheimer chronicles one pro-technology decision after another. A school district in Union City, California, spent $37 million to purchase new tools for 11 schools, and paid for it by cutting science equipment and field trips. Montgomery Blair High School in Maryland, one of the first schools to be wired (in 1989), enjoyed Internet service provided by the National Institutes of Health. The Kittridge Street Elementary School in Los Angeles dropped its music program in order to afford a "technology manager." In 2001, Henrico County Public Schools in Virginia distributed Apple laptops to every high school student in the system, and a year later the State of Maine gave one to each seventh- and eighth-grade student in the state, along with their teachers. New Technology High School in Napa, California, received $300,000 from the U.S. Department of Education and $250,000 from the California Department of Education for its pioneering, super-wired facilities. (One of the school's slogans is, a teacher tells Oppenheimer, "It doesn't matter what you know. It matters what you show.")

Overall, in 2006, public schools across the country purchased $1.9 billion of electronic curricular materials, a rise of 4.4 percent from 2005, and the momentum shows no signs of slowing. The fervor extends to powerful foundations and education firms, whose reform proposals always assign technology a critical role in public school improvement. A 2003 report by the National Commission on Writing, *The Neglected 'R': The Need for a Writing Revolution*, began with the observation that "the teaching and practice of writing are increasingly shortchanged throughout the school and college years." It also noted that "today's young people, raised at keyboards and eager to exchange messages with their friends, are comfortable with these new technologies and eager to use them." So, we have a contradictory situation, poor writing in school and energetic writing at home online. Instead of pausing to consider a relationship between popular technologies and poor writing skills, though, the report careens in another direction. It advises that a National Educational Technology Trust "be explored, perhaps financed through federal-state-private partnerships, to pay for up to 90 percent of the costs associated with providing hardware, software, and training for every student and teacher in the nation."

Reading Next: A Vision for Action and Research in Middle and High School Literacy, a 2004 report sponsored by the Carnegie Corporation, likewise cites the problems, for example, the low reading skills of high school dropouts and graduates. Nevertheless, its 15-point plan for improvement sets "A Technology Component" at number eight, asserting blankly that "technology is both a facilitator of literacy and a medium of literacy." Nowhere does it consider how technology in the lives of adolescents promotes or retards the development of verbal skills—technology as actually used by them, not ideal visions of what technology might do best. Instead, the document invokes the standards of the times: "As a topic, technology is changing the reading and writing demands of modern society. Reading and writing in the fast-paced, networked world require new skills unimaginable a decade ago." The overheated qualifier "unimaginable" reveals how firmly the education sector has adopted the revolutionary, epochal thinking of hi-tech activists.

Higher education, too, joins the trend. In 2004, Duke University passed out iPods to every freshman, and in 2005 Clemson required entering freshmen to purchase a laptop. The Clemson digital assistance Web site explains why:

We had a four year pilot laptop computer program which investigated the benefits of a laptop computer environment

from both practical and pedagogical points of view. The
results are clear—our laptop students are completely
convinced this is the only way to go!

Taking the enthusiasm of 18-year-olds as a measure of educational
benefits may sound like a dicey way to justify such a sweeping change
in classroom practices, but many studies out to evaluate e-learning
do precisely that. When the Maine laptop program mentioned on
page 117 commissioned a midyear progress report, researchers af-
firmed that it "is having many positive impacts on teachers and their
instruction, and on students' engagement and learning." The evidence, as cited in *eSchool News:* "By an overwhelming margin, sev-
enth graders who received laptop computers last fall say the
computers have made schoolwork more fun," and "83 percent of the
students said the laptops improve the quality of their work." A 2002
report by the Corporation for Public Broadcasting titled *Connected
to the Future* found that using the Internet has made Hispanic and
African-American students "like school more," and that "these positive attitudes from children and parents in under-served populations
underscore the potentially vital role that the Internet can play in
children's education."

Pro-technology forces play up the better attitudes as signs of
progress, and who doesn't want a happier school population? When
we isolate actual learning, however, the self-reported happiness of
the kids begins to make sense in an altogether opposite way. Digital
technology might brighten the students' outlook not only for the
obvious reason that it gives them mouses and keyboards to wield,
but also because it saves them the effort of acquiring knowledge and
developing skills. When screens deliver words and numbers and images in fun sequence, digital fans assert, the students imbibe the embedded lessons with glee, but, in fact, while the medium may raise
the glee of the students, we have little evidence that the embedded
lessons take hold as sustained learning in students' minds. For, in the

last few years several studies and analyses have appeared showing little or no achievement gains once the schools went digital. Various digital initiatives have fallen short, quite simply, because students who were involved in them didn't perform any better than students who weren't.

- In 2000, Kirk Johnson of the Heritage Foundation analyzed NAEP data on students who used computers in the classroom at least once a week and on students who used them less than once a week. Controlling for the major demographic factors, as well as the qualifications of the teachers, Johnson created a statistical model and applied it to NAEP's nationwide sample of fourth- and eighth-graders who took the reading test in 1998. His conclusion: "Students with at least weekly computer instruction by well-prepared teachers do not perform any better on the NAEP reading test than do students who have less or no computer instruction." (Johnson)

- In 2004, two economists at the University of Munich analyzed data from the 2000 Programme for International Students Assessment (PISA), the achievement test for 15-year-olds discussed in chapter one. They compared test scores for students in 31 countries with background information collected on PISA questionnaires regarding home and school computer use. Their conclusion: "Once other features of student, family and school background are held constant, computer availability at home shows a strong statistically negative relationship to math and reading performance, and computer availability at

school is unrelated to performance." (Fuchs and
Woessmann)

- In winter 2006, two University of Chicago economists
  published an appraisal of E-Rate, the federal program of
  subsidies to public schools for Internet access. E-Rate
  revenues started to reach schools in 1998, climbing to
  $2.1 billion by 2001, and the researchers wanted to find
  out if the program did, indeed, improve learning
  outcomes. Focusing on California, which administered
  regular achievement tests to students and maintained
  records on computers in classrooms, they determined
  that from 1997 to 2001, the portion of schools with
  Internet access in at least one classroom leaped from
  55 percent to 85 percent. Some gain in student learning
  should have emerged. Yet, the authors conclude, "the
  additional investments in technology generated by E-
  Rate had no immediate impact on measured student
  outcomes." Furthermore, more time online didn't help:
  "When we look at the program's impact after two years,
  the estimated effects go down, not up." (Goolsbee and
  Guryan)

- As part of the Technology Immersion Pilot, in 2004 the
  Texas Education Agency directed $14 million in federal
  funds toward wireless technology in selected middle
  schools in the state. Teachers and students received
  laptops, teachers underwent professional development,
  and technical support was ongoing. The program
  included an evaluation component concentrated on
  student achievement. When the evaluation appeared in
  April 2006, it reported improvements in parental

support, teacher productivity, and student behavior, but it said this about academic outcomes: "There were no statistically significant effects of immersion in the first year on either reading or mathematics achievement." Furthermore, the "availability of laptops did not lead to significantly greater opportunities for students to experience intellectually challenging lessons or to do more challenging school work." (Texas Center for Educational Research)

• In March 2004, the Inspectorate of Education in Scotland produced an evaluation of information and communications technology (ICT) in the public schools. Over the preceding five years, Scotland had invested £150 million to integrate computers into all areas of student work, and the report resounded with cheers for the aims and progress. "The potential to transform patterns and modes of learning and teaching is clear," the chief inspector intoned, and dozens of assertions in the report back him up, such as "Use of ICT by learners encourages independence in learning" and "Learners use ICT well to develop their understanding of the world in which they live." But several skeptical remarks keep popping up, almost as afterthoughts. "This did not often lead to enhanced learning in the subject area," goes one, and another: "The burden placed on teachers by the need to monitor the content of learners' personal pages on [networking] sites led some teaching staff to question the net value of these services but all learners found them valuable and enjoyable to use." The most damning judgment comes at the end in a decisive summation: "Inspectors found no evidence of increased attainment, in formal qualifications or against nationally defined levels, that could be directly attributed to the use of ICT in learning and teaching." (Scotland Inspectorate)

• In March 2007, the National Center for Education Evaluation and Regional Assistance issued an evaluation report entitled *Effectiveness of Reading and Mathematics Software Products: Findings from the First Student Cohort.* Mandated by the No Child Left Behind Act, the report examined the use and effectiveness of selected technologies in different elementary and secondary school classrooms. Fully 132 schools participated in the study, and Mathematica Policy Research and SRI International conducted it. Vendors of the products trained teachers in their use, and researchers used control groups and conditions to meet scientific standards. Student achievement was measured mainly with test scores, and yielded an unambiguous first finding: **"Test Scores Were Not Significantly Higher in Classrooms Using Selected Reading and Mathematics Software Products"** (emphasis in original). Even though the research team chose 16 products out of a competitive review of 160 submissions, identifying them partly for evidence of effectiveness (12 of them had received or been nominated for awards), the products didn't raise or lower student performance at all. *Education Week* drolly observed, "The findings may be disturbing to the companies that provided their software for the trial" (see Trotter). The conclusions are not decisive, as some of the control groups implemented other technologies in their work. But the fact that the most popular and respected technologies in reading and math education produced no significant differences calls into question the millions of dollars invested by the federal government.

- In May 2007, the *New York Times* reported a policy change in a New York State school district that was one of the first to outfit students with laptops. Responding to teacher feedback and learning outcomes, "the Liverpool Central School District, just outside Syracuse, has decided to phase out laptops starting this fall, joining a handful of other schools around the country that adopted one-to-one computing programs and are now abandoning them as educationally empty—and worse" (see Hu). The school board president explained, "After seven years, there was literally no evidence it had any impact on student achievement—none." The story also cited other hi-tech failures. A Richmond, Virginia, high school "began eliminating its five-year-old laptop program last fall after concluding that students had failed to show any academic gains compared with those in schools without laptops," and in 2005 Broward County, Florida, ended a $275 million program to provide laptops to 260,000 students after finding that the cost would exceed $7 million to lease the computers in only four schools.

Given the enormous sums of money at stake, and the backing of the highest political and business leaders, these discouraging developments should enter the marketplace of debate over digital learning. They are not final, of course, but they are large and objective enough to pose serious questions about digital learning. The authors of the studies aren't Luddites, nor are school administrators anti-technology. They observe standards of scientific method, and care about objective outcomes. Their conclusions should, at least, check the headlong dash to technologize education.

All too often, however, the disappointment veers toward other, circumstantial factors in the execution, for instance, insufficient usage by the students and inadequate preparation of the teachers. In the 2006 *ECAR Study of Undergraduate Students and Technology*, when researchers found that most of the younger respondents and female respondents wanted less technology in the classroom, not more, they could only infer that those students "are comparatively unskilled in IT to support academic purposes." It didn't occur to them that those students might have decent IT skills and still find the screen a distraction. Several education researchers and commentators have mistrusted technophilic approaches to the classroom, including Larry Cuban, Jane Healy, and Clifford Stoll, but their basic query of whether computers really produce better intellectual results is disregarded. On the tenth anniversary of E-Rate, for instance, U.S. senators proposed a bill to strengthen the program while tightening performance measures—but they restricted the tightening to financial and bureaucratic measures only, leaving out the sole proper justification for the costs, academic measures. The basic question of whether technology might, under certain conditions, hinder academic achievement goes unasked. The spotlight remains on the promise, the potential. The outcomes continue to frustrate expectations, but the backers push forward, the next time armed with an updated eBook, tutelary games the kids will love, more school-wide coordination, a 16-point plan, not a 15-point one . . . Ever optimistic, techno-cheerleaders view the digital learning experience through their own motivated eyes, and they picture something that doesn't yet exist: classrooms illuminating the wide, wide world, teachers becoming twenty-first-century techno-facilitators, and students at screens inspired to ponder, imagine, reflect, analyze, memorize, recite, and create.

They do not pause to consider that screen experience may contain factors that cannot be overcome by better tools and better implementation. This is the possibility that digital enthusiasts must face before they peddle any more books on screen intelligence or commit $15 million to another classroom initiative. Techno-pushers hail digital learning, and they like to talk of screen time as a heightened "experience," but while they expound the features of the latest games and software in detail, they tend to flatten and overlook the basic features of the most important element in the process, the young persons having the experiences. Digital natives are a restless group, and like all teens and young adults they are self-assertive and insecure, living in the moment but worrying over their future, crafting elaborate e-profiles but stumbling through class assignments, absorbing the minutiae of youth culture and ignoring works of high culture, heeding this season's movie and game releases as monumental events while blinking at the mention of the Holocaust, the Cold War, or the War on Terror. It is time to examine clear-sightedly how their worse dispositions play out online, or in a game, or on a blog, or with the remote, the cell phone, or the handheld, and to recognize that their engagement with technology actually aggravates a few key and troubling tendencies. One of those problems, in fact, broaches precisely one of the basics of learning: the acquisition of language.

WHEN RESEARCHERS, educators, philanthropists, and politicians propose and debate adjustments to education in the United States, they emphasize on-campus reforms such as a more multicultural curriculum, better technology, smaller class size, and so on. At the same time, however, the more thoughtful and observant ones among them recognize a critical but outlying factor: much of the preparation work needed for academic achievement takes place not on school grounds but in informal settings such as a favorite reading spot at home, discussions during dinner, or kids playing Risk or chess. This is especially so in the nontechnical, nonmathematical areas, fields in which access to knowledge and skill comes primarily through reading. Put simply, for students to earn good grades and test scores in history, English, civics, and other liberal arts, they need the vocabulary to handle them. They need to read their way into and through the subjects, which means that they need sufficient reading-comprehension skills to do so, especially vocabulary knowledge. And the habits that produce those skills originate mostly in their personal lives, at home and with friends, not with their teachers.

Everything depends on the oral and written language the infant-toddler-child-teen hears and reads throughout the day, for the amount of vocabulary learned inside the fifth-grade classroom alone doesn't come close to the amount needed to understand fifth-grade textbooks. They need a social life and a home life that deliver requisite words to them, put them into practice, and coax kids to speak them. Every elementary school teacher notices the results. A child who comes into class with a relatively strong storehouse of words races through the homework and assembles a fair response, while a child without one struggles to get past the first paragraph. No teacher has the time to cover all the unknown words for each student, for the repository grows only after several years of engagement in the children's daily lives, and the teacher can correct only so much of what happens in the 60+ waking hours per week elsewhere. That long foreground, too, has a firm long-term consequence. The strong vocabulary student learns the new and unusual words in the assigned reading that he doesn't already know, so that his initial competence fosters even higher competence. The weak vocabulary student flails with more basic words, skips the harder ones, and ends up hating to read. For him, it's a pernicious feedback loop, and it only worsens as he moves from grade to grade and the readings get harder.

The things they hear from their parents, or overhear; the books and magazines they read; the conversation of their playmates and fellow students; the discourse of television, text messages, music lyrics, games, Web sites . . . they make up the ingredients of language acquisition. It is all too easy to regard out-of-school time only as a realm of fun and imagination, sibling duties and household chores, but the language a child soaks up in those work and play moments lays the foundation for in-school labor from kindergarten through high school and beyond. And so, just as we evaluate schools and teachers every year, producing prodigious piles of data on test scores, funding, retention, and AP course-taking, we should appraise the verbal media in private zones too. Which consumptions build vocabulary most effectively?

We can't follow children around and record the words they hear and read, but we can, in fact, empirically measure the vocabulary of the different media children and teens encounter. The discrepancies are surprising. One criterion researchers use is the rate of "rare words" in spoken and written discourse. They define "rare words" as words that do not rank in the top 10,000 in terms of frequency of usage. With the rare-word scale, researchers can examine various media for the number of rare words per thousand, as well as the median-word ranking for each medium as a whole.

The conclusions are nicely summarized in "What Reading Does for the Mind" by education psychologists Anne E. Cunningham and Keith E. Stanovich, who announce straight off, "What is immediately apparent is how lexically impoverished most speech is compared to written language." Indeed, the vocabulary gap between speech and print is clear and wide. Here is a chart derived from a 1988 study showing the rare-word breakdown for print materials.

	Rank of median word	Rare words per 1000
• newspapers	1690	68.3
• adult books	1058	52.7
• comic books	867	53.5
• children's books	627	30.9
• preschool books	578	16.3

And the same for oral materials.

- prime-time adult TV shows   490   22.7
- prime-time children's shows   543   20.2
- *Sesame Street*   413   2.0
- conversation by college grads   496   17.3

Print far exceeds live and televised speech, even to the point that a book by Dr. Seuss falls only slightly beneath the conversation of intelligent adults on the rare-word-per-thousand scale. And when compared to a television show for the same ages, *Sesame Street*, pre-school books outdo it by a hefty factor of eight. Adult books more than double the usage of rare words in adult TV shows, and children's books beat them on the median-word ranking by 137 slots. Surprisingly, cartoons score the highest vocabulary of television speech. (I do recall the voice of Foghorn Leghorn as more lyrical and the discourse of Mr. Peabody more intellectual than anything from Rachel and Monica or Captain Frank Furillo.)

The incidence of rare words is a minute quantitative sum, but it signifies a crucial process in the formation of intelligent minds. Because a child's vocabulary grows mainly through informal exposure, not deliberate study, the more words in the exposure that the child doesn't know, the greater the chances for growth—as long as there aren't too many. If someone is accustomed to language with median-word ranking at 1,690 (the newspaper tally), a medium with a median-word ranking of 500 won't much help. Young adults can easily assimilate a discourse whose every word is familiar. While that discourse may contain edifying information, it doesn't help them assimilate a more verbally sophisticated discourse next time. Exposure to progressively more rare words expands the verbal reservoir. Exposure to media with entirely common words keeps the reservoir at existing levels.

Years of consumption of low rare-word media, then, have a dire

intellectual effect. A low-reading, high-viewing childhood and adolescence prevent a person from handling relatively complicated
texts, not just professional discourses but civic and cultural media
such as the *New York Review of Books* and the *National Review*. The
vocabulary is too exotic. A child who reads children's books encounters 50 percent more rare words than a child who watches children's
shows—a massive discrepancy as the years pass. Indeed, by the time
children enter kindergarten, the inequity can be large and permanent. Education researchers have found that children raised in print-
heavy households and those raised in print-poor households can
arrive at school with gaps in their word inventories of several thousand. Classroom life for low-end kids ends up an exercise in pain,
like an overweight guy joining a marathon team and agonizing
through the practice drills. It doesn't work, and the gap only grows
over time as failure leads to despair, and despair leads to estrangement from all academic toil. A solitary teacher can do little to change
their fate.

This is why it is so irresponsible for votaries of screen media to
make intelligence-creating claims. Even if we grant that visual media
cultivate a type of spatial intelligence, they still minimize verbal intelligence, providing too little stimulation for it, and intense, long-
term immersion in it stultifies the verbal skills of viewers and
disqualifies them from most every academic and professional labor.
Enthusiasts such as Steven Johnson praise the decision-making value
of games, but they say nothing about games implanting the verbal
tools to make real decisions in real worlds. William Strauss and Neil
Howe, authors of *Millennials Rising: The Next Great Generation*
(2000), claim that the Millennial Generation (born after 1981) is
optimistic, responsible, ambitious, and smart, and that, partly because of their "fascination for, and mastery of, new technologies,"
they will produce a cultural renaissance with "seismic consequences
for America." But Strauss and Howe ignore the lexical poverty of
these new technologies, and they overlook all the data on the millen-

nials' verbal ineptitude. Unless they can show that games and shows and videos and social networking sites impart a lot more verbal understanding than a quick taste of *Grand Theft Auto* and *Fear Factor* and *MySpace* reveals, sanguine faith in the learning effects of screen media should dissolve.

Young Americans suffer the most from their endorsement, even as they adopt the vision and testify to the advantages of digital tools. Here one of the disabling tendencies of youth gains ground. The evaluators of digital-learning programs accept the enthusiasm of eighth-graders for computers in the classroom as a reliable indicator of academic benefit. Pro-technology voices in public life interpret the 18-year-old at a screen blogging and gaming, intensely interactive, as a revolutionary figure, a "Netizen" wielding what Will Richardson terms "new disruptive technologies that are transforming the world." Their judgment flatters the juniors, doing what admirers of youth have done ever since Jean-Jacques Rousseau and William Wordsworth wrote their paeans more than two centuries ago: ennobling the diversions of youth. While the rhetoric of pro-technology voices soars, however, the reality of adolescent Web practices—the nine out of ten postings and game sessions and messages—is just what we should expect, the adolescent expressions and adolescent recreations of adolescents.

Indeed, the contrast between hype and reality would be comical were it not for the severe costs. In his national tour of digital schools, Todd Oppenheimer recounts one ludicrous mismatch after another. Visiting a high school in Maryland "whose budget for technology is so lavish that it has earned the school fame for being one of the most wired in the nation," he wanders through a classroom with a teacher and sees the students entering data into spreadsheets. But when he passes through by himself he spies the same students on the Dallas Cowboys Web site, joining a news exchange on favorite sodas, and checking out Netscape headlines.

Here is Emily Nussbaum profiling a teen blogger in the *New York*

Times Magazine: "When M. gets home from school, he immediately logs on to his computer. Then he stays there, touching base with the people he has seen all day long, floating in a kind of multitasking heaven of communication." All evening long M. checks his blog for responses from readers, then composes "wry, supportive commentary to their observations" and "koanlike observations on life." Another teen blogger Nussbaum profiles is J., a high schooler in Westchester County, New York. "In his online outpourings," Nussbaum applauds, "J. inveighed hilariously against his parents, his teachers and friends who had let him down." But read her specimen of J.'s blogger wit: "'Hey everyone ever,' he wrote in one entry, 'stop making fun of people. It really is a sucky thing to do, especially if you hate being made fun of yourself. . . . This has been a public service announcement. You may now resume your stupid hypocritical, lying lives.'"

To praise such postures as "wry" and "hilarious," and to overlook the puerile sentiments, is to reinforce the simultaneously self-negating and self-aggrandizing adolescent bearings. A more circumspect glance finds that bad grammar, teen colloquialisms, and shallow ironies litter the blogs, comment threads, and social networking sites, raising the vocabulary problem cited earlier. Just as weak-vocabulary encounters don't inculcate stronger reading-comprehension skills, so weak-vocabulary writing doesn't yield better composition skills. Teen blog writing sticks to the lingo of teens—simple syntax, phonetic spelling, low diction—and actually grooves bad habits. Nevertheless, instead of telling J. and other teens heavy into Web 2.0 to pull away from the screen and devote a few more hours to algebra, chemistry, and French, Nussbaum and other adult observers marvel at the depth and pace of their immersion. They give adolescents just what they want, a rationale for closing their books, hanging out online, and jockeying with one another. Teenagers don't want to spend Tuesday night on science tasks or *1984*. With the screen luring them all the time with the prospect of a new contact in the last hour, the payoff for homework looks too distant, the effort too dull. AOL is more honest about the contrast. Among the options on its teen page (www.teens.aol.com) sits "Look at Pretty Pictures," a file of celebrity photos whose main attraction appears in the subtitle: "Because it's better than homework."

THE ENHANCED CONNECTIVITY, and the indulgence of teachers and journalists, feed yet another adolescent vice that technophiles never mention: peer absorption. Educators speak about the importance of role models and the career pressures facing kids, but in truth, adolescents care a lot more about what other adolescents think than what their elders think. Their egos are fragile, their beliefs in transition, their values uncertain. They inhabit a rigorous world of consumerism and conformity, of rebellious poses and withering group judgments. Boys struggle to acquire the courage and strength of manhood, girls the poise and strength of womanhood. They tease one another mercilessly, and a rejection can crush them. Life is a pinball game of polarized demands—a part-time job that requires punctuality and diligence, pals who urge them to cut up in class; a midterm forcing them to stay home and study, a friend who wants to catch a horror flick. For many of them, good standing with classmates is the only way to secure a safe identity, and so they spend hours on the channels of adolescent fare searching out the latest in clothes, slang, music, sports, celebrities, school gossip, and one another. Technology has made it fabulously easier.

And so, apart from all the other consequences of digital breakthroughs, for the younger users a profound social effect has settled in. Teens and young adults now have more contact with one another than ever before. Cliques used to form in the schoolyard or on the bus, and when students came home they communicated with one another only through a land line restricted by their parents. Social life pretty much stopped at the front door. With the latest gadgets in their own rooms and in the libraries, however, peer-to-peer contact never ends. Email and Instant Messaging maintain high school friendships long after graduation. Social networking sites produce virtual buddies who've never met in person and live 3,000 miles apart, but who converse intimately from one bedroom to another. School secrets and bullying get amplified on a saucy sophomore's blog, and two dozen others chime in. As soon as one class ends, undergraduates scurry across the quad for their next class but still take time to check cell phones for messages. Twitter technology (debuting in March 2006) enables users to send short updates on the spur of the moment through mobile phones and pocket PCs to others' devices, or to a profile page that forwards the message to every registered friend slated to receive them. The "tweets" can go out every few minutes and be as mundane as "Well, I'm still stuck in traffic," the rationale, according to *twitter.com*, stemming from one simple query: "What are you doing?" That is the genuine significance of the Web to a 17-year-old mind, not the universe of knowledge brought to their fingertips, but an instrument of nonstop peer contact.

Votaries of screen media and the Web start from the truism that the Web delivers a phenomenal body of data, stories, facts, images, and exercises. A column by education writer Joel Turtel advises "Let's Google and Yahoo Our Kids' Education" for that very reason. While in-class exercises drown students in overscheduled drudgery, he argues, search engines permit his daughter to "explore any subject" and put "the whole world at her fingertips." Studying is joyful and economical. "She can learn about tulips, cooking, dinosaurs, fashion, arithmetic, model airplanes, how to play the piano, or story books by thousands of authors," Turtel enthuses. "When she is older, she can search dozens of Internet libraries, including the Library of Congress, for information on any subject under the sun."

He's right, it's all there, the great books, masterpieces, old maps, encyclopedia entries, world newspapers, science facts, and historical events. But that's not where the kids go. Caesar conquered Gaul,

Cleopatra seduced him, and Antony took his place after the assassination, but young Americans prefer to learn about one another. In Nielsen//NetRatings for October 2006, nine of the top ten sites for 12- to 17-year-olds offered content or support tools for social networking. Chief Nielsen analyst Ken Cassar noted with surprise "the extent to which a wide array of supporting Web sites has developed in conjunction with these bigger, more well-known Web destinations. MySpace and YouTube have spawned a vibrant online ecosystem." The National School Boards report "Creating and Connecting" opens, "Online social networking is now so deeply embedded in the lifestyles of tweens and teens that it rivals television for their attention." It counted nine hours a week of networking time. For college students, the numbers are no better. In 2002, Pew Research issued a "data memo" on Web sites and college kids. It found: "Seven of the top 20 Web sites focus on apparel, four focus on movies and event tickets, and three are music related. Other popular sites focus on posters and artwork, video games and consumer electronics" ("College Students and the Web"). In early 2006, when Northwestern University communications professor Esther Hargittai polled 1,300 students at University of Illinois–Chicago on their online time and favorite destinations, their choices were all too predictable. At number one stood *Facebook* (78.1 percent), followed by *MySpace* (50.7 percent). Only 5 percent regularly checked a blog or forum on politics, economic, law, or policy. Only 1 percent had ever perused the leading left-wing blog *dailykos.com*.

The acclaimed empowerment that Web 2.0 has fostered goes almost entirely toward social stuff. Teens and young adults like email and Instant Messaging and pornography, not www.si.edu (Smithsonian Institution). The Web offers wondrous information and images, but why would a high school senior download them when he can read what his classmates say about what happened over the weekend? People can watch shows from the PBS series *NOVA* online or find on *YouTube* a clip of Thelonious Monk playing "Blue Monk" while Count Basie grins in front of the piano, but those clips pale before the thrill of composing something about yourself, posting it online, having someone, somewhere, read it and write something back. That's the pull of immaturity, and technology has granted young Americans ever more opportunities to go with it, not outgrow it. Back in 2001, Pew Research issued a report titled "Teenage Life Online," and almost the entire document focused on social matters, friendships, and messaging. The word *knowledge* appeared only once in the entire 46 pages, when it mentioned that one-quarter of teens use the Internet to "get information about things that are hard to talk to other people about." Instead of opening adolescents and young adults to worldly realities, acquainting them with the global village, inducting them into the course of civilization, or at least the Knowledge Economy, digital communications have opened them to one another—which is to say, have enclosed them in a parochial cosmos of youth matters and concerns.

Maturity comes, in part, through vertical modeling, relations with older people such as teachers, employers, ministers, aunts and uncles, and older siblings, along with parents, who impart adult outlooks and interests. In their example, they reveal the minor meaning of adolescent worries, showing that the authentic stakes of life surpass the feats and letdowns of high school and college. The Web (along with cell phones, teen sitcoms, and pop music), though, encourages more horizontal modeling, more raillery and mimicry of people the same age, an intensification of peer consciousness. It provides new and enhanced ways for adolescents to do what they've always done in a prosperous time: talk to, act like, think like, compete against, and play with one another. Social life is a powerful temptation, and most teenagers feel the pain of missing out—not invited to the party, not having the right clothes, not making the sports team, not having a date for the dance. Digital technology is both a way into it and a way out. It keeps popular teens in the know and in the clique, providing connections that stabilize their popularity—midnight phone calls to

exchange gossip, message boards to announce impromptu gather-
ings, news feeds on the reigning youth icons, etc. And it gives unpop-
ular teens an outlet and an audience, for instance, the nerd who
opens a blog and gripes nightly on the day's displeasures, the reclu-
sive gamer who joins chat rooms on his favorite games, the shy sophomore hoping an understanding voice responds to her profile, etc.

In both cases, the absorption in local youth society grows, and adolescence appears ever more autonomous. For all of them, popular
youths and marginal ones, the celebrated customization power of
digital technology is disabling. Ordinary 18-year-olds love digital
technology because it allows them to construct a reflexive surround-
ing. The part-time job tires them and the classroom irks them to
death, but the blogs, games, shows, videos, music, messages, updates, phone calls . . . they mirror their woes and fantasies. It's a pre-
packaged representation of the world, a "Daily Me," a rendition of
things filtered by the dispositions of young users. All of them groove
the input, and the screen becomes not a vein of truth but a mirror of
desire. Google News sends daily links to stories on topics of their
choice. RSS feeds keep them abreast of favorite Web sites, and only
those sites. Edgy blogs anchor their outlook, and they never hear a
dissenting word. Mark Zuckerberg reveals to the *Wall Street Journal*
the secret of the site he founded, *Facebook:* "That's kind of what we
are doing here, but with 'What's going on in the world with these
people that I care about'" (see Kessler). The things that bother and
bore them are blocked out. The people they don't know and don't
want to know they don't have to meet. A coup may have erupted in
Central America, a transportation bill passed the House, a food scare
just started, but if they don't care about them they don't have to
hear about them. Reality is personalized, and the world outside
steadily tallies the ego inside. A 16-year-old panelist at the 2006 Online News Association convention summed it up perfectly. When a
journalist in the audience asked if sticking solely to RSS feeds made
her miss the "broader picture," she snapped, "I'm not trying to get a

broader picture. I'm trying to get what I want." For most adolescents that means the horizon ends with their friends, music, TV shows, games, and virtual contacts. The adult realities of history, politics, high art, and finance can wait.

The psychological delights are intellectually stultifying. For education to happen, people must encounter worthwhile things outside their sphere of interest and brainpower. Knowledge grows, skills improve, tastes refine, and conscience ripens only if the experiences bear a degree of unfamiliarity—a beautiful artwork you are forced to inspect even though it leaves you cold; an ancient city you have to detail even though history puts you to sleep; a microeconomic problem you have to solve even though you fumble with arithmetic. To take them in, to assimilate the objects intelligently, the intellectual tool kit must expand and attitudes must soften. If the first apprehension stalls, you can't mutter, "I don't get it—this isn't for me." You have to say, "I don't get it, and maybe that's *my* fault." You have to accept the sting of relinquishing a cherished notion, of admitting a defect in yourself. Poet Rainer Maria Rilke's simple admonition should be the rule: "You must change your life."

Nobody savors the process, but mature adults realize the benefits. Adolescents don't, and digital connections save them the labor of self-improvement. These connections answer to concerns of young users, and in each application they reinforce an existing sensibility. The screen and the cell bombard adolescents with youth trifles, and the sporadic brush with challenging objects that recall their shortcomings is quickly offset by a few minutes back in virtual comfort zones. The opportunity costs are high, for what might happen if they converted half the hours at the screen to reading essays, conjugating foreign verbs, supporting a local politician, or disassembling an old computer? Three years might pass and they would stand well above their peers in knowledge and skills, but the adolescent doesn't think that far ahead. With the screen offerings, the intellectual barriers are low and the rewards immediate.

This is precisely why young adults claim technology as their own, and why we should reconsider the basic premise of digital learning: that leisure time in front of screens forms an educational progress. Not reject the premise, but examine it again, slow it down, set it in light not only of the promise of technology, and its inevitability, but in light of a demonstrable and all-too-frequent outcome. For most rising users, screen time doesn't graduate them into higher knowledge/skill states. It superpowers their social impulses, but it blocks intellectual gains.

With poor results in evidence, we should reassess the novel literacies hailed by techno-cheerleaders and their academic backers, compare them to the old ones in terms of their effects, and determine whether the abilities acquired in game spaces and Read/Write Web sites transfer to academic and workplace requirements. Too many assumptions pass unexamined. The Federation of American Scientists report on video games cited earlier maintains, "The success of complex video games demonstrates [that] games can teach higher-order thinking skills such as strategic thinking, interpretative analysis, problem solving, plan formulation and execution, and adaptation to rapid change . . . the skills U.S. employers increasingly seek in workers and new workforce entrants." But for all the popularity of games among teens and the faith among experts that they instill "higher-order thinking skills," U.S. employers complain relentlessly about "lower-order" thinking skills, the poor verbal and numerical competencies of incoming workers. The Federation report itself notes that only some games prove beneficial ("educational games") and that they affect only "some aspects of learning." "Strategic thinking" and "interpretative analysis" sound like advanced cognitive talents, but do games help students read and multiply better than traditional methods do?

Many leading education researchers, assuming that the information economy commands that learning be digitalized, nonetheless press forward without judging the quality of the outcomes. As

Donald Leu, endowed professor of literacy and technology at the University of Connecticut and former president of the National Reading Conference, put it in 2000:

> If it is already clear that the workplace and higher education
> have become dependent upon such technologies, why do
> we require efficacy studies in school classrooms? Research
> time might be better spent on exploring issues of how to
> support teachers' efforts to unlock the potentials of new
> technologies, and not on demonstrating the learning gains
> from technologies we already know will be important to
> our children's success.

The sense of inevitability—technology's here to stay, so we might as well go with it—prompts researchers to accept the practices technology fosters, to tolerate and respect the habits young people develop as a serious and catholic literacy. One article from 2002 in *The Reading Teacher*, a major journal in the field, nicely exemplifies that approach. The author, a communications professor in Australia, observes and interviews students in classrooms reading and writing on screens, then outlines in bullet points the mental broadening that Web reading produces:

- permits nonlinear strategies of thinking;
- allows nonhierarchical strategies;
- offers nonsequential strategies;
- requires visual literacy skills to understand multimedia components;
- is interactive, with the reader able to add, change, or move text; and
- enables a blurring of the relationship between reader and writer. (See Sutherland-Smith.)

We might inquire whether the hasty browsing through Google-searched Web sites, the adolescent repartee of teen blogs, and the composition of *MySpace* profiles really amount to "strategies of thinking." And we might wonder whether visual elements in the multimedia environment highlight or obscure the print elements, which is to say, whether acute visual literacies might or might not interfere with verbal literacy. Not here, though. The author casts Web reading as a supplement to book reading, not a better or worse medium, just a different one, and so she interprets the Web as a mind-expanding forum. "The Internet provides opportunities to extend thinking skills beyond the hierarchical, linear-sequential model that serves so well in the world of print text," she concludes.

Recent trends in reading habits among teens and young adults, though, alter the relationship. Screen reading isn't a supplement anymore, is no longer an "extension" of thinking skills beyond the "linear-sequential model." It's the primary activity, and the cultivation of nonlinear, nonhierarchical, nonsequential thought patterns through Web reading now transpires on top of a thin and cracking foundation of print reading. For the linear, hierarchical, sequential thinking solicited by books has a shaky hold on the youthful mind, and as teens and young adults read linear texts in a linear fashion less and less, the less they engage in sustained linear thinking. Nonlinear, nonhierarchical thinking sounds creative and individualized, but once the Web dominates a student's intellectual sphere, does it change value, sliding into a destructive temptation to eschew more disciplined courses of thinking, to avoid reading a long poem line by line, tracking a logical argument point by point, assembling a narrative event by event . . . ? The other effects, too, might prove harmful. If students grow up thinking that texts are for interactivity—to add, to delete, to cut and paste—do they acquire the patience to assimilate complex texts on their own terms, to read *The Iliad* without assuming that the epic exists to serve their purposes? If the Web blurs the reader-writer relationship, what happens to a Web-saturated young adult when he enters a workplace that sets limits on a writer's identity and opinions and needs, for instance, in journalism?

Those questions don't crop up in establishment academic inquiry, and they certainly don't preoccupy the digital-learning advocates. There is, however, an instructive ongoing research project far from the education sector that does address the nature and effectiveness of screen habits and Web reading in ways that bear directly upon the youth-screen interface. Nielsen Norman Group is a consulting firm headquartered in Fremont, California, led by Jakob Nielsen, a former Sun Microsystems engineer, and Don Norman, a cognitive scientist with distinguished service in academic and private research, including tenure as vice president of the Advanced Technology Group at Apple Computer. For several years, Nielsen Norman has executed controlled testing of Web experiences, analyzed the consumer aspect of new technologies, questioned the prevailing wisdom of Web design, and issued regular industry "alerts" on the findings that enjoy 11 million page views per year, according to the company Web site.

Ten years ago, the *New York Times* termed Nielsen "the guru of Web page 'usability'" and identified the core aim of the firm: to make Web pages easier to use and read and trust. That's the service Nielsen Norman offers its clients from General Motors to Merck to the Getty Museum to the U.S. Navy—a better Web site, better graphics, and better text. Nielsen has no stake in grand pronouncements about the Digital Age, and no speculations about "new literacies" or "digital natives" or "learning styles" surface in his reports. Instead, he bestows concrete, evidence-based recommendations regarding site design, for instance, how to make on-screen text more inviting, how to craft effective banners and headings, how to keep recipients from deleting messages and e-newsletters, and how to balance visual and verbal formats. Nielsen doesn't emphasize the creativity of Web design experts or the characteristics of products for sale or items to peruse on the site. He consults a more mundane factor, the habits and reactions of regular users in their routine usage, customers the Web site hopes to attract and hold.

That means Nielsen Norman must devise testing sessions with ordinary subjects, observing how they "see" different pages, move from site to site, and register images, prose, color, headlines, layout, and font. In the standard setup, people sit before a screen and testers ask them to visit certain sites and perform certain functions, then encourage them to explore the site as they wish and to voice immediate impressions of the things they encounter. Testers go silent while users think out loud as they navigate and read. "Don't like the color," "Borrrrrrring," "Too much stuff," "I'm stopping here," they mutter, and the observers record them faithfully. The procedure monitors more than opinions, too. Because, Nielsen insists, "you have to watch users *do* things," the trials include an eyetracking component, a technique that detects eye movements and charts where on the Web page vision moves and rests, and for how long.

Fifteen years of tests, analyses, retests, reports, and consultations have crystallized into an unexpected but persuasive model of Web users and Web page usability. It begins with accounts of how people actually read a page on the screen. Using the eyetracker in successive studies from the early 1990s through 2006, Nielsen has reached a set of conclusions regarding how users take in text as they go online and browse, and they demonstrate that screen reading differs greatly from book reading. In 1997, he issued an alert entitled "How Users Read on the Web." The first sentence ran, "They **don't**" (emphasis here and in later citations original). Only 16 percent of the subjects read text on various pages linearly, word by word and sentence by sentence. The rest scanned the pages, "picking out individual words and sentences," processing them out of sequence. The eyetracker showed users jumping around, fixating on pieces that interest them and passing over the rest. This is what the screen encourages users to do, Nielsen observes. The Web network goads users to move swiftly through one page and laterally to another if nothing catches their eye. Web designers who assume that visitors, even motivated ones, read their prose as it is written misconstrue their audience.

A similar study of Web reading came out of Nielsen's "Alertbox" in April 2006 with the title "F-Shaped Pattern for Reading Web Content." Here the eyetracker picked up a curious movement in user scanning. "F for *fast*," it opened. "That's how users read your precious content. In a few seconds, their eyes move at amazing speeds across your website's words in a pattern that's very different from what you learned in school." The pattern looks like the capital letter F. At the top of the page, users read all the way across, but as they proceed their descent quickens and horizontal movement shortens, with a slowdown around the middle of the page. Near the bottom of the page, the eyes move almost vertically, forming the lower stem of the F shape. The pattern varied somewhat with each of the 232 user-subjects, but the overall trajectory from wide-to-narrow as the eyes slid from top to bottom held steady. Whatever content businesses want to communicate to visitors better not be concentrated in the lower-right portions of the screen, Nielsen advised.

In between those two studies, Nielsen reported the findings of another, more specialized eyetracking project conducted by the Poynter Institute in 2000. Poynter concentrated on newspaper sites and selected subjects who gathered news online at least three times a week. The exercises the 67 participants completed in the test, therefore, largely replicated their normal reading habits at home. Two tendencies of online newsreaders, it became clear, revealed salient features of screen reading. One, users preferred news briefs to full articles by a factor of three to one. As Nielsen generalized, even in news environments "the most common behavior is to hunt for information and be ruthless in ignoring details." Furthermore, the eyetracker revealed, on those occasions when users read the full article, they "saw" only about 75 percent of the complete text. Two, urged to go online just as they do normally, users in the Poynter study frequently engaged in "interlaced browsing," that is, opening several windows and hopping back and forth, reading a bit on one site, then a bit on another, then returning for more to the original, then opening a new window, etc. Nielsen's inference: "Users are not focused on any one single site." They like to move around, and they want what they read on one site to gel with the text on the others. They regard the Web not as a collection of discrete sites with high walls and idiosyncratic characteristics, but as a network of related sites with enough similarities to make cross-reading run smoothly.

When users receive news information they supposedly care about, their concentration doesn't much improve. In 2006, Nielsen performed its own eyetracking study of user news consumption, this time examining how users take in email newsletters and RSS news feeds ("Email Newsletters: Surviving Inbox Congestion"). People receive newsletters and feeds because they have asked for them, subscribing to newsletters and personalizing the feeds so that their inbox fills with content matched to their professional and leisure interests. But their interests barely affected their reading habits. When email newsletters arrive, Nielsen discovered, users allot only 51 seconds to them. "'Reading' is not even the right word," he writes, "since participants **fully read only 19% of newsletters**." Recipients ignored the introductory material (67 percent of them "had zero fixations within newsletter introductions"), glanced at the main content, then moved on to something else. News feeds are popular with young adults, personalizing portals and filtering out uninteresting news. But "Our eyetracking of users reading news feeds," Nielsen reports, "showed that people **scan headlines** and blurbs in feeds even more ruthlessly than they scan newsletters." They typically read only the first two words of headlines, and if nothing in the list sparks their attention in a half-second's time, they pass on.

These inquiries into Web reading don't try to distinguish individuals by group markers, but in a couple of cases Nielsen did in fact single out participants by age and literacy. A 2005 alert reported findings for lower-literacy users, which Nielsen estimates constitute fully 30 percent of all Web users. In tests for this group, the reading pattern both slowed down and sped up. On one hand, their smaller vocabularies forced them into linear processing. "They must **read word for word**," Nielsen writes, "and often spend considerable time trying to understand multi-syllabic words." They don't scan in the way middle- and high-literacy users do, and so they don't reach enough information to make nuanced choices. Furthermore, when the page gets too complicated, they don't hop through it—they skip it entirely. Hence the flip side of their usage, the acceleration. In both cases, comprehension suffers.

A few months before the lower-literacy alert, Nielsen reported on the other group tested—teenagers. Testers monitored 38 13- to 17-year-olds as they visited 23 Web sites, performed assigned tasks, and voiced their immediate responses, the findings published in the Alert "Usability of Websites for Teenagers." Nielsen remarks upon the standard conceptions of young users, that they live "wired lifestyles," wield technology better than their elders, and are "technowizards who surf the Web with abandon." In this case, however, "our study refuted these stereotypes." Overall, teens displayed reading skills, research procedures, and patience levels insufficient to navigate the Web effectively. They harbor the same traits of other Web surfers, only more so. Their success rate for completing ordinary tasks online reached only 55 percent, significantly short of the 66 percent success rate that adult users achieve. Teenage users scan skippingly like older users, though a bit faster, and they likewise struggle to stay on point as they travel from page to page. They favor cool graphics and clean design, and businesses hoping to draw teen traffic to their Web site better find ways to entertain them. "Being boring is the kiss of death in terms of keeping teens on your site," Nielsen says. "That's one stereotype our study confirmed: teens have a short attention span and want to be stimulated." A site that demands close attention to words sends them packing, for the simple fact is: "**Teenagers don't like to read a lot on the Web**. They get enough of that at school."

Interestingly, Nielsen paused in the teen alert to criticize common overestimations of teen agility online. First of all, he noted, too many projects and commentaries rely on self-reported behavior instead of close observation of actual behavior by testers and by eyetracking technology. Second, Web experts come from the "high end of the brainpower/techno-enthusiasm curve," and the teens they encounter do, too. Surrounded by youths skilled in technology, they take them as the norm, misjudging the vast majority of young users. "Rarely do people in the top 5 percent spend any significant time with the 80 percent of the population who constitute the mainstream audience," Nielsen chided. Furthermore, Web experts tend to remember the "super-users in the bunch," the ones who performed unusual feats, not the rest who did what everyone else does. Recall James Gee's focus on "kids who have redesigned the family computer, designed new maps and even made mods, designed Web sites, written guides, and contracted relationships with people across the world," as if such standouts filled every high school. Only the insulation of researchers in an advanced Web world leads them to judge such youths typical, or to believe that with more challenging screen time many, many more teens can rise to their level. Nielsen's study suggests a different set of talents to improve the other 80 percent: not more computer literacy and screen time, but more basic literacy and more patience, things better attained elsewhere.

NIELSEN'S RESEARCH is an impartial and skeptical commentary on the sanguine visions of digital learning and screen-based education that we've heard, and it recasts the entire intellectual meaning of Web technologies. Although Nielsen's experiments are limited, nonetheless they record vital screen habits that affect screen experience of all verbal kinds. Web reading and Web learning on average, Nielsen demonstrates, are far less creative, complex, literate, and inquisitive than techno-enthusiasts claim. People seek out what they already hope to find, and they want it fast and free, with a minimum of effort. They judge what they see not on objective traits of the content delivered, the quality of language and image, but on subjective traits of familiarity and ease. The fluent passage from one site to the next often counts more than the unique features of one site and another, and the more a site seems self-contained, as with PDF files, the less users approve it. Indeed, as Nielsen stated in the 2003 alert "PDF: Unfit for Human Consumption," the more Web pages look like book pages, the less people read them. A big, linear text lacking ordinary navigation features, a PDF strikes users as a "content blob," and anybody motivated to read it usually prints it to paper first. In general, the content encountered and habits practiced online foster one kind of literacy, the kind that accelerates communication, homogenizes diction and style, and answers set questions with information bits. It does not favor the acquisition of knowledge, distinctive speech and prose, or the capacity to reason in long sequential units. It does not cultivate the capacity to comprehend dense texts such as a legal contract or a logical proof or an Elizabethan sonnet. In fact, hard texts irritate young people, for they've spent years clicking away from big blocks of prose and thick arguments, and losing the freedom to do so (say, in a classroom) doesn't stir them to think harder and read more closely. Forming reading and thought patterns through screens prepares individuals for only part of the communications demands of the twenty-first century, the information-retrieval and consumer-behavior parts. The abilities to concentrate upon a single, recondite text, to manage ambiguities and ironies, to track an inductive proof . . . screen reading hampers them.

Digital Age devotees contend, of course, that Web 2.0 can inspire both. Yes, young users will continue the hasty browsing and juvenile pleasures, they affirm, but with better games and sites, and more intelligent interactivity, users will upgrade their cognition and open their perception. As technology improves and screens grow more portable and reader-friendly, people will play more, read more, and learn more. Minds will soar upward, they predict, and at the core of their vision lies an assumption about the malleability of human nature, a dream of perfectibility with a long utopian tradition behind it.

Nielsen regards the prospect differently, not from the viewpoint of educators tied to a scheme of human progress and industry figures who stand to profit from digital learning, but from that of an independent researcher interested in what works. Given the routine behavior of ordinary users, what must businesses do to survive in online environments? he asks, and the entire thrust of Nielsen Norman's consultation assumes a reverse process for the Web/user future. Instead of young minds and sensibilities adapting to the Web's smarter elements, the people and businesses purveying Web content need to adapt to the interests and impatience of youths. Human nature is more resistant to change than the enthusiasts think, and the Web offers too many choices for experts and mental engineers to steer human behavior in one direction. Inertia and familiarity rule a user's actions, not long-term learning goals, and the tendency holds most especially with adolescents. If presented with a series of sites with more and less challenging content, users do what nature inclines them to do: patronize the least taxing and most customary zones. Web designers and Web-prone educators who hold out for higher-order thinking tasks and who try to control user usage will find their products neglected and forgotten.

This is the reality Nielsen highlights. The Web is a consumer habitat, not an educational one. Digital-learning advocates might restrict one sphere of usage in a classroom or through homework, and parents might invest in educational games for their children, but whatever benefits the assignments and programs provide will dissipate in the many more hours students spend online alone. Nobody can overcome the imbalance, not conscientious parents and not multimilliondollar foundations, and the more that young Americans read, write, view, listen, shop, gossip, play, role-play, design, and emote online, the more the educational aims will vanish. The habits young people form after school, on weekends, and over the summer are pleasing—fast scanning, page hopping, sloppy writing, associative thinking, no unfamiliar content—and while they undermine the values and demands of the classroom and the workplace (scrupulous reading, good grammar, analytic thinking), these habits won't go away.

With observed online consumer habits ever in hand, Nielsen drafts a series of recommendations for site design that anticipate the future of screen experience. Survival in the hypercompetitive climate of the Web depends on securing and holding a limited resource, the attention of meandering users. To make their sites rank high in search queries, to make sites a regular stop in a user's daily travels, to lengthen that pause, Nielsen advises, Web designers must alter the language and format of their pages. Here are some specifics:

- Because users visit one page *through* other pages, and rely on that one page to lead them profitably to other pages as well, the one page should downplay its distinctiveness. To ease inter-site movement, Nielsen writes, "users prefer your site to work the same way as all the other sites they already know" ("End of Web Design"). A site whose language reflects that of other sites facilitates a user's flow and will yield higher traffic. A site whose language attains a style and vocabulary superior to others doesn't inspire more and longer visits. It interrupts the flow and sends users elsewhere.

- To attract lower-literacy users, sites should key their
  language to specific literacy levels, a sixth-grade reading
  level on the home page, Nielsen counsels, and an eighth-
  grade level for other pages. If diction and syntax rise
  above middle-school competence, sites automatically
  exclude visitors/customers/members solely on grounds of
  readability. A fair portion of visitors will come and never
  return, a risk businesses can't run in such a competitive
  market.

- To draw a steady stream of new visitors, sites must
  optimize their "searchability." "Unless you're listed on the
  first search engine results page," Nielsen observes, "you
  might as well not exist." Because users usually type
  common words into the search box, a site whose
  keywords are technical terms, marketese, or any kind of
  exotic or sophisticated diction drops down the results
  list. Novel vocabulary restricts site visits, and so, Nielsen
  urges in the title of a 2006 alert, "Use Old Words when
  Writing for Findability."

- To mirror the fast scanning style of Web reading, sites
  should contain writing that is eminently scannable. Each
  paragraph should contain only one idea, Nielsen says,
  and each should comprise half the word count of
  conventional writing. Keywords should be highlighted
  through typeface and color variations so that they serve
  as convenient markers for the scurrying reader. Language
  should sound objective and evidence-based so that users
  don't suffer the added cognitive burden of distinguishing
  fact from bias and exaggeration. Finally, the more
  designers can break the text up into units through

subheadings, bullets, and boxes, the more easily users can identify its relevance.

- In a corollary to "scannability," text and image should have high visibility for a variety of tools. In particular, Web pages must charm users through the least reader-friendly screens, as do cell phones and other mobile devices. That calls for even shorter sentences, more highlighted and simple keywords, and more schematic aids such as subheads and bullet lists.

These recommendations follow directly from the observed behavior of ordinary people in action online. Their screen reading, surfing, and searching habits dictate the terms of successful sites, and they mark an obdurate resistance to certain lower-order and higher-order thinking skills, most important, the capacity to read carefully and to cogitate analytically. When a site contains edifying material that doesn't echo their active interests, users don't stick around, settle in, and undergo an on-screen lesson. They return to the search results to find a site that does meet their needs, immediately, without burdening themselves with learning anything else. When a page slows them down, as PDF files tend to do, users don't slow down for long. They click out. When they encounter big words on a page, they don't reach for a dictionary. They hurdle them, and if too many big words show up, they leave the scene entirely. When they need information, users seek out the simplest, straightest rendition, not a nuanced, contextualized, qualified version. The mind online drifts toward simplicity, familiarity, and visibility. It wants the greatest amount of content for the least amount of work.

That's the momentum of screen reading, especially so with younger users, and it has an objective counterpart in virtual spheres. The Web evolves through usage, and traffic volume steers the evolution. If that's how users behave, the Web responds. When AOL posted a Q&A page on its Red service for teens, it crafted a pertinent title: "Truth or Crap." A standard heading such as "True or False" wouldn't appeal to the target audience, explained Malcolm Bird, vice president of AOL's youth area. "You have to speak to them in relevant terms," he told the *Wall Street Journal* in 2005 (see Zaslow), relevance including the prevailing verbal conventions. And so, a few idioms dominate. One of them is the teen lingo of social networking sites, teen blogs, and IM exchanges. Go to *MySpace*, click on "browse," click on any photo, and the amateur glamour shots and trifling chit-chat unfurl. On one of them I just picked at random the comment sequence runs: "what up chik how you been mine was allright holla at me some time," "Hey girlie! Just stopping by to show some luv," "HA! I popped your comment cherry!! I love you baby :)."

Another idiom is the flat, featureless, factual style of *Wikipedia* entries. The site incorporates the brains of thousands, and one might assume that so many contributors and editors would create a hetero-geneous repository of learning, the style changing as much as the in-formation from page to page. In fact, though, read a few *Wikipedia* entries and the pat verbal formula stands out, the prose drained of almost every distinguishing trait. It's a wonderful resource for a quick fact or figure, but use it more extensively and after a while the en-tries all sound the same. Note, for example, the sentences on George Washington's presidency: "Although he never officially joined the Federalist Party, he supported its programs and was its inspirational leader. By refusing to pursue a third term, he made it the enduring norm that no U.S. President should seek more than two. Washing-ton's Farewell Address was a primer on republican virtue and a stern warning against involvement in foreign wars." The information suf-fices, but it rolls off the screen in flinty tones, the phrases sounding like cue cards flipped one by one. And yet *Wikipedia* stands as the prime academic reference for students. Its popularity has a corollary effect: *Wikipedia* prose sets the standard for intellectual style. Stu-dents relying on *Wikipedia* alone, year in and year out, absorb the prose as proper knowledge discourse, and knowledge itself seems blank and uninspiring.

We have a plus and minus effect. The language of popular knowledge sites conveys helpful information, but it is too dull to break the grip of adolescent speech on the young mind. Knowledge-language and social-language stand apart, far apart, and young users throw all their energy to the latter. Now and then the Web helps youth knowledge grow, to be sure. *Facebook* founder Mark Zuckerberg explains to the *Wall Street Journal* how the network rescued him once in an art history class. "For the final exam, we had to learn the historical significance of something like 500 pieces of art from that period," he recalls. "Having not really read that stuff, I was in a lot of trouble, spending my time building Facebook instead of studying." Zuckerberg's diction suggests why he would struggle in a humanities class, but in this case his initiative carried through. He downloaded images of all the artworks, posted them on the site with a comment box, then forwarded it to every other student in the class. The ensuing feedback kept him working for hours, and he ended up acing the class. But let's be clear about the players—an ingenious young entrepreneur communicating with fellow Harvard undergrads, the best of the best, a minuscule elite. For 99 percent of the rest of their age group, *Facebook* and other social networking sites have no knowledge aims at all. Sites are for socializing, and they harden adolescent styles and thoughts, amplifying the discourse of lunchroom and keg party, not spreading the works of the Old Masters.

I see the results every semester, and in my own classes I often ask students to conduct an experiment in their daily lives. The next time you sit down to dinner with three friends, I tell them, try something unusual. In the midst of conversation, toss in a big word, a thesaurus word, casually as you sip your Coke. Instead of grumbling, "Yeah, so-and-so is really a jerk," say, "Ah, what a truculent boor." Don't utter *nice*, say *congenial*; not *cheap*, but *pecuniary*; not *hard*, but *arduous*;

not *strong*, but *ardent* or *fervent* or *Herculean*. When I rattle off the higher words, they laugh not just at the words alone, but at what they foresee will happen, too. "If I talk like that to my friends," one student joshed the other day, "I won't have any friends."

If he's right, it demonstrates that the social settings of adolescence actually conspire against verbal maturity. Peer pressure and peer judgment discourage wit, word play, and eloquence, and what impresses others in a job interview, a cocktail party, or an office meeting only alienates their buddies. The occasional high-toned term and periodic sentence that mark one as intelligent and thoughtful in adult situations mark one as pretentious and weird in adolescent situations. The verbal values of adulthood and adolescence clash, and to enter adult conditions, individuals must leave the verbal mores of high school behind.

The screen blocks the ascent. Given the online habits of young users, the popular sites and prevailing reading patterns, digital technology caters to youthfulness and haste. If Nielsen is right, more sites will adjust to their lesser literacies and leaping eyes, and sites that proffer elevated terms and elegant sentences will serve micro-niche audiences or disappear altogether. Sites want to maximize visitors, to become bookmarks, to convert every online traveler passing by into a daily reader, customer, member, subscriber, commenter. Learned content and eloquent style are not the way to attract them. The proliferation and competition of .com pages yield paradoxical effects that we've seen already—not more variety, but more homogeneity, not a race for quality, but a slide to the least common denominator. This doesn't rule out digital learning, to be sure, but it does indicate that as young people extend their leisure pursuits online, diving into peer society and grooving scan habits, screen time turns anti-intellectual. Going online habituates them to juvenile mental workouts. Can we expect them to shift cognitive gears whenever an educational page appears on the screen? With diversionary hours online far exceeding edifying hours, when digital learning moments arise, we may assume that students bring all their diversionary tics and expectations along with them.

YOUNG PEOPLE have too much choice, too much discretion for educators and mentors to guide their usage. By the time they enter classrooms outfitted for e-learning, they've passed too many hours doing their own e-thing, grooving non-learning routines too firmly. And once again, in Nielsen's consumer logic, the trend will only increase. Fast scanning breeds faster scanning, and more scannable online prose. Social networking promotes more social networking and more personal profile pages. Adolescents are imitative creatures, and digital technology makes their models come almost entirely from their own ranks. Techno-enthusiasts extol Web 2.0 for precisely its individualist empowerment, the freedom of citizens to roam in a populous virtual universe, to follow pathways into museums, theaters, and performance spaces, to map and view faraway places, to write back to reporters and politicians, and so on. But liberated teenagers don't follow the group blog *History News Network*, or download the essays on *Arts & Letters Daily*, or view masterworks from the Metropolitan Museum of Art. They visit the amusement parks of youth expression, and if one site disappoints them, they have countless others to discover.

In a word, the gain in consumer choice and talkback capacity brings a parallel loss. Digital technology provides so many new and efficient ways to communicate, enables so much personalization and customization, that almost all the material encountered depends on the preferences of the users. The vendors of Web content have to anticipate consumer interests like never before, and their traditional duty to inform as well as delight has collapsed. Thirty years ago, granted a place on the airwaves, each purveyor assumed a responsibility to entertain and to instruct, to offer an *ABC News* along with

Charlie's Angels, 60 Minutes with *One Day at a Time*. In pre-cable, pre-Internet times, competition was limited, and viewers sometimes watched programs that didn't jibe with their likings. The mismatch could be frustrating, but it occasionally served an edifying purpose: forcing people to recognize other peoples, different tastes, distant knowledge . . . if they wanted to tune in at all. Yes, the concentration of media in a few hands sometimes engendered a cultural arrogance among the producers and an ideological narrowness in the programming. But it also introduced young minds to what they might have missed if they had obeyed only their own dispositions.

I remember coming home to Maryland for Christmas break after spending my first term at UCLA in 1977. I looked forward to sleeping in and hanging out, playing basketball in a cold gym before lunch, seeing friends at night, and watching *Star Trek* reruns in the afternoon. But the TV schedule had changed, and my only options from two to four were soap operas, *The Gong Show*, a talk show (Mike Douglas, I think it was, or Donahue), and a special series on PBS. The PBS offering was unusual, a lineup of American and foreign films from the silent era forward that went by the name (I think) the Janus Film Series. Soap operas were out, and the Unknown Comic and Chuck Barris got old quickly. I stuck with the movies, and in the subsequent three weeks I watched for the first time *La Strada, Metropolis, Wild Strawberries, The Battleship Potemkin, L'Avventura, The 400 Blows,* and *The Rules of the Game.* Parts of them I didn't understand, and I certainly couldn't share the experience with my friends, but when the soldiers marched down the Odessa steps, when the Parisian boy reached the sands of the coastline and the camera froze on his face, when the day-trippers combed the island for the lost Anna . . . the screen imparted something unavailable on the b-ball court or over the phone. My empty afternoons and PBS programmers airing shows unlikely to garner a large afternoon audience came together to deliver odd and haunting tales and sightings to an idle mind. It wasn't always enjoyable—the petty intrigues of Renoir's

aristocrats at a rural estate hardly excited me—but the impression
that in these films a serious enterprise was under way, that film could
yield a different space and time, light and perspective, was entranc-
ing. I returned to UCLA a novice, taking several film courses and hit-
ting the revival houses (as they were called then) every other week.
The experience lingers today, but here's the important lesson: if I
had had a hundred screen options to choose from, it never would
have happened.

For today's young users, it doesn't. Their choices are never limited, and the initial frustrations of richer experiences send them elsewhere within seconds. With so much abundance, variety, and speed,
users key in to exactly what they already want. Companionship is
only a click away. Congeniality fills their inboxes. Why undergo the
labor of revising values, why face an incongruent outlook, why cope
with disconfirming evidence, why expand the sensibility . . . when
you can find ample sustenance for present interests? Dense content, articulate diction, and artistic images are too much. They don't
challenge young users to learn more and heighten taste. They remind them of their deficiencies, and who wants that? Confirma-
tion soothes, rejection hurts. Great art is tough, mass art is easy.
Dense arguments require concentration, adolescent visuals hit home
instantly.

The Web universe licenses young Americans to indulge their
youth, and the ubiquitous rhetoric of personalization and empowerment—*MySpace, YouTube*, etc.—disguises the problem and implants
false expectations well into adulthood. They don't realize that success in popular online youthworlds breeds incompetence in school
and in the workplace. With no guidance from above, with content
purveyors aiming to attract audiences, not educate them, young users think that communications come easy. With fewer filters on people's input and output, young users think that their opinions count
and their talents suffice. They don't realize what it really takes to do
well. Bill Joy's further remarks at the Aspen Institute panel point-

edly identify this unfortunate combination of open access and mistaken self-evaluation:

> People are fooling themselves that they're being creative in these spaces, that the standard of creativity in the world to be competitive and to be a great designer is very hard. You have to go to school, you have to apprentice, you have to do hard things. It's not about your friends like something you did. . . . And so, I think this is setting a false expectation you can create your little island and people can come to it in a video game. . . . The real problem is, by democratizing speech and the ability to post, we've lost the gradation for quality. The gradation for quality always was based on the fact that words have weight, that it costs money to move them around, so there was back pressure against junk.

The back pressure is waning, and even if nobody looks at their blog entries and self-made videos, if nobody heeds their talkback, young people nonetheless may spend after-school hours in an online youthworld, running up opportunity costs every time they check their *MySpace* page and neglect their English homework, paying for them years later when they can't read or write well enough to do academic work or qualify for a job, or know enough to answer simple questions about scientific method, Rembrandt, or Auschwitz. Kids will be kids, and teens will be teens. Without any direction from the menu, they stick with what they know and like. They have no natural curiosity for the historical past and high art, and if no respected elder introduces them to Romanticism and the French Revolution, they'll rarely find such things on their own. With the read/write/film/view/browse/message/buy/sell Web, adolescent users govern their own exposure, and the didactic and artistic content of smarter sites flies by unseen and unheard.

This is not to say that young people should never play and chat and view and post online. It's a question of balance. As long as adolescent concerns didn't take up every leisure hour of the day, as long as mentors now and then impressed the young with the importance of knowledge, as long as book reading held steady, intellectual pursuits maintained some ground in the out-of-school lives of kids. They weren't required for work or school, but they still contributed to a young person's formation. They included reading for fun, visiting museums, listening to what music educators call "art music," browsing in libraries and bookstores, attending theater and dance performances, joining extracurricular groups (such as French Club), and participating in politics, say, by volunteering in a campaign. Such activities exposed young people to complex artistic forms, imparted historical tales and civic principles, and excited moral judgment and ideological fervor. They provided a background knowledge transcending a sophomore's social world.

In an average 18-year-old's life, these pursuits can't come close to rivaling video games, cell phone calls, and Web diversions. Young Americans are no less intelligent, motivated, ambitious, and sensitive than they ever were, and they are no less adolescent and fun-loving, either. It's not the under-30-year-olds who have changed. What has changed is the threshold into adulthood, the rituals minors undergo to become responsible citizens, the knowledge and skill activities that bring maturity and understanding. Outside the home, the classroom, library, bookstore, museum, field trip, employer, and art space hosted the rituals and fostered the activities. The digital realm could do it, too, but not in the way young Americans use it. When the Internet arrived, video games grew more interactive and realistic, cable reached 300 channels, handhelds and wireless hit the market . . . a new age of hyper-epistemology was heralded, and the adaptive intellects of teens, encased in the cachet of supersmarts, were projected to push thought past the pre-digital frontier. But young Americans did something else, and still do. The popular digital practices of teens and 20-year-olds didn't and don't open the world.

They close the doors to maturity, eroding habits of the classroom, pulling hours away from leisure practices that complement classroom habits.

And that isn't all the fault of the juniors, or the technophiles and Web site purveyors. Nor should we put all the blame on the parents who plunk their infants in front of the screen so they might have an hour of rest, or who install a computer in the kids' bedrooms and expect it to be a learning tool. Parents like technology because it eases the demands of parenting, but they might be a little less inclined to do so if they weren't led to believe in the intellectual benefits of screen time. When it comes to education, parents take their cue from others, people who set learning standards and legitimize different exposures.

This leads us to another group: the custodians of culture, the people who serve as stewards of civilization and mentors to the next generation. They maintain the pathways into knowledge and taste—the school curriculum, cultural institutions, and cultural pages in newspapers and magazines—guarding them against low standards, ahistoricism, vulgarity, and trendiness. If the pathways deteriorate, don't blame the kids and parents overmuch. Blame, also, the teachers, professors, writers, journalists, intellectuals, editors, librarians, and curators who will not insist upon the value of knowledge and tradition, who will not judge cultural novelties by the high standards set by the best of the past, who will not stand up to adolescence and announce, "It is time to put away childish things." They have let down the society that entrusts them to sustain intelligence and wisdom and beauty, and they have failed students who can't climb out of adolescence on their own.

CHAPTER FIVE

THE BETRAYAL OF
THE MENTORS

A few years ago, an activist nonprofit organization, Partners for Livable Communities, sponsored a study of community arts programs for troubled and underserved youth. The project wasn't much different from many other social inquiries into arts education in and out of school, and during the two years I worked at the National Endowment for the Arts I came across similar surveys and write-ups that had noteworthy backing and wide circulation upon their release but later sat undisturbed in offices and libraries. In this case, the main authors, Shirley Brice Heath and Laura Smyth, produced two artifacts, a resource guide and a video documentary both titled *ArtShow: Youth and Community Development*. With support from the U.S. Department of Education, Carnegie and MacArthur foundations, and General Electric, among others, they documented enterprises in Louisville, the Bronx, Boston, and Cotati, California, chronicling their efforts to rescue dropouts, interviewing their students, and outlining the elements of their success. In several cases, they showed, students failing in school entered the programs and found themselves, channeling their energies in constructive ways, taking inspiration from arts training and overcoming estrangement from math, English, and biology. More than that, the students became entrepreneurs, offering artistic services—as illustrators, muralists, photographers—to individual and corporate customers.

Artists for Humanity in Boston, for instance, started in 1990 with six paid young artists teaching small groups of urban kids, but by the publication of *ArtShow* in 1999, it boasted 50 young artist-teachers paid to mentor 300 students. And instead of operating as a social service organization, Artists for Humanity acted as a nonprofit business, with participants contracting to design T-shirts for Gillette, the Red Sox, and MIT; murals for Fleet Bank; and calendars for small local firms. In 1998, it sold nearly $200,000 in artwork, although its operating expenses exceeded $400,000.

The financial progress is impressive, but in such programs, *ArtShow* maintains, the real measure of success lies elsewhere. The long-term value stems from their human capitalization, the conversion of marginal young Americans into self-sufficient, confident, creative citizens. The resource guide rightly points out the wasted hours of young people's off-campus lives, emphasizing the lack of elder contact. "Thrown back on either peer interaction or social isolation," it regrets, "young people during those years most critical for moral development miss repeated and consistent immersion in activities framed within and around pro-social and pro-civic values orientations." Left to themselves, teens have no forward direction. Their goals contract and blur into meeting friends and "doing stuff," and the prospect of becoming a positive contributor to their neighborhood never even crosses their minds. The circle of peers maps their horizon, and the day's gratifications fulfill their ambition. With no wider understanding of their own prospects or their community, city, or nation's health, they slide all too inevitably into the desolate portion of teens—close to 30 percent—who enter ninth grade and never make it through twelfth.

The community projects *ArtShow* describes turn these kids around, transforming the empty hours of adolescence into working, learning, maturing routines. Parents are absent, school's a drag, and jobs pay little, leaving a vacuum that pulls unassisted teens down into dereliction. The projects fill it with constructive, esteem-building activities. Older youths teach younger youths, and as the programs unfold they design and execute concrete art objects they can see and hear and feel. Most important, they observe others doing the same, enjoying a thrill of satisfaction when outsiders actually pay money for what they have created. Trinia works at a fast-food restaurant and helps her ill mother care for eight siblings, but she still sets off for theater rehearsals three times a week. After four years with the troupe she has landed the lead role in an upcoming production. The following September, she hopes to enroll in a local business college. Marcus dropped out of school two years earlier after his older brother went to prison for armed robbery. After several months in and out of detention centers, he now has part-time security and moving jobs, along with a one-year-old daughter. Nevertheless, he attends a youth choral society three times a week, practicing for a solo part in the next season. Marcus, too, aims for college in the fall, a technical school, if he can earn his GED in time. These individuals stand at the cusp of adulthood, and they can go either way. The arts programs prove to be deciding factors, structuring the weeks and disciplining their energy, adding positive accomplishments to the discouraging circumstances at home.

The *ArtShow* inquiry showcases methods of handling the degenerating young lives of Trinia, Marcus, and hundreds more, and it singles out most of all an adjustment in the approach to youth. Instead of regarding youngsters as inferior minds and unformed egos in need of tutoring, educators should treat them as colleagues in creativity, voices at the community table with a unique perspective. The guest preface in the resource guide bears the title "Young People as Partners," and advocates "taking youth on as serious and necessary partners in sustaining momentum in our learning—individually and organizationally." The introduction complains that "Few put young people shoulder-to-shoulder with adults in taking on responsibility for the moral, civic, and learning climates of their communities." Media images of troubled youth spread the skepticism, which has a self-fulfilling effect. The more we mistrust youths, the more youths reject adult guidance. The attitude must change. We should acknowledge, the authors insist, "that young people can lead the way in helping us [adults] see how differences—of talent, culture, and creative preferences—add value to communities." Indeed, the central lesson of neighborhood programs applies more to elders than to students: "The theories, practices, and illustrative cases given here will help adults gain the confidence and know-how necessary to accept leadership from young people," to believe in them as "mentors for their younger peers."

Young people cited in the guide and filmed in the video offer personal testimony to the benefits. A rural girl in Kentucky's Governor's School for the Arts found it "weird" to be "working with people that have already focused and have already got their own body of work—enough to call it 'their work' and things like that. Well, I realized that I had a lot of talent but I also realized that I needed to focus." A California student illustrator confesses, "I'm just thrilled to have my artwork in the window here. People driving by, people walking around asking me questions about it." The co-founder of Artists for Humanity assures, "When we see a project go from pencil and paper to the customer, everyone gets a rush," and his colleague recalls, "Artists for Humanity gave me a voice when no one else would give me a thought." Their confidence and creativity mark a jubilant contrast to the dead-end vision of kids stuck on the streets and tuning out in class.

And so, as one pores over the *ArtShow* materials, it is somewhat jarring to hear in one of the video interviews a young artist/mentor sound a stiff negative note about the work. At one point, he remem-

THE BETRAYAL OF THE MENTORS   167

bers the difference between regular art classes in high school and exercises at Artists for Humanity, and as he speaks a proud disdain spills forth.

> You go to school, you know, and I'm sitting in class and I, you
> know, go to the illustration department, and I see kids
> drawing and painting, everybody draws the exact same
> boring, traditional way trying to be Picasso or Rembrandt or
> whoever else, you know, and I'm just trying to be Carlo
> Lewis, you know, I don't really care, I don't want to be
> Rembrandt, you know, I'm a black guy from [words garbled],
> that's who I am.

We don't know how deeply the attitude runs, or where he got it, or how staunchly the young man shall grip his irreverence in the future, but he plainly finds the contrasts enabling. The factors are antagonistic—great precursors vs. himself, conventional models vs. individual expression—not *and* but *versus*. Tradition and individuality stand opposed, and it doesn't occur to him that absorbing the former might actually inspire and enhance the latter. Indeed, tradition for him isn't dormant or neutral. It's a threat. Originality comes from within, he believes, and only when his individual experience is sheltered from dead influences will it spring forth faithfully. It's as if he had to clear away the artistic lineage, to reduce the pantheon of artists to "Picasso or Rembrandt or whoever else" in order to create his own space. Regular art class was boring and homogenizing, and studying the masters only alienated the pent-up self. "Imitation is suicide," Ralph Waldo Emerson decreed in "Self-Reliance," and a young urban guy 170 years later heeded the rule and cast his art not as devotion to craft or union with a pedigree of creators, but as a way to be himself and nobody else.

The episode marks a dramatic segment in the film, but it has an ironic import. The statement makes a claim to individuality, but in truth the young artist merely expresses a customary adolescent stance, and his disregard follows logically from his age and era. It is the nature of adolescents to believe that authentic reality begins with themselves, and that what long preceded them is irrelevant. For 15-year-olds in the United States in the twenty-first century, the yardstick of pertinence is personal contact, immediate effects. Space and time extend not much further than their circumstances, and what does Holbein's portrait of Sir Thomas More have to say to a kid who works at Wendy's, struggles with algebra, and can't find a girl-friend? The attitude marks one of the signal changes of the twenti-eth century in the United States. It insists that a successful adolescence and rightful education entail growing comfortable with yourself, with who you are at age 17. Many generations ago, adolescent years meant preparation for something beyond adolescence, not authentic selfhood but serious work, civic duty, and family responsibility, with parents, teachers, ministers, and employers training teens in grown-up conduct. Adolescence formed a tenuous middle ground between the needs of childhood and the duties of adulthood, and the acquisi-tion of the virtues of manhood and womanhood was an uncertain progress. It did not terminate with an acceptance and approval of the late-teen identity. The shrewdest approach was not to prize the in-terval but to escape it as efficiently as possible.

Not anymore. For a long time now, adolescence has claimed an independent value, an integrity all its own. The rise of adolescence is too long a story to tell, but the stance of teachers and researchers that fostered it may be indicated by a few highlights. In one of its first authoritative expressions, Professor G. Stanley Hall, president of Clark University and head of the American Psychological Associa-tion, composed a massive volume outlining the uniqueness of the stage. In *Adolescence: Its Psychology and Its Relations to Physiology* . . . (1904), he observed in glorious cadences, "Self-feeling and ambition are increased, and every trait and faculty is liable to exaggeration and excess. It is all a marvelous new birth, and those who believe that

nothing is so worthy of love, reverence, and service as the body and
soul of youth, and who hold that the best test of every human institution is how much it contributes to bring youth to the ever fullest
possible development, may well review themselves and the civilization in which we live to see how far it satisfies this supreme test."

Hall's model shifted the burden of maturity entirely to adults,
and it only takes a small step to pass from his effusions to one of the
youth Bibles of the latter twentieth century, Charles Reich's *The
Greening of America* (1970), a long, animated discourse on the cata-
clysmic energies of young Americans. A leader of the Free Speech
Movement, Jack Weinberg, famously advised, "Don't trust anyone
over thirty," a slogan handily dismissed as sophomoric cheek. Reich,
a 42-year-old Yale law professor, converted the defiant antics and
rash flights of youth into a World Historical advent, and his publications in *The New Yorker* and the *New York Times* weren't so easily ignored, especially when *The Greening of America* climbed the
best-seller list. "There is a revolution coming," Reich prophesied. "It
will not be like revolutions of the past. . . . This is the revolution of
the new generation. Their protest and rebellion, their culture, clothes,
music, drugs, ways of thought, and liberated life-style are not a passing fad or a form of dissent and refusal, nor are they in any sense ir-
rational." Reich interpreted youth lifestyle as a serious expression
with deep political, social, and moral content, however flippant and
anti-intellectual it appeared, and while his book comes off today like
little more than a dated artifact in a time capsule, shorn of the radical, Bacchic 1960s rhetoric, the outlook he promoted carries on.

A cover story in *Time* magazine exemplifies it well (24 Jan 2005).
The article profiles a new youth phenomenon, an unforeseen generational sub-cohort termed the "Twixters." This curious social outcrop-
ping rests in a novel cluster of demographic traits. Twixters:

- are 22 to 30 years old;
- have a college degree, or substantial college coursework;

- come from middle-class families; and
- reside in cities and large suburban centers.

These features embody nothing unusual, certainly, but where they lead is surprising. What makes the Twixters different from other people with the same demographics from the past is the lifestyle they pursue after college. Consider the typical choices they have made:

- Instead of seeking out jobs or graduate studies that help them with long-term career plans—internships, for instance, or starting low in a company in which they plan to rise—they pass through a series of service jobs as waiters, clerks, nannies, and assistants.

- Instead of moving into a place of their own, they move back home with their parents or into a house or large apartment with several Twixter peers. In fact, *Time* reports, 20 percent of 26-year-olds live with their parents, nearly double the rate in 1970 (11 percent).

- Instead of forming a long-term relationship leading to marriage, they engage in serial dating. They spread their significant personal contact across many friends and roommates and sex partners, who remain deeply important to them well beyond college.

Despite their circumstances, Twixters aren't marginal youngsters sinking into the underclass. They drift through their twenties, stalled at work and saving no money, but they like it that way. They congregate just as they did before college, hopping bar to bar on Friday night and watching movies on Saturday. They have achieved little, but they feel good about themselves. Indeed, precisely along the lines of Reich's understanding, they justify their aimless lifestyle as a journey of self-discovery. Yes, they put off the ordinary decisions of adulthood (career, marriage), but with a tough job market and so many divorced parents, their delays mark a thoughtful desire to "search their souls and choose their life paths," to find a livelihood right for their "identity." So Lev Grossman, the author of the story, phrases it. Social scientists quoted in the article, too, ennoble the lifestyles, judging Twixter habits (in Grossman's paraphrase) "important work to get themselves ready for adulthood." These young people take adulthood "so seriously, they're spending years carefully choosing the right path into it." University of Maryland psychologist Jeffrey Arnett dislikes the "Twixter" label, preferring "emerging adulthood." They assume no responsibilities for or to anyone else, he concedes, but that only permits them "this wonderful freedom to really focus on their own lives and work on becoming the kind of person they want to be." Sociologist James Côté blames their delay on the economy: "What we're looking at really began with the collapse of the youth labor market," he says, which persists today and means that young people simply can't afford to settle down until their late twenties. Marshall Heskovitz, creator of the television shows *thirtysomething* and *My So-Called Life*, gives the problem a social/emotional angle: "it's a result of the world not being particularly welcoming when they come into it. Lots of people have a difficult time dealing with it, and they try to stay kids as long as they can because they don't know how to make sense of all this. We're interested in this process of finding courage and one's self." And a Dartmouth neuroscientist backs the economic and social resistances with brain chemistry: "We as a society deem an individual at the age of 18 ready for adult responsibility. Yet recent evidence suggests that our neuropsychological development is many years from being complete."

Their comments apply a positive spin to what less sympathetic elders would call slacker ways. But even if we accept the characterizations—their brains aren't ready, the cost of living is high, they take marriage too seriously to plunge into it—there is something missing from the expert observations in the article, an extraordinary absence in the diagnosis. In casting Twixter lifestyle as genuine exploration and struggle, neither the author nor the researchers nor the Twixters themselves whisper a single word about intellectual labor. Not one of the Twixters or youth observers mentions an idea that stirs them, a book that influenced them, a class that inspired them, or a mentor who guides them. Nobody ties maturity to formal or informal learning, reading or studying, novels or paintings or histories or syllogisms. For all the talk about life concerns and finding a calling, none of them regard history, literature, art, civics, philosophy, or politics a helpful undertaking. Grossman speaks of Twixter years as "a chance to build castles and knock them down," but these castles haven't a grain of intellectual sand in them. As these young people forge their personalities in an uncertain world, they skirt one of the customary means of doing so—that is, acquainting themselves with the words and images, the truths and beauties of the past—and nobody tells them they have overlooked anything. Social psychologists don't tell them so, nor do youth experts and educators, but the anti-intellectual banality of their choices is stark. What is the role of books in the Twixter's world? Negligible. How has their education shaped their lives? Not at all. This is what the Twixters themselves report. One of them remarks, "Kids used to go to college to get educated. That's what I did, which I think now was a bit naïve. Being smart after college doesn't really mean anything."

In a word, the Twixter vision aligns perfectly with that of their wired younger brothers and sisters. It's all social, all peer-oriented. Twixters don't read, tour museums, travel, follow politics, or listen to any music but pop and rap, much less do something such as lay out a personal reading list or learn a foreign language. Rather, they do what we expect an average 19-year-old to do. They meet for poker, buy stuff at the mall, and jump from job to job and bed to bed. The maturity they envision has nothing to do with learning and wisdom, and the formative efforts that social scientists highlight don't include books, artworks, ideologies, or Venn diagrams. For the Twixters, mature identity is entirely a social matter developed with and through their friends. The intellectual and artistic products of the past aren't stepping-stones for growing up. They are the fading materials of meaningless schooling.

The Twixter piece illustrates a softer version of the outlook we witnessed above, the Arts for Humanity mentor-artist who doesn't give a darn about Rembrandt and Picasso. He merely supplies a clear and distinct expression of the self-oriented, present-oriented, anti-tradition, knowledge-indifferent posture of his contemporaries. And the authors of the *ArtShow* study likewise reflect the judgment of Grossman's social scientists and youth experts. Keep in mind that the filmmakers chose to insert the "I'm just trying to be Carlo Lewis, you know" avowal into the video, that among the many testimonials they filmed, this one survived the final cut. They must have liked it, and his disposal of artistic masters served their pedagogical point. In fact, if you read through the 95 pages of the resource guide, you can't find a single assertion of the value of precursors, canonical models, aesthetic concepts, and artistic traditions. The list of 10 "Youth-Based Organizational Goals" includes "Working with every young person's sense of self," "Promoting dynamism and creativity to model on-going habits of learning, self-assessing, and project critiquing," and "Helping young people engage realistically with prejudicial behaviors that target youth." It has nothing like "Introduce students to important artistic styles and movements" or "Have students visit local museums and select works to copy," and it never recognizes that "project critiquing" of an intelligent kind requires artistic standards and knowledge. Moreover, it won't acknowledge that the best way to combat stereotypes of youth as ignorant and irresponsible is for youths to demonstrate the opposite. The truth is that nothing endorses arts education better than educated student-artists, and in neglecting tradition *ArtShow* overlooks one of art's strongest claims, the cultural authority of artistic heritage. An earnest student who speaks engagingly about Impressionism exhibits the value of after-school arts programs a lot more effectively than a research report filled with grandiloquent abstractions about learning and selfhood. But *ArtShow* cares more about the feelings of youths than the judgments of adults.

I watched the *ArtShow* video for the first time in the company of four arts educator/researchers, and when it ended one of them smiled and exclaimed how much he enjoyed precisely the complaint about kids in art class all having to copy the same Rembrandt painting. He concurred with the oppressiveness of it. I asked him whether he really thought that this was a good educational outcome. He blinked in reply, not sure what I meant. I said that such a disrespectful attitude toward artistic tradition was bound to limit the young man in his career. Not at all, the others disputed, and look at how far he's already come. "Okay, then," I relented. "Still, does the young man's growth have to assume such an adversarial pitch?" Does tradition have to retire so conspicuously in order for the adolescent self to come into its own?

Nobody else worried about the polarity, though, and my question seemed to arrive from out of the blue. It's not an atypical response. Spend some hours in school zones and you see that the indulgent attitude toward youth, along with the downplaying of tradition, has reached the point of dogma among teachers, reporters, researchers, and creators in arts and humanities fields, and pro-knowledge, pro-tradition conceptions strike them as bluntly unpleasant, if not reactionary and out of touch. Indeed, the particular mode of sympathy for the kids has taken such a firm hold that offering education as a fruitful dialectic of tradition and individuality looks downright smothering. Uttered so rarely in education circles, a modest opinion in favor of tradition comes across to experts and mentors as an aggression against the students, a curmudgeon's grievance. For many of

them, the power of cultural tradition sounds authoritarian and retrograde, or aligned with a Eurocentric, white male lineage, their view
recalling the Culture Wars of the 1980s when conservative activists
battled liberal professors over the content of the curriculum in English classes. In truth, however, the indulgence crosses ideological
boundaries, touching generational feelings that mix widely among
liberals and conservatives alike. It's not a political conflict. It's a cultural condition, a normative sentiment positioning young people in
relation to a past and a future, the cultural inheritance and their pro-
spective adulthood. Instead of charting as Left or Right, it charts as
traditionalist or self-centered (or youth-centered, present-fixated,
individualist). And while traditionalists lean toward conservative
opinion, many liberals feel a similar respect for the past and impatience with youth self-absorption, and many conservatives no longer
set their moral values, religious faith, and civic pride under the long
shadow of great books and thoughts and artworks.

In other words, the youth-ist attitude is just that, not an outlook
but a reflex, not political correctness but generational correctness.
The *ArtShow* researchers and the Twixter experts adopt youth sym-
pathies as a mannerism, a custom of their expertise. What makes
someone say to an adolescent, "Before you sally forth into the world,
heed the insight of people long dead who possessed a lot more talent
and wisdom than you," is more a personal ethic than a political creed.
The ethic has seeped down to the level of etiquette, so that when a
dissenting voice calls for more traditional knowledge, it sounds not
just wrong, but wrongheaded, mean-spirited, bad form. The intellectual force of the call is obscured by its impropriety. This is the natural course of a norm. It begins as a fresh and unusual idea, then
passes through the stages of argument, clarification, revision, and acceptance. It may have been radical or controversial once, but over
time, adopted by more and more people, it turns into common sense
and its distinctiveness dims. When an idea becomes a habit, it stops
sparking thought. When everybody accepts it, it abides without

evidence. At that point, the idea acts as a tacit premise, like travel directions you print out from Mapquest when taking a trip for the first time. You follow the route and arrive at Point B. You don't ponder alternatives. In a traditional classroom from way back when, a youth-centered approach might have appeared iconoclastic and provocative, triggering disputes over learning, maturity, and selfhood. Now it passes without a murmur.

THE PROCESS was complete decades ago, and like so many dominant cultural attitudes today, the final ennobling of youth motives and attribution of youth authenticity derive from the revolutionary heat of the 1960s. And they advanced, as the conversion of ideas into norms often does, not mainly through logic and evidence, but through intimidation. A host of analyses dating from that time to our own ranging from Morris Dickstein's *Gates of Eden* to Christopher Lasch's *The Culture of Narcissism* to Allan Bloom's *The Closing of the American Mind* to Roger Kimball's *The Long March* document the fiery forensics of that moment, and they vividly portray the youth spirit of the age. But here we focus upon something else—the notable, mainstream, middle-aged mentor's posture toward them. The kids and their idols forged a radical youth culture on and off the campus, but what concerns us here is how the conventional stewards of tradition, the intellectuals and teachers in authority, reacted to it.

One particularly eloquent and vigorous exposition illustrates the position well. It appeared in the October 1968 issue of *The Atlantic Monthly*, at the same time that youth activism was cresting, roiling college campuses everywhere. That month, for instance, the House Un-American Activities Committee subpoenaed Jerry Rubin for hearings on demonstrations in Chicago during the recent Democratic Convention. Co-founder of the Youth International Party (Yippies), Rubin showed up bereted and shirtless, sporting a bandolier of live cartridges and a toy M-16 rifle. Meanwhile, at Berkeley, students and administrators negotiated over a series of ten lectures to be delivered by Black Panther Eldridge Cleaver in a course on racism. The same week, a few miles south at Stanford University, Cleaver provided an audience a sample of his rhetoric:

> America is the oppressor of humanity . . . America the torturer, America the ugly, the successor of Nazi Germany.
>
> I challenge Ronald Reagan to a duel because Reagan is a punk, a sissy and a coward. . . . He can fight me with a gun, a knife, or a baseball bat. I'll beat him to death with a marshmallow.

In this temperature of youth fury the *Atlantic Monthly* article weighed in. The author was 42-year-old Rutgers University English professor and World War II veteran Richard Poirier, and it bore the histrionic title "The War Against the Young." The heading in the magazine cites him as a distinguished author, editor (*Partisan Review*), and academic, but the essay drifts far from his scholarly field and into the cauldron of 1960s adolescence, which he terms "that rare human condition of exuberance, expectation, impulsiveness, and, above all, of freedom from believing that all the so-called 'necessities' of life and thought are in fact necessities." Indeed, that Poirier should have taken up the generation gap at all would surprise colleagues and students from years later who knew him as a renowned scholar of American literature devoted to literary memory and canonical writers. In 1979, he co-founded the Library of America, a still-running, award-winning venture providing handsome editions of classic American writing. According to its Web site, the Library of America "seeks to restore and pass on to future generations our nation's literary heritage," and the founders' aim was to ensure that those works remained in print for those generations. Before that, Poirier had produced commanding interpretations of American literature, and for graduate students in the 1970s and 1980s, knowing the thesis of his *A World Elsewhere: The Place of Style in American Literature* was essential. One would expect him to defend cultural institutions even while sympathizing with the political messages of the young. Few individuals represented the virtues of tradition and knowledge better than Poirier.

All of which runs against the argument of the *Atlantic Monthly* essay. It starts with a patent fact: "The rebellion has broken out." To the dismay of their parents, "the youth of the world almost on signal have found local causes—economic, social, political, academic ones—to fit an apparently general need to rebel." Young Americans have rejected the society they stand to inherit, the "system" *in toto*, and they insist upon a full-scale "cultural revolution" as a "necessary prelude even to our capacity to think intelligently about political reformation." They won't be put off, Poirier warns, and they scorn the blandishments of middle-class success. Poirier does not supply examples of the revolt, however, nor does he demonstrate the revolutionaries' fitness to arraign, try, and sentence the "governing system." Youth rebellion proceeds in fitful ways, and as sideburns lengthen, rock 'n' roll spreads, ROTC flees the campus, and Vietnam escalates, the Youth Movement grows more militant and sweeping. In early October, the FBI warned that the "New Left" is bent on sabotage, and judged Students for a Democratic Society a "forerunner in this nihilist movement." Poirier has his eye on something more dangerous, however, an insidious counterrevolutionary force gathering against it.

It comes from the seniors. Surprisingly, he doesn't mean the FBI or those aged ogres launching "patronizations, put-downs, and tongue-lashings" at the young, "the likes of Reagan and Wallace." Poirier identifies a milder, no less effective enmity: the rational, moderate-sounding Establishment intellectuals who decry the belligerent rhetoric and inflated self-image of the Movement. People such as Columbia professor and Hubert Humphrey advisor Zbigniew Brzezinski, Soviet "containment" theorist George Kennan, and Amherst English professor Benjamin DeMott object to the verbal violence, the "revolutionary fervor" and "spirit of over-kill" suffusing the leading voices of youth in America. From their Olympian power centers, Poirier observes, they compose calm but withering analyses in *Time* and *The New Republic* targeting the young as foolhardy and shrill. That's the elders' tactic, and Poirier finds it abhorrent.

He concedes that the young are "inarticulate" and "foolish," but he doesn't care to test the accuracy of the intellectuals' judgment. What matters is the style of their speech. In their overall demeanor, he says, they speak in the idiom of adulthood, the language of "responsible, grown-up good sense." Poirier describes it as "a language that is intellectually 'cool,' a language aloof from militant or revolutionary vocabularies." While youth leaders sound riotous and raving, censorious commentators such as DeMott prefer "a requisite dispassion," their "uses of language . . . almost wholly abstracted from the stuff of daily life." The moderate tone lays all good sense on the side of adults, and youth sympathizers stand exposed, visibly impolite, erratic, and extreme. The very rationality of the discourse denies any credibility to youth protest. This leads to the extraordinary thesis of Poirier's essay. However civil, thoughtful, and reasonable it comes off, he declares, the discourse of counterrevolutionary intellectuals amounts to, precisely, a "war against the young." Their sensible moderation constitutes an assault, a "more subtle method of repression," "yet another containment policy, this one for youth."

Note the equation. "Containment" was a geopolitical strategy, a Cold War way of combating Soviet expansion. Here it turns inward on one portion of the U.S. population, the younger set. The putatively rational and prudent judgments by levelheaded thinkers in fact repeat the foreign policies of the U.S. government, including the harshest ones. "The intellectual weapons used in the war against youth," Poirier proclaims, "are from the same arsenal—and the young know this—from which war is being waged against other revolutionary movements, against Vietnam." The very values that youth fail to embody—rationality, moderation—are themselves the rightful object of youth fury, Poirier says, for they undergird the killing tactics unfolding in Southeast Asia. Their rationality merely rationalizes the status quo, and their moderation moderates the indignation of young people idealistic enough to reject the Establishment. The protocols of civil society serve incongruous aims—to resolve dissent in peaceful ways *and* "to suppress some of the most vital elements now struggling into consciousness." If that's true, Poirier reasons, youth irresponsibility is a mode of critique, youth intemperateness the stoppage of a vile system. Their protest doesn't target one policy or another. It dives deeper into fundamental values, the grounds of civility, respect, propriety—and properly so if civility itself acts to screen planned degradations across the globe. This is why the Youth Movement is not a reform agenda. It's a cultural revolution.

Immaturity has its purpose, then, juvenile excess a liberatory end, and if we recoil at the sight of youths invading campus quads and burning cars, we should ponder first the grounds of our recoil. *We* have to change, Poirier insists, deep down. We must "learn to think differently." The burden sits all on the adults.

> In thinking about the so-called generation gap, then, I suggest that people my age think not so much about the strangeness of the young but about their own strangeness. . . . Only when the adult world begins to think of itself as strange, as having a shape that is not entirely necessary, much less lovely, only when it begins to see that the world, as it has now been made visible to us in forms and institutions, isn't all *there*, maybe less than half of it—only then can we begin to meet the legitimate anguish of the young with something better than the cliché that they have no program. . . . For what the radical youth want to do is to expose the mere contingency of facts which have been considered essential. That is a marvelous thing to do.

The conventional poles reverse. Youth teach elders, not vice versa, and the real world isn't so real after all. The established knowledge of the past, "facts which have been considered essential," has no present clout. And as the facts of life melt under the inquisitive anguish of the young, the normal lives of middle-class adults come to seem every bit as temporal and partial as the lifestyle experiments of hippies. Or rather, even more so, for 1960s youths are willing to question social existence, while 1960s adults conform to it. "Radical youth," caustic and restless, gets all the concessions, the "adult world," sober and rational, all the suspicion. Only the adult world needs fixing.

POIRIER'S ESSAY MARKS a signal case of the generational romance, the transformation of youth from budding egos into attuned sensibilities. His argument models a different mentoring, an approach that may have respected the students but yielded a terrible outcome. Over the years, the indulgence of youth circulated among educators and settled into a sanctioned pedagogy with a predictable result: not an unleashing of independent, creative, skeptical mental energies of rising students, but what we have seen in previous chapters, routine irreverence and knowledge deficits.

The radical youth argument did its work all too well. From the 1960s to the 1980s, with movies, music, television, and fashion drifting steadily down the age ladder, the college campus stood as one of the last ties to tradition, where canonical knowledge prevailed over youth concerns. But if the uprising called for a wholesale cultural revolution, the campus stood squarely in its sights. As Poirier surmised, to meet the youth challenge, "the universities need to dismantle their entire academic structure, their systems of courses and requirements, their notion of what constitutes the proper fields and subjects of academic inquiry." And once a distinguished scholar writing in an eminent intellectual magazine interpreted the presiding civilization as a factitious social fabric accountable to the disordered, exigent scrutiny of teenagers, lesser academics could hardly hold back. If Richard Poirier could ennoble youth motives and denigrate adult standards, if a renowned academic could renounce a hierarchy at whose top he stood, if the momentum of culture beyond the campus surged headlong on the same course, what junior colleagues would object? The continuity of tradition was always a fragile thing, and it wouldn't take much for generation-to-generation handoffs to go wrong, but when the things that ensured it fell under reproach—classrooms and teachers themselves—adolescents could add a brand-new moral weapon to their resistance. If sensible adult judgment complemented bombing raids in Vietnam, adult critics of youth weren't just cranky pedants. They were creepy plotters, and they might as well join hands with Pentagon strategists and corporate bosses. This was argument by stigmatization, guilt by far-flung association. American society relied on learned professors and high-brow periodicals to maintain intellectual ideals, but here they commended youth subversion. Poirier characterized "youth in its best and truest form" not as modesty, studiousness, and respect, but as "rebellion and hope." Anyone who stood in its way fell into the camp of reactionaries.

It didn't take long for Poirier's provocative sallies to become professional observance. By the 1980s, the rebellious, anti-Establishment posture of young adults had become the creed of America's educational institutions. These days, rarely does a tenth-grade English teacher say to a class, "If you don't read Homer, Shakespeare, Wordsworth, or Austen, you will be an incomplete person and lead an incomplete life." In 1959, political philosopher Leo Strauss defined liberal education as "the counter-poison to mass culture." A history professor who agrees with this view today becomes a fuddy-duddy in his own department. Adolescence claimed a distinct mindset and moral position, and enlightened, hip mentors echoed the call. Nobody liked the tags *reactionary, conservative,* or *dinosaur,* and for teachers charged with grading and disciplining students, and thus vulnerable to the charge of authoritarianism, indulgence of youth became an effective way to parry them. One could hardly imagine a more adult-oriented publication than the *New York Review of Books,* and its contributors reside in the most eminent institutions. Listen to one of its regulars, though, Anthony Grafton, professor of history at Princeton, describing the activities of American college kids.

> Undergraduates do all sorts of things at universities. They play computer games, they eat pizza, they go to parties, they have sex, they work out, and they amuse each other by their pretensions. What most fiction has ignored is that a lot of them also spend vast amounts of time alone, attacking the kinds of intellectual problems that can easily swallow lifetimes. In the perilous months of their last years at good colleges and universities, seniors parachute into mathematical puzzles, sociological aporiae, and historical mysteries that have baffled professionals. With the help—and sometimes the hindrance—of their teachers, but chiefly relying on their own wits and those of their close friends, they attack Big Questions, Big Books, and Big Problems.

Observe the aside on teachers "hindering" the students, and the hint of novelists who "ignore" their better habits, along with the observation of almost-graduates tackling problems that have "baffled" adult experts for decades and longer. Indeed, the objects of their searches are momentous enough to merit capital letters. College seniors, Grafton attests, pursue questions and puzzles that "swallow lifetimes," even though their final months on campus are "perilous." The teachers help, sometimes, but usually students consult "their own wits," and the input of their "close friends" matters more than in-class lectures.

The summary draws a remarkable picture of undergraduate life, and the fact that it comes from an accomplished historian, not a minor instructor who likes to hang out with the kids, underscores the distortion. The rhetoric overreaches. How many college kids pick up Big Books and Big Questions? According to Grafton, "a lot of them," but in truth that figure falls way down into minuscule portions of young Americans, even among those at better institutions. Grafton notices some of his charges engaged in high-flown inquiries (a few Princeton students, cream of the cream) and he makes a trend out of it—a pure case of Ivy League insularity. On top of the exaggeration, too, he piles a dreamy bombast. Grafton doesn't just say that his students learn the remote details of history. They probe history's "mysteries." They don't just pore over math puzzles. They "parachute" into them. The gap between fact and verbiage widens, the rhetorical space filled precisely by the indulgence of youth. A description so elevated, so melodramatic, aims more for affect than information. The phenomenon Grafton portrays is a lot rarer than he says, but no matter. The attitude it requires, the tender regard for youth, is, one assumes, no less apt. It's an injunction, so ready and fitting that an exacting and erudite historian/intellectual, writing in a hard-edged Manhattan biweekly, goes soft when talking of 20-year-olds.

The sentimentality justifies mentors in downgrading their mentoring task. They can't produce much solid evidence of youth brilliance and drive, and so they resort to lofty and flushed language to make the case. "Young adults are fiercely individualistic. . . . They are still incredibly open to new ideas and they want to dabble and experiment." So enthuses a report from the Advertising Council (with funding from MTV and the Pew Research Center), though providing little evidence of the good of their "dabbling." The *Philadelphia Inquirer*'s columnist Jane Eisner acknowledges the embarrassing voting rates of 18- to 29-year-olds, but shifts the issue: "Only if we address the structural reasons that young people don't vote can we begin to count on them to infuse our democracy with the ideas and idealism for which young Americans have always been prized" (Sept 2004). "Always been prized" for their "ideas and idealism"? Since 1965, perhaps, but not before.

Young people pick up these rationalizations and run with them. For a study of news consumption entitled *Tuned Out: Why Americans Under 40 Don't Follow the News* (2005), journalist David Mindich interviewed hundreds of young adults who told him that "the political process is both morally bankrupt and completely insulated from public pressure," a sentiment whose truth is doubtful—how do *they* know?—but that saves them the trouble of civic action. In a 1999 survey by Northwestern University's Medill School of Journalism ("Y Vote 2000: Politics of a New Generation"), 69 percent of 15- to 24-year-olds concurred with the statement "Our generation has an important voice, but no one seems to hear it." The cliché is so hollow it could rank with the statement "Our generation has sexual desires, but no one satisfies them," but it has acquired a seriousness that 50 years ago would have been inconceivable. It is normal for young people, temporarily, to act disaffected and feel unheard, but for the mentors to turn this condition into an injustice is to downgrade their position, with youths only too eager to play along. No matter how benevolent the rhetoric of the mentors, though, the thing it bestows—intellectual independence—does the majority of youths no favors. And this isn't only because most youths aren't ready to exercise it wisely, to their long-term benefit. It's also because, while the indulgence emancipates the young mind, it sends an implicit and far-reaching message, too, one the kids handily discern. It sabotages something that may, perhaps, be more fragile than the transmission of knowledge from old to young, namely, the simple, sturdy conviction that knowledge itself is worth receiving, the conviction that traditions remote from their daily circumstances have any bearing.

When teachers stand before the young and assure them of the integrity and autonomy of what adolescents think and say and write, teachers expect the young to respond affirmatively, to seek out knowledge and truth on their own. And maybe that works for the upper-crust students, those contending zealously for a place at Yale or an internship on the Hill. But beyond that talented tenth or twentieth student, something different happens. All of them expect the mentors to enter the room with credentialed authority, some know-how that justifies their position, even if some of the kids begrudge and reject it. When the mentors disavow their authority, when they let their discipline slacken, when they, in the language of the educators, slide from the "sage on the stage" to the "guide on the side," the kids wonder what goes. They don't consider the equalizing instructor a caring liberator, and they aren't motivated to learn on their own. They draw another, immobilizing lesson. If mentors are so keen to recant their expertise, why should students strain to acquire it themselves?

The opposite of what the indulgers intend sets in. Knowledge and tradition are emptied of authority. Ronald Reagan once declared, "Freedom is never more than one generation away from extinction," but a more elemental rule may be, "Knowledge is never more than one generation away from oblivion." If the guardians of tradition claim that the young, though ignorant, have a special perspective on the past, or if teachers prize the impulses of tenth-graders more than the thoughts of the wise and the works of the masters, learning loses its point. The thread of intellectual inheritance snaps. The young man from Boston who announces with pride that he cares nothing about Rembrandt and Picasso typifies the outcome. His disregard follows from the mentors' disregard, their own infidelity to tradition, and the transfer affects all students more or less, the best and brightest as well as the dropouts. The indulgers assume that their approval will bring teachers and students closer together, throwing students further into academic inquiry, inspiring them to learn and study, but the evidence shows that this does not happen.

One pertinent measure of the trend appears as an item on the

National Survey of Student Engagement (NSSE), the national survey cited in chapters one and two. The question tallies how many first-year and senior undergraduates "Discussed ideas from your readings or classes with faculty members outside of class." The activity goes beyond course requirements, the tests and papers, and thus charts how many students are inspired by lectures and homework to confer with the instructor on their own. The numbers are disappointing. In 2003, fully 40 percent of the first-year respondents "Never" exchanged a word with a teacher beyond the classroom. Seniors that year displayed more engagement—only 25 percent responded "Never"—although that is still too high a figure after three years of coursework. Normally, as students proceed, they pursue more specialization in a major and form shared interests and career concerns with teachers. Nevertheless, one quarter of all seniors ignore their professors outside the classroom. Worse, three years later, both ranks increased their disengagement. In 2006, first-year students raised the "Never talk to my teacher" rate to 43 percent, and seniors to 28 percent. More students tune their professors out once the hour is up, and the engagement score gap between seniors and freshmen still stands at only 15 points—a sign that the curriculum hasn't improved.

Notwithstanding the disengagement numbers, however, researchers summarizing the 2003 NSSE survey commend precisely the pedagogical methods of the indulgers. The report observes,

> One of the pleasant surprises from the first few years of
> NSSE findings was the substantial number of students
> engaged in various forms of active and collaborative learning
> activities. This shift from passive, instructor-dominated
> pedagogy to active, learner-centered activities promises to
> have desirable effects on learning.

A nice prediction, but wholly without support. As "instructor domination" dwindles, as "learner-centered" classrooms multiply, then students should feel empowered to hunt down their profs at other times and places. But while "active, learner-centered" pedagogies have proliferated, more student-teacher contact hasn't happened, as subsequent NSSE reports show. In a "passive" mode, with an authoritative teacher before them, students may feel more secure and encouraged to consult one-on-one. Once "activated" by power-sharing profs, though, students head elsewhere. A paradox may have set in: the more equal and accessible the teachers, the less accessed they are by the students. Nonetheless, NSSE researchers buy the "learner-centered" assumption. They assert that youth-approving teaching strategies "take students to deeper levels of understanding and meaning," but if deeper understanding entails closer engagement with instructors, their own data don't correlate with the theory.

The researchers could find other noncorrelations elsewhere, too. For instance, *Your First College Year,* a survey of first-year students sponsored by the Higher Education Research Institute at UCLA, provided the following summary in 2005:

> Although most respondents studied and discussed their
> courses with other students during the first year, findings
> suggest that many remain disengaged from their coursework:
> over half "frequently" or "occasionally" came late to class;
> almost half turned in course assignments that did not reflect
> their best work or felt bored in class; and approximately one-
> third skipped class at least "occasionally" in the first year.

College delinquency of this kind says nothing about these students' intelligence. It marks an attitude, a sign of disrespect, and we may blame several influences for its spread. When colleges treat students as consumers and clients, they encourage it, as does pop culture when it elevates hooky-playing tricksters such as Ferris Bueller into heroes. College professors complain all the time about it, but they have their own part in the students' negligence, for they pass it along whenever they esteem the students' knowledge and de-authorize their own.

That isn't what they think they do, of course, but the effect is the same. Many indulgers believe that teacher-centered instruction bores the kids into diffidence or proves too difficult to handle, and that student-centered instruction will inspire the lesser-caliber students to work harder and stay in school, but in fact those lesser students say otherwise. In a National Governors Association poll of 10,378 teenagers (reported in July 2005), nearly 90 percent intended to graduate, and more than one-third of them stated that high school has been "easy" (less than 10 percent called it "very hard"). Surprisingly, the future dropouts scored similarly on the "hardness" index. Of the 11 percent who admitted that they didn't intend to graduate from high school, only one in nine gave as a reason, "schoolwork is too hard." At the top, at 36 percent, was the claim that they were "not learning anything," 12 points higher than sheer "hate" for the school they attend. The reactions of delinquent college students are less extreme than that, but they echo the high school dropouts' motives. When "instructor-domination" decreases, a few students step up their learning, but most of them cut their discipline, now and then blowing off in-class duties and all the time ignoring their teachers out of class. A 2005 report sponsored by Achieve, Inc., on college and workplace readiness heard less than one-quarter of high school graduates say that they were "significantly challenged and faced high expectations" (*Rising to the Challenge: Are High School Graduates Prepared for College and Work?*). In the *First-Year* study, only 30 percent of students studied 11 or more hours per week, and 39 percent did six hours or less. Only 24 percent "frequently" felt that their courses inspired them "to think in new ways." Half the students (49 percent) visited an instructor's office hours a sorry two times or fewer per term. Let the students guide themselves, and they'll do so happily.

As they glide through their courses, they seem unaware of the long-term disadvantages. Here, too, the abnegation of the mentors plays a role, for in releasing students from the collective past they deny students a resource to foster a healthy and prosperous future. Dissociated from tradition, with nobody telling them that sometimes they must mute the voices inside them and heed instead the voices of distant greatness, young people miss one of the sanative, humbling mechanisms of maturity. This is the benefit of tradition, the result of a reliable weeding-out process. At any present moment, a culture spills over with ideas and images, sayings and symbols and styles, and they mingle promiscuously. Many of them arise passing only a commercial standard, not a critical or moral one, and in the rush of daily life it's hard to discriminate them, the significant from the insignificant, trendy from lasting, tasteful from vulgar. As time goes by, though, the transient, superficial, fashionable, and hackneyed show up more clearly and fall away, and a firmer, nobler continuity forms. We think of jazz, for instance, as the tradition of Armstrong, Ellington, Parker, Monk, Fitzgerald, Getz, and the rest, but at the time when they recorded their signature pieces, jazz looked much different. The cream hadn't fully risen to the top, and "Parker's Mood" and "Blue 7" appeared amid a thousand other, now forgotten songs in the jazz landscape. Only with the passage of time does the field refine and settle into its superior creations.

The tradition-making process, then, somewhat distorts the actual historical genesis of its ingredients. But it serves a crucial moral and intellectual function. Tradition provides a surer standard, a basis for judgment more solid than present comparisons, than political, practical, and commercial grounds. Young Americans exist amidst an avalanche of input, and the combination overwhelms their shaky critical sense. Tradition provides grounding against and refuge from the mercurial ebb and flow of youth culture, the nonstop marketing of youth products to youths. The great nineteenth-century critic Matthew Arnold explained the benefits of connecting to "the ancients" in precisely these "steadying" terms:

> The present age makes great claims upon us: we owe it
> service, it will not be satisfied without our admiration. I know
> not how it is, but their commerce with the ancients appears
> to me to produce, in those who constantly practice it, a
> steadying and composing effect upon their judgment, not of
> literary works only, but of men and events in general.

Contact with the past steadies and composes judgment of the present. That's the formula. People who read Thucydides and Caesar on war, and Seneca and Ovid on love, are less inclined to construe passing fads as durable outlooks, to fall into the maelstrom of celebrity culture, to presume that the circumstances of their own life are worth a Web page. They distinguish long-term meanings in the sequence of "men and events," and they gamble on the lasting stakes of life, not the meretricious ones.

Nobody likes a scold, but the critical filter has never been more needed. The rush of the "present age" noted by Arnold in 1853 has cascaded into a deluge. Digital technology has compounded the incoming flow, and young adults flounder in it the most. Their grandparents watch them at the keyboard, on the cell phone, with the BlackBerry, etc., and it looks like delirium. All the more reason, then, to impart the unchanging and uncompromising examples, in Arnold's words, the "best that is known and thought in the world." Without the anchor of wise and talented men and women long gone, of thoughts and works that have stood the test of time, adolescents fall back upon the meager, anarchic resources of their sole selves. They watch a movie—say, *Pretty Woman*—and see it in the light of real and imagined high school romances instead of, in this case, fairy tales and 1980s finance wizards. Asked for a political opinion, they recall the images they catch on television, not the models of Washington, Churchill, and Pope John Paul II. Instead of understanding the young adult roller coaster of courtship and rejection with the help of novels by Jane Austen, they process their miasmic feelings by themselves or with sympathetic friends. And why should they do otherwise when the counsel of mentors, not to mention the avalanche of movies, music, and the rest, upholds the sovereignty of youth perspective? The currents of social life press upon them hourly, while the pages within *The Decline and Fall of the Roman Empire* and *Wuthering Heights* seem like another, irrelevant universe. They don't know much about history and literature, but they have feelings and needs, and casualty figures from Shiloh and lines from Donne don't help.

No wonder psychological assessments show rising currents of narcissism among Americans who haven't yet joined the workforce. In one study publicized in early 2007, researchers analyzed the responses of more than 16,000 college students on the Narcissistic Personality Inventory going back to the early 1980s. Undergraduates in 2006, it turned out, scored 30 percent higher than students in 1982 on the narcissism scale, with two-thirds of them reaching above-average levels. The researchers traced the rise directly to self-esteem orientations in the schoolroom, and lead author Jean Twenge groused, "We need to stop endlessly repeating, 'You're special,' and having children repeat that back. Kids are self-centered enough already."

The behavioral features of narcissism are bad enough, but a set of other studies demonstrates just how disabling it proves, particularly with schoolwork. One consequence of narcissism is that it prevents young people from weighing their own talents and competencies accurately. Narcissists can't take criticism, they hate to hand power over to others, and they turn disappointments into the world's fault, not their own. These are the normal hurdles of growing up, but for narcissists they represent a hostile front advancing against them. It's a distorted and destroying mirror, as Narcissus himself showed when he fixed upon his own reflection in the pool and snubbed the calls of love and caution he'd heard before, unable to leave his lovely countenance until the end. Education requires the opposite, a modicum of self-doubt, a capacity for self-criticism, precisely what the narcissist can't bear.

The attitude is even more harmful than the knowledge deficiencies we've seen earlier. An ignorant but willing mind can overcome ignorance through steady work and shrewd guidance. Read a few more books, visit a museum, take some classes, and knowledge will come. An unwilling mind can't, or won't. It already knows enough, and history, civics, philosophy, and literature have too little direct application to satisfy. For many young Americans, that translates into a demoralizing perception problem, a mismatch of expectation and ability. An October 2005 report by the U.S. Department of Education drew the distinction in gloomy forecasts. Titled *A Profile of the American High School Senior in 2004: A First Look*, it culled four traits out of the academic lives of more than 13,000 students from across the country. They were: tested achievement, educational intentions, reasons for choosing a particular college, and life goals. Set alongside each other, the first two characteristics settled so far apart as to signal a national pathology. The study focused on student achievement ratings on math scores and derived the usual abysmal picture. Only "a third (35 percent) showed an understanding of intermediate-level mathematical concepts," and 21 percent of them could not perform "simple operations with decimals, fractions, powers, and roots." More than one-third of high school seniors (37.6 percent) could not complete "simple problem solving, requiring the understanding of low-level mathematical concepts," and a tiny 3.9 percent reached proficiency in "complex multistep word problems."

A troubling outcome, but no shocker. The surprise comes with the second trait, the students' expectations. The survey asked high school seniors how much education they expected to complete—not *wanted* to complete, but would successfully complete—and their answers bounded far beyond trait #1. Fully 69 percent of the respondents "expected to complete college with a 4-year degree," and of that group 35 percent believed that they would proceed further to earn a professional or postbaccalaureate degree. Of the others, 18 percent predicted that they would earn a two-year degree or attend college for some period of time. That left 8 percent who had no prediction, and only 5 percent who admitted that they would never attend college.

Broken down by proficiency, the expectations looked downright heartbreaking. Nearly one-third (31.7 percent) of the students who expected to graduate from college could handle, at best, simple problem solving, and one-fifth of those anticipating an advanced degree could do no better. Only 7.6 percent of the I-expect-an-advanced-degree group reached advanced proficiency in mathematics, while 9.4 percent of graduate-degree intenders compiled a transcript with the highest mathematics coursework as pre-algebra or lower.

In the National Governors Association poll cited on page 189, similar misestimations came up. When asked "How well do you think your high school prepares you in each of the following areas?" 80 percent replied "Excellent/Good" in basic reading skills and math skills—a number far exceeding the actual percentage. Three-quarters of them claimed "Ability to read at a high level," and 71 percent boasted excellent/good algebra talents. Furthermore, they demanded more courses in senior year "related to the kind of job I want," not realizing that they can't proceed to more specialized courses until they improve their basic proficiencies in standard subjects.

The same exaggerations show up in younger grades as well. As we saw in chapter one, the 2003 *Trends in International Math and Science Study* (TIMSS) provided sharp comparisons between fourth- and eighth-graders in the United States and in other countries in math achievement. The TIMSS also asked qualitative questions, such as how much participants agree or disagree with the statements "I usually do well in mathematics" and "I enjoy mathematics." When researchers at the Brookings Institution compared these confidence and enjoyment measures with actual performance, they uncovered a curious inverse correlation among different nations. Its 2006 report, *How Well Are Students Learning?*, concluded that

> countries with more confident students who enjoy the
> subject matter—and with teachers who strive to make
> mathematics relevant to students' daily lives—do not do as
> well as countries that rank lower on indices of confidence,
> enjoyment, and relevance.

The numbers are clear. While confident students perform better than un-confident students *within* nations, *between* nations the relationship overturns. The 10 nations whose eighth-graders score lowest in confidence include the best performers in the world—Singapore, Korea, and Hong Kong, among others—while the highest-confidence eighth-graders come from some of the worst performers. Nearly half of the students in Jordan "Agree a lot" that they "do well," but their national score was 424, 165 points lower than students in Korea, only 6 percent of whom agreed "a lot" that they "do well." Just 4 percent of Japanese students believed that they "do well," and they scored 570, while 43 percent of Israeli students rated themselves highly, and the nation as a whole scored much lower than Japan, 496 points. For students in the United States, the inverse relationship wasn't much better. Two-fifths of them (39 percent) had high confidence, but with a score of 504 points they fell well behind the point totals of Korea, Japan, Hong Kong, Singapore, the Netherlands, and Chinese Taipei, even though those countries lagged well behind the United States on the confidence scale. Only 5 percent of the U.S. respondents "Disagreed a lot" with the "do well in math" assertion, even though fully 93 percent of the U.S. eighth-graders failed to achieve an advanced score (625) on the test.

In enjoyment ratings, the same inverse relationship held. Students in every one of the 10 highest "enjoy math" nations fell below the international average in math aptitude. At 54 percent, students in the United States slightly beat the international enjoyment average, but the enjoyment rating of the highest performers (Korea, etc.) stood at least 23 points lower than the U.S. rating.

In other words, enjoyment and achievement have no necessary relation. This is not to say that teachers should implement an anti-confidence, anti-enjoyment pedagogy. The Brookings researchers caution that the pattern has no positive lessons to offer, but it does suggest that "the American infatuation with the happiness factor in education may be misplaced." Confidence and enjoyment don't guarantee better students. Furthermore, they prevent the students from forming one of the essential ingredients of long-term success: an accurate, realistic appraisal of their present capacities.

Indeed, when comparing the self-image of the students and the knowledge/skill deficits that emerge whenever they undergo objective tests, one has to wonder: What are they thinking? Optimism is nice, but not when it reaches delusional limits. Soon enough, the faulty combo of aptitude and ambition will explode, and the teenagers won't understand why. Michael Petrilli of the Fordham Foundation terms it "the reality gap between students' expectations and their skills" (see McCluskey), and the illusion gets punctured all too readily not long after high school graduation. General education requirements in college include a math course, and any degree in the sciences entails more than that. One week in calculus sends them scurrying to drop/add, and many end up in remediation or disappear altogether. It doesn't make sense. The math skills they lack are requisite for the degrees they expect, but they don't make the connection. They must get their college readiness conceits from somewhere besides test scores and coursework, partly, no doubt, from teachers who, with the best intentions, tell middling students that they're doing great, that they should follow their dreams, be all they can be . . .

All too often, the mentors don't see the results of their indulgence, which emerge only after students leave their class, leaving teachers unaware of how the approach misleads their charges. A recent study of teachers' expectations touches one of the significant thresholds in a person's educational life: graduation. When a student graduates from high school, the diploma is supposed to signify a certain level of skill and knowledge, but the teachers who have graded them don't seem to realize the levels actually expected of students at the next stage. Instead, high school teachers consistently assess the skills of their graduating students much more highly than college teachers assess the skills of their entering students. That's the finding of companion surveys sponsored by the *Chronicle of Higher Education* in 2006, one of them directed at high school teachers, the other at college professors (see *Chronicle of Higher Education*, "What Professors and Teachers Think"). Researchers asked 746 high school teachers and 1,098 college professors specifically about the college readiness of the kids they instructed, and the variance was huge. On the general question "How well prepared are your students for college-level work?" 31 percent of the teachers stated "Very well," while only 13 percent of professors stated "Very well." In the "Not well" category, professors doubled the teacher score, 24 percent to 12 percent, meaning that while only one in eight high school teachers found among the students "large gaps in preparation" that left them "struggling," one in four college teachers found them. In certain subject areas, the discrepancy between high school and college perceptions increased to a ratio of nine to one. In mathematics, fully 37 percent of teachers estimated that the students were "Very well prepared," while a meager 4 percent of professors agreed. For science, 38 percent of teachers gave them "Very well prepared," but only 5 percent of professors did. In writing, nearly half the professors (44 percent) rated the freshman class "Not well prepared," while only 10 percent of teachers were equally judgmental. Interestingly, for motivational traits the discrepancy shrank significantly, for example, with teachers and professors differing by only three points in judging students "Very well prepared" to "work hard." The decrease indicates that the problem lies not in the students' diligence but in their intellectual tool kits, and that the energy students devote to schoolwork (and leisure play) often dodges activities that build college-level knowledge and skills.

One of the most precious tools they lack does not appear in predominant education philosophies, however, nor does it shape training programs for teachers and professors, nor does it arise in discussions of American competitiveness and innovation among business leaders and politicians interested in education. When foundation personnel talk of school improvement and education officers announce academic outcomes, they cite test scores, retention rates, school choice plans, technology, and a dozen other topics, but not this one. And if it were posed to intellectuals, academics, educators, and journalists, a few might seize it as crucial but most would give it a limp nod of approval, or stare blankly, or reject it outright. It sounds fainthearted to them, or outmoded, moralistic, or irrelevant. The tool is precisely what has been lost in the shifting attitude in favor of youth: self-criticism in the light of tradition.

ADOLESCENTS ARE painfully self-conscious, to be sure, and they feel their being intensely, agonizing over a blemish on the cheek and a misstep in the lunchroom. But the yardstick of their judgment comes not from the past but from the present, not from wise men and women but from cool classmates, not from art and thought through the ages but from pop culture of the moment. They pass through school and home ever aware of inadequacy, but the ideals they honor raise them only to the condition of peer respect. Their idols are peer idols, their triumphs the envy of friends, not adults. Their self-criticism isn't enlightened and forward-looking, nor is it backward-looking. It's social and shortsighted.

What young Americans need isn't more relevance in the class-room, but less. A June 2006 op-ed in *Education Week* on student dis-engagement in class, "The Small World of Classroom Boredom," concludes, "Instead of responding to our students as individuals with their own interests and knowledge, the school curriculum is, by and large, remote, providing little connection between the classroom and students' lives" (see Schultz). Yes, the coursework is remote, but in-stead of blaming the curriculum and offering more blather about sparking "intellectual curiosity" and "independent thinking," as the author does, let's blame "students' lives" for stretching the divide. Young people need mentors not to go with the youth flow, but to stand staunchly against it, to represent something smarter and finer than the cacophony of social life. They don't need more pop culture and youth perspectives in the classroom. They get enough of those on their own. Young Americans need someone somewhere in their lives to reveal to them bigger and better human stories than the sa-gas of summer parties and dormitory diversions and Facebook sites.

In slighting the worth of tradition, in allowing teenagers to set their own concerns before the civilization of their forebears, mentors have only opened more minutes to youth contact and youth media. And not just school time, but leisure time, too, for the betrayal of the mentors ripples far beyond the campus. In the past, as long as teach-ers, parents, journalists, and other authorities insisted that young people respect knowledge and great works, young people devoted a portion of out-of-class hours to activities that complement in-class work. These include the habits we've already charted: books for fun, museums, "art music," dance and theater, politics. They didn't have to reach high seriousness to do their quasi-educational work, either. Historical curiosity needn't demand a reading of Thomas Carlyle's *The French Revolution: A History* (1837). An afternoon trip to a local landmark might do. Reading comprehension tested in class could be enhanced by detective stories and romance novels at home at night. Not all reading had to equal classic Victorian novels. The activities had a sustaining effect, too, for they helped young people increase their store of knowledge and cultivate the critical eye, which in turn made their leisure habits improve.

The more mentors have engaged youth in youth terms, though, the more youth have disengaged from the mentors themselves and from the culture they are supposed to represent. To take one more example: in 1982, 18- to 24-year-olds made up 18.5 percent of the performing arts attendance. In 2002, the portion fell to 11.2 percent, a massive slide in audience makeup, and an ominous sign for the future of arts presenters (National Endowment for the Arts, *Survey of Public Participation in the Arts*).

The decline of school-supporting leisure habits—lower reading rates, fewer museum visits, etc.—created a vacuum in leisure time that the stuff of youth filled all too readily, and it doesn't want to give any of it back. Digital technology has fostered a segregated social reality, peer pressure gone wild, distributing youth content in an instant, across continents, 24/7. Television watching holds steady, while more screens mean more screen time. What passes through them locks young Americans ever more firmly into themselves and one another, and whatever doesn't pass through them appears irrelevant and profitless. Inside the classroom, they learn a little about the historical past and civic affairs, but once the lesson ends they swerve back to the youth-full, peer-bound present. Cell phones, personal pages, and the rest unleash persistent and simmering forces of adolescence, the volatile mix of cliques and loners, rebelliousness and conformity, ambition and self-destruction, idolatry and irreverence, know-nothing-ness and know-it-all-ness, all of which tradition and knowledge had helped to contain. The impulses were always there, but the stern shadow of moral and cultural canons at home and in class managed now and then to keep them in check. But the guideposts are now unmanned, and the pushback of mentors has dwindled to the sober objections of a faithful few who don't mind sounding unfashionable and insensitive.

The ingredients come together into an annihilating recipe. Adolescent urgings, a teen world cranked up by technology, a knowledge world cranked down by abdicating mentors . . . they commingle and produce young Americans whose wits are just as keen as ever, but who waste them on screen diversions; kids whose ambitions may even exceed their forebears', but whose aims merge on career and consumer goals, not higher learning; youths who experience a typical stage of alienation from the adult world, but whose alienation doesn't stem from countercultural ideas and radical mentors (Karl Marx, Herbert Marcuse, Michel Foucault, etc.), but from an enveloping immersion in peer stuff. Their lengthening independence has shortened their mental horizon. Teen material floods their hours and mentors esteem them, believing the kids more knowledgeable and skilled than they really are, or, perhaps, thinking that assurance will make them that way.

Few things are worse for adolescent minds than overblown appraisals of their merits. They rob them of constructive self-criticism and obscure the lessons of tradition. They steer their competitive instincts toward peer triumphs, not civic duty. They make them mistrust their guides, and interpret cynically both praise and censure. They set them up for failure, a kind of Peter Principle in young people's lives whereby they proceed in school and in social circles without receiving correctives requisite to adult duties and citizenship. They reach a level of incompetence, hit a wall in college or the workplace, and never understand what happened. The rising cohort of Americans is not "The Next Great Generation," as Strauss and Howe name them in their hagiographic book *Millennials Rising.* We wish they were, but it isn't so. The twenty-first-century teen, connected and multitasked, autonomous yet peer-mindful, marks no great leap forward in human intelligence, global thinking, or "netizen"-ship. Young users have learned a thousand new things, no doubt. They upload and download, surf and chat, post and design, but they haven't learned to analyze a complex text, store facts in their heads, compre-

hend a foreign policy decision, take lessons from history, or spell correctly. Never having recognized their responsibility to the past, they
have opened a fissure in our civic foundations, and it shows in their
halting passage into adulthood and citizenship. They leave school,
but peer fixations continue and social habits stay the same. They join
the workforce only to realize that self-esteem lessons of home and
class, as well as the behaviors that made them popular, no longer apply, and it takes them years to adjust. They grab snatches of news and
sometimes vote, but they regard the civic realm as another planet.
And wherever they end up, whomever they marry, however high
they land in their careers, most of them never acquire the intellectual tools they should have as teenagers and young adults. Perhaps
during their twenties they adapt, acquiring smarter work and finance
habits. But the knowledge and culture traits never catch up. It's too
late to read Dante and Milton. There is too little time for the French
Revolution and the Russian Revolution. Political ideas come from
a news talk guest or a Sunday op-ed, not a steady diet of books old
and new.

A few years of seasoning in the American workplace may secure
their income and inculcate maturity in private life, but it won't sustain the best civic and cultural traditions in American history. If
young people don't read, they shut themselves out of public affairs.
Without a knowledge formation in younger years, adults function
as more or less partial citizens. Reading and knowledge have to
enter their leisure lives, at their own initiative. Anayzing Pew Research data from 2002 and 2004, political scientists Stephen and
Linda Bennett lay out the simple fact: "People who read books for
pleasure are more likely than non-readers to report voting, being
registered to vote, 'always' voting, to pay greater attention to news
stories about national, international, and local politics, and to be better informed."

As the rising generation reaches middle age, it won't re-create the
citizenship of its precursors, nor will its ranks produce a set of com-

mitted intellectuals ready to trade in ideas, steer public policy, and espouse social values on the basis of learning, eloquence, and a historical sense of human endeavor. This is one damaging consequence of the betrayal of the mentors that is often overlooked. When people warn of America's future, they usually talk about competitiveness in science, technology, and productivity, not in ideas and values. But the current domestic and geopolitical situation demands that we generate not only more engineers, biochemists, nanophysicists, and entrepreneurs, but also men and women experienced in the ways of culture, prepared for contest in the marketplace of ideas. Knowledge-workers, wordsmiths, policy wonks . . . they don't emerge from nowhere. They need a long foreground of reading and writing, a home and school environment open to their development, a pipeline ahead and behind them. They need mentors to commend them when they're right and rebuke them when they're wrong. They need parents to remind them that social life isn't everything, and they need peers to respect their intelligence, not scrunch up their eyes at big words. It takes a home, and a schoolhouse, and a village, and a market to make a great public intellectual and policy maker. The formula is flexible, but with the Dumbest Generation its breakdown is under way, and with it the vitality of democracy in the United States.

CHAPTER SIX

NO MORE
CULTURE WARRIORS

E veryone knows the story of Rip Van Winkle. The tale of a Dutch American villager who saunters into the woods for a 20-year nap has endured for 190 years, sliding comfortably up and down the cultural scale from college English classes to afternoon cartoons in dozens of renditions. The vignette entertains young and old, and the idea of waking up to find everything changed must exercise some deep timeless appeal, for the outlines of the story long preceded Washington Irving's version. When Irving adapted the age-old tale to a Hudson River setting in the eighteenth century, however, he added a political element, and it may explain why "Rip Van Winkle" has remained so popular a token of American literary history.

Irving's addition centers on the time frame of the plot. Rip lives in a small village in the Catskills, a quiet hamlet founded more than a century earlier by Dutch colonists roving up the Hudson. At the hub sits a small inn where the elders sit in the shade of a large tree and beneath a portrait of King George III, puffing pipes while they "talk listlessly over village gossip, or tell endlessly sleepy stories about nothing." Sometimes an old newspaper falls into their hands, and "how sagely they would deliberate upon public events some months after they had taken place." Rip enjoys his seat on the bench, for he is "a simple, good natured man" of creature comforts, and the children and dogs toy with him daily. Indeed, his only dislike is "profitable labour," for while he will help a neighbor husk corn or pile rocks, his own fences go unmended, his garden unweeded, his fowling piece unfired. Rip would while away his life in easeful penury, in fact, letting his inherited land dwindle to ruin if not for his wife, a hardworking, long-suffering woman who scolds her husband for his laziness until he slinks away with a timid sigh.

Then comes the fateful autumn afternoon. Rip sets out for the hills half in search of game, half of peace. An hour of squirrel shooting leaves him panting. On a precipice above the river, he muses on the setting sun and the reception he expects at home when a voice calls out his name. A peculiar hairy fellow approaches dressed in "antique Dutch fashion" and hauling a keg on his shoulder. Rip follows him up the ravine until they reach a hollow where a company of more men like him mingle and drink with melancholy expressions on their faces, playing "nine pins" over and over. They refill their flagons from the fresh keg and Rip imbibes as well. "One taste provoked another," Irving writes, until his eyes roll and Rip slides into a deep sleep.

The next paragraph directly begins, "On awaking, he found himself on the green knoll . . ." Rip worries he might have slept through the night. His dog has disappeared, and instead of his well-oiled gun a rusty firelock lies in the grass beside him. He rises and moans, his joints stiff and tender, and he's terribly hungry.

Stumbling back to the village, he faces the first shock. He doesn't recognize anybody. They pass by with blank looks, touching their chins as they peer at him. He does the same and discovers "his beard had grown a foot long!" Strange children cluster around as Rip presses on seeking a familiar face or landmark. The hills rise just where they used to, and the silver Hudson flows where it always had, but "The very village seemed altered." Unfamiliar faces lean out of unfamiliar doorways, and dogs bark suspiciously. When he reaches his own grounds, he finds a decrepit, abandoned house with no wife and no children. He rushes to the old inn down the road only to encounter a rickety structure with broken windows and "The Union Hotel, by Jonathan Doolittle" painted over the door. The shade tree is gone, and in its place stands a tall pole with an odd flag at the top, a "singular assemblage of stars and stripes." He recognizes only one thing, "the ruby face of King George" still beaming upon his minions, but now wearing a blue coat instead of a red one, a sword in hand, not a scepter, a cocked hat on his head, and a different title: "GENERAL WASHINGTON."

The signs place the moment roughly in time. Rip has slept through the American Revolution. He leaves a colonial village and returns to a new nation, missing out on a providential sequence in world history. Independence has been declared, a bloody war has been fought, a government has been formed, and a Constitution has been ratified. The villagers have lived through a cataclysm, but Rip knows nothing about it.

People surround him, "eyeing him from head to foot, with great curiosity." Rip gazes back and notes that the changes in the village go beyond countenances and dwellings. "The very character of the people seemed changed," Irving narrates. "There was a busy, bustling, disputatious tone about it, instead of the accustomed phlegm and drowsy tranquility." No local sages recline in the shade telling and retelling homespun yarns. Rip always found their society soothing, and public life for him meant respite from private cares and tasks. But now, the public square rings with command. A man with pockets stuffed with handbills cries out to the rest, "haranguing vehemently about rights of citizens—election—members of congress—liberty—Bunker's hill—heroes of seventy-six—and other words, that were a perfect Babylonish jargon to the bewildered Van Winkle." He

spies Rip and queries "which side he voted?" Rip stares uncomprehendingly when another man sidles up and inquires "whether he was
Federal or Democrat."

The terms pin down the actual year, 1796, and isolate the foun-
dational act of the new nation, a national election. Rip has come
back home only to step into party politics, Federalists vs. Democrats
(Adams vs. Jefferson in the '96 race), and the men want him to de-
clare himself accordingly. He doesn't understand, and when another
man asks him if he's brought a gun to an election with a "mob" in
tow in order to "breed a riot," Rip can only splutter, "I am a poor
quiet man, a native of the place, and a loyal subject of the King, God
bless him!"

"A tory!" they yell. "A spy!" Hardly, but "subject" is the only public
identity Rip has ever known, and it's a thin, reflex one. He can't
elaborate, and his only rejoinder is personal. He asks about his com-
rades, but they've mostly died, some in battle. He calls out his own
name, and the people point to a young man slouching beneath a tree,
careless and ragged, who looks just like him, or like he used to, and
it turns out to be his son. The answers overwhelm him, the sights are
too much, and he mumbles in a swoon,

> "I'm not myself—I'm somebody else—that's me yonder—
> no—that's somebody else, got into my shoes—I was myself
> last night, but I fell asleep on the mountain, and they've
> changed my gun, and everything's changed, and I'm changed,
> and I can't tell what's my name, or who I am!"

The disorientation is funny, the comic tension lying in the contrast between Rip's old-world indolent ways and the vigorous public
mores of a post-Revolution village. But a serious issue underlies the
humor. Irving singles out 1776 to 1796 as the absent years, making
Rip's return represent not just one individual's experience, but a nation's experience, illuminating just how much things have changed

for everyone. If Irving chose 1755 to 1775, the changes would have been all local, the persons and place alone, not the very *character* of things. Rip's sojourn would have no political or civic meaning, just a private one. The selected time frame, then, highlights the advent of democracy itself, and what it does to people deep down. Irving dramatizes the transformation by throwing a simple-minded colonial denizen of a remote village into the newly formed United States at its most political moment, Election Day. How better to illuminate the civic burdens thrust upon the people?

Thus the amusing tale of a 20-year sleep becomes a parable of civic life. Rip's vertigo discloses the taxing responsibilities of American citizenship. Before, the villagers were subjects. Now they are political agents, voters, and they tell Rip that he, too, is "now a free citizen of the United States." Rip used to dwell wholly within the immediate circumstances of his life, all in the present, but the times now demand that he attend to faraway affairs, and to remember formative events of the past ("heroes of seventy-six" etc.). Before, villagers found an old newspaper and debated public matters months after they had played out, but now they participate directly in those outcomes. In fact, one of his old cronies sits in Congress, an elevation Rip cannot even imagine. The public square is no longer a place for idle talk and an afternoon smoke, the people relating on common, natural interests. They gather beneath a political sign, the American flag, not a giant swaying shade tree, and the discourse divides them into partisans.

And the community won't let him alone. In the polling booth, one must take sides, and if Rip can't then he isn't quite a full and legitimate citizen. Only his confusion holds them back, and they realize that the newfound ideals of citizenship don't mean anything to him. A few old folks in the crowd recognize him, and one of them recalls his disappearance 20 years earlier. Rip recounts his experience with the weird Dutch band in the hills, and the villagers smile and shake their heads, judging him either loony or lying. In any case, "the company broke up and returned to the more important concerns of the election." Rip's wife has died—"she broke a blood vessel in fit of passion at a New-England pedlar"—but his daughter takes him in, and with time he settles back into idleness happier than before. Still, the villagers try to make him "comprehend the strange events that had taken place during his torpor," Irving's language emphasizing not the glory of the Revolution but its radical adjustments. Rip didn't live through them, however, and the latest civic realities never sink in, for "the changes of states and empires made but little impression upon him." The others fill in the lost decades, explaining how "there had been a revolutionary war—that the country had thrown off the yoke of old England," but the knowledge affects him not. It's as if the assumption of democratic citizenship requires many years of adaptation, for this is a change of character, not just circumstances, and a change of character in the people will happen only through daring and hardship.

Nevertheless, the villagers find a significant place for him in the civic life of things. He represents the past, pure and simple. Rip doesn't much care about what's happened, the knowledge of recent history and contemporary politics, but he does serve as a reminder of what the villagers have left behind—a "subject" identity. He becomes a throwback, "a chronicle of the old times 'before the war.'" That's his role, or counter-role, a pre-citizen who assumes none of the political duties of the present, but who reminds the others of a contrasting past.

The knowledge factor is crucial, not for Rip, but for the others, and it extends the meaning of democratic citizenship. The villagers explain to him what has happened, recounting revolutionary events one by one as part of their own need to remember, to arrange a sequence of changes that ensures continuity with the past. That makes the abrupt independence of the States a bit less overwhelming. We assume today the freedom-loving, self-reliant, don't-tread-on-me spirit of early American citizens, but Rip's quick identification as a

NO MORE CULTURE WARRIORS 211

subject of King George shows its flip side, and that not every New World inhabitant aimed to live free or die. For even the most rebellious colonists, not to mention Rip and similarly contented subjects, losing that symbolic father was a psychic blow, and the patient instruction of the villagers serves to lighten it. As the literary scholar Donald Pease puts it, "While apologists for the Revolution may have claimed that it liberated America from her past, that liberation was more easily managed in their abstractions than in the lives of many Americans. As a figure in transition from a town life before the war, Rip enabled the townspeople to elaborate upon the changes the war made in their lives."

In the post-War village, they vote, they declaim, they assume powers, and the highest laws and central documents of the land encourage them. It's a heady charge, prone to drift, as the Founders understood, especially with no long-established institutions to regulate it and nothing but the fuzzy concept of "We the people" to contain it. Knowledge helps guarantee its beneficence. That's why the electioneer isn't just grabbing votes when he recalls Bunker Hill and "seventy-six" in his harangue to the populace. Yes, he acts as a partisan, but he also ties the day's voting to a historical legacy, demonstrating that democratic action must unfold in the shadow of civic ideals lest it descend entirely into cheap self-interest. No longer subjects of any kind, citizens have gained their freedom but lost a measure of guidance. They don't have King or Landowner or Church to tell them what to do and how to think. In the United States, aristocratic lineages are dubious, families are mobile, and the churches too splintered and dissenting to convey a dominant civic tradition. People must do and think for themselves without the counsel of institutions that have presided for centuries.

Civic knowledge fills the void left by Old World institutions whose authority has collapsed. This is why Thomas Jefferson counted so heavily on public schools to ensure the continuance of the Republic. Only the broad education of each generation would sustain the nation, "the diffusion of knowledge among the people," he wrote in 1786. If "we leave the people in ignorance," he warned, old customs will return, and "kings, priests and nobles . . . will rise up among us." Indeed, Jefferson would have it that no person would qualify as "a citizen of this commonwealth until he or she can read readily in some tongue, native or acquired." Education would preserve the sovereignty of the people, and without it the very system designed to represent them would descend into yet another tyranny in the dismayingly predictable course of nations. He even relied on public schools to identify promising young men of merit but lacking wealth and birth, who would be supported in higher education by public funds. They would join a vigilant citizenry in tracking the actions of leaders and setting them against the ideals and examples of the Founders, a lineage passed along through books and in schoolrooms. Without watchful constituents, officials in power would stray and government would no longer reflect the will of the people. Jefferson, Madison, and the other Founders expected men in government to behave all too humanly, letting the influences they wield tempt them away from public goods and toward special interests. The scrutiny of informed citizens checked their opportunism, which is why the Founders valued a free press. In truth, they despised journalists, but they acknowledged the essential watchdog role newspapers played. They are the eyes and ears of the people, popular informants keeping vested powers under inspection. A free electorate pledges to safeguard civic life, not only promoting some candidates and interests over others, but also guarding its prerogatives against any infringement, consciously controlling the powers their representatives assume. To do so, they need information they cannot obtain on their own.

Hence the essential connection of knowledge and democracy. Democracy requires an informed electorate, and knowledge deficits equal civic decay. The equation poses a special problem in that democracy does not force citizens to participate. One of the ever present potentials of a free society is for its citizens to decide *not* to follow public affairs, to determine that keeping apprised and ready takes too much effort with too little personal payoff. A paper by George Mason University professor Ilya Somin, titled "When Ignorance Isn't Bliss: How Political Ignorance Threatens Democracy," analyzes the problem in precisely these terms. "If voters do not know what is going on in politics," Somin asserts, "they cannot rationally exercise control over government policy." When government grows too complex and the effects of policy drift down into individual lives in too delayed and circuitous a way, citizenship knowledge appears an onerous and impractical virtue. "Only political professionals and those who value political knowledge for its own sake have an incentive to acquire significant amounts of it," Somin says. Who wants to read through all of the prescription-drug-benefit additions to Medicare, or break down the latest reauthorization of the Higher Education Act? Who can endure an hours-long school board meeting? Why spend weeks listening to candidates and sorting out the issues, then standing in line for two hours to vote, when a single vote never makes a difference in the outcome? No ordinary citizen has to if he doesn't want to. Individual freedom means the freedom not to vote, not to read the newspaper, not to contemplate the facts of U.S. history, not to frequent the public square—in a word, to opt out of civic life.

The data Somin invokes come from the National Election Study, Pew Research Center, and numerous social scientists, and they all reach the same depressing conclusion. In Somin's paraphrase, "Most individual voters are abysmally ignorant of even very basic political information." Ever since the first mass surveys from the 1930s, too, voter knowledge has risen only slightly, despite enormous gains in education and media access. Foreseeing no improvements ahead, Somin advises another solution, a smaller government, which would reduce the amount of knowledge necessary for the electorate to fulfill its observant and controlling duties. Intellectuals and educators, however, can't bypass the knowledge needs of the citizenry, and they must attend to the minds of the young. And one factor that might overcome their intransigence and make them more engaged citizens, one thing that will upset the quite rational calculation by young Americans of the meager practical benefits of civic behavior, is precisely the ingredient Jefferson considered essential.

Again we return to knowledge—knowledge of current events and past events, civic ideals and historical models. It supplies a motivation that ordinary ambitions don't. Voting in every election, reading the op-ed pages, sending letters to politicians, joining a local association . . . they don't advance a career, boost a paycheck, kindle the dating scene, or build muscle and tan skin. They provide a civic good, but the private goods they deliver aren't measured in money or prospects or popularity. Instead, they yield expressive or moral satisfactions, the pleasure of doing something one knows is right, and those vary with how much cultural memory each person has. Consistent voters vote because voting is simply the right thing to do. Rather than suffer the shame of not voting, they leave work and stand in line, and feel better for it. People take the time to send emails to talk show hosts because not speaking their minds is more painful than speaking their minds is inconvenient. They join a boycott even though they like the things boycotted.

Knowledge heightens the moral sense that sparks such profitless commitments. It draws people out of themselves and beyond the present, sets their needs in a wider setting than private circumstances and instant gratification. Tradition raises conviction over consumption, civic duty over personal gain. Past models, whether religious, political, literary, etc., lift the bar of daily conduct. Tradition also holds leaders to higher standards. When citizens disregard the best exemplars of the past, they judge present leaders on partisan and material grounds alone, and leaders behave accordingly. But when they compare what leaders do and say today with what they said and did yesterday and long ago, they add posterity to current events and legacy to a leader's performance. Citizens need a yardstick reaching back in time measuring actions and policies not only by their immediate effects, but also by their relation to founding principles and to divergences from them through history.

A healthy democracy needs a vigilant citizenry, and a *healthily* vigilant citizenry needs a reservoir of knowledge. Traditions must be there at hand, with citizens maintaining a permanent sense of what America is about. A roster of heroes and villains, a record of triumphs and catastrophes, a corpus of principles . . . they impart a living past that adds noncommercial, nonsocial stakes to the individual lives of otherwise private persons. An inheritance unfolds that every citizen may claim, the books, essays, and tales they read linking their separate existences to a regional, political, ethnic, religious, or other context and story within an American scheme.

The inspiring lines and climactic moments and memorable figures are ever available. It may be the words of Thoreau quietly explaining, "I went to the woods because I wished to live deliberately, to front only the essential facts of life, and see if I could not learn what it had to teach, and not, when I came to die, to discover that I had not lived." Or Emerson urging, "Build, therefore, your own world." Or the fateful stand of Frederick Douglass, a teenage slave, worked and whipped into servility by his master until he resolves to fight back, introducing the turnabout with, "You have seen how a man was made a slave; you shall see how a slave was made a man." Or the sober spiritual musings of Emily Dickinson:

> There's a certain Slant of light,
> Winter afternoons—
> That oppresses, like the Heft
> Of Cathedral Tunes— . . .

Heavenly Hurt, it gives us—
We can find no scar,
But internal difference,
Where the Meanings, are—

None may teach it—Any—
'Tis the Seal Despair—
An imperial affliction
Sent us of the Air—

When it comes, the Landscape listens—
Shadows—hold their breath—
When it goes, 'tis like the Distance
On the look of Death—

We have two former candidates for the presidency meeting on a July morning in 1804 on the banks of the Hudson River for an affair of honor, the final encounter after years of political sparring. We have two failing ex-presidents holding on until July 4, 1826, exactly 50 years after they had signed the Declaration of Independence, one of them muttering as his last words, "Thomas Jefferson survives." And there is the contemporary scene every summer afternoon at the Lincoln Memorial when families in bunches climb the steps and gaze at the monumental figure in his chair, then turn to the North wall and join other Americans in a silent read of the words inscribed there:

With malice toward none; with charity for all; with firmness in the right, as God gives us to see the right, let us strive on to finish the work we are in; to bind up the nation's wounds; to care for him who shall have borne the battle, and for his widow, and his orphan—to do all which may achieve and cherish a just and lasting peace, among ourselves, and with all nations.

These are the materials of a richer existence, and they come from a narrow slice of time and one nation only. They raise personal experience to impersonal civic levels, and inspire citizens toward higher ambitions. They elevate popular discourse and rebut the coarseness of mass culture. They correct the dominance of passing manners and tastes. They provide everyone an underlying American-ness, a common lineage uniting citizens in the same way the king does in a monarchy, a church does in a theocracy, a dictator does in a dictatorship, and the Party does in communist states. Except that the American patrimony is evolving and ideal and accessible, the nation being "conceived in liberty, and dedicated to the proposition that all men are created equal." It remains for the people to keep those conceptions and propositions alive.

Because the American tradition lies in the hands of the populace, it does not demand conformity, nor does it homogenize different cultural, political, and ethnic strains in U.S. history. In fact, the opposite happens. People read and study the same things, but their knowledge amplifies differences at the same time that it grants them a shared inheritance. The more people know, the more they argue. They quarrel over, precisely, what America is about, over who the heroes are and who the villains are. They honor the Bill of Rights and respect electoral processes and revere Lincoln, but they wrangle endlessly over the Second Amendment, immigration, and the size of government. They select certain traditions as central, others as marginal or errant, classify certain outlooks as essentially American, others as un-American, and reinterpret the probity of annexations, Reconstruction, the Populist Movement, the New Deal, the Cold War, Reagan . . .

Knowledge breeds contention, then, but that's how a pluralistic, democratic society works through rival interests and clashing ideologies. Disagreements run deep, and messy pursuits and cravings for power cloud the ideas and values in conflict. But the battles that ensue solicit the intelligence and conviction and rightness of the adversaries, and they collide armed with the ammunition of ideas and phrases, works of art and lessons in philosophy and religion, episodes from history and literature. An informed contentiousness serves a crucial function, forcing each antagonist to face potent dissenters, to come up with more evidence and stronger arguments. When values, ideas, and customs collide in an open public contest, one side wins and the other retires, not returning for further contest until it amends its case. And the winning side gains, too, for a steady and improving adversary keeps it from slipping into complacency and groupthink. Good ideas stay fresh by challenge, and bad ideas go away, at least until they can be modified and repackaged.

Knowledgeable antagonists elevate the process into a busy marketplace of ideas and policies, and further, at critical times, into something many people dread and regret, but that has, in truth, a sanative influence: a culture war. Culture wars break out when groups form that renounce basic, long-standing norms and values in a society and carry their agenda into mass media, schools, and halls of power. The battle lines aren't just political or economic, and people don't fight only over resources and access. They attack and defend the "hegemony," that is, the systems of ideals, standards, customs, and expectations that govern daily affairs by ordinary people and big decisions by public figures. Defenders experience the system almost unconsciously as simply the way things are and ought to be, while attackers suffer it as a dynamic, oppressive, and ubiquitous construct. The conflict veers toward psycho-political and religious terrain where minds don't easily meet and common grounds are lacking. The war is ideological, a trial of fundamental assumptions about justice, truth, beauty, and identity, and its outcome is sweeping. When local politicians raise property taxes in a county, they can alter real estate values, hire more schoolteachers, and shift millions of dollars from private to public use. But they don't ignite a culture war. The change is too much a matter of degree, and the nuts and bolts of bureaucratic process obscure whatever cultural discords arise. But when a school district changes the reading list for sophomore English classes, deeper moral and spiritual meanings are activated. People who ignore the deliberations of school boards and pay no attention to changes in their property-tax assessments respond instantly pro and con to a teacher stating in the newspaper, "We need more works by women of color on the high school syllabus." The decision implicates sensitive core values, and the fervor on both sides reflects how far tacit and dearly held beliefs have left the place of common sense and entered the swarm of controversy.

Not many people relish the warfare—who likes to hear basic faiths and values scorned and displaced?—and outside the ranks of intellectuals, artists, journalists, advocacy/interest groups, and other regular partisans, culture wars often appear as gratuitous and overblown occasions sowing disunity in the nation. Most likely, to parents waking up in the morning, rushing to feed the kids and drop them at school before heading to the office, the sight of a headline in the newspaper at the breakfast table trumpeting the latest flare-up strikes them as a distraction, not a battle cry. But in a larger view, not day-to-day but in the full scope of a century, culture wars serve a vital purpose in the sustenance and renewal of democratic affairs. They open new testing grounds for prevailing opinions and ideological challenges. They lift ideals out of the commonplace, positing that if ideals can't survive debate then something must be wrong with them, or with the people who embrace them. They prevent living inspirations from hardening into routine doctrines, in the words of John Stuart Mill, into "a mere formal profession" instead of a "real and heartfelt conviction." They shake up and realign political parties. They break down some institutions (single-sex colleges, for instance) and inaugurate others (for example, periodicals such as *Dissent* and *The Public Interest*).

Our society is so parceled out into professional and political niches that direct and open ideological combat infrequently takes place. Intellectuals operate in restricted settings—teachers in classrooms, professors at scholarly conferences, editors in editorial offices, foundation and think tank personnel at headquarters, bloggers at home . . . Professors talk to other professors in a stilted, quasi-technical language, and in spite of their disputatiousness, they mirror one another more than they realize, agreeing on Big Questions and quibbling over small ones. Advocacy groups deliberate in rooms filled with members only, letting the ideas that unify them go fallow and flat, the discussion turning ever to tactics, not premises. Web-based intellectuals develop an audience of agreeable minds, and the comment rolls in blog entries sound like an echo chamber. Many newsrooms and publishing ventures constitute a monoculture, a subtle ideological radar passing within as objectivity but in fact typecasting the content workers address in their jobs before they are even conscious of it.

Culture wars break down the walls. They don't stop the sectarianism, and they can aggravate group commitments, but they also pierce the insulation of each group. Insiders may grow more polarized, but they have to face the arguments and strategies of outsiders. If they ignore them, keeping to themselves and shoring up turf, not articulating underlying values, they lose the war, for the theater has spread to the public square, and combatants can't rely on the rhetoric that suffices within familiar niches. Twenty years ago, for example, when William Bennett, Allan Bloom, and other traditionalist conservatives attacked the campus for its leftist bias and abandonment of the classics, it did the professors no good to retort and deny in committee rooms and conference papers. Bennett spoke from the National Endowment for the Humanities, and politicians and journalists listened. Bloom's *The Closing of the American Mind* lingered on best-seller lists for more than a year, selling one million copies in the months after its publication. The author even appeared on *Oprah*. To respond effectively, professors had to plead their case at the microphone and in the op-ed page, and they failed miserably. They had grooved their idiom in the mannered zones of academia, and they couldn't revise it for public presentation.

The customary rites of professionalism and rehearsals of group identity didn't work, and college professors have been nervous about public attention ever since. Academics resented the publicity Bloom, Bennett, and other traditionalists received, while traditionalists grumbled that it had no effect on the campus. (Ten years after writing the foreword to *The Closing of the American Mind*, Saul Bellow stated, "I'm certain it has affected persons. I don't think it's affected departments or institutions, to judge by the going trend.") But while none of the contenders were satisfied, the episode demonstrates the value of culture wars operations. Academia had grown too complacent and self-involved. The professors had become too caught up with themselves, and they needed a shake-up. Any group pledged to uphold or to dismantle certain values and norms should never grow too comfortable with its agenda, or too closed in its deliberations. Insularity is unhealthy. It gives insiders false pictures of the world and overconfidence in their opinions. It consoles them on all sides with compliant reflections. But the comforts of belonging don't prepare them to leave the group, to enter the marketplace of ideas and defeat adversaries with the weapons of the intellect, not the devices of group standing, party membership, accreditation, and inside information. However intelligent they are, people who think and act within their niche avoid the irritating presence of ideological foes, but they also forgo one of the preconditions of learning: hearing other sides. Hearing them, that is, in earnest and positive versions, not through the lens of people who don't endorse them. They develop their own positions, tautly and intricately, but can't imagine others'. Again, in the words of John Stuart Mill: "They have never thrown themselves into the mental position of those who think differently from them." A paradoxical effect sets in. The more secure they feel, the more limited their horizons and the more parochial their outlook.

Culture wars intrude upon the parishes. They slow the impetus toward specialization. They don't end partisanship, to be sure, but they do check the influence of one-note interest groups and narrow experts. And the rancor they evoke shouldn't cancel the galvanizing challenges they pose. Opportunists and zealots join the fray, yes, but that's the cost a society pays to ensure pluralism and fend off bias.

The process can slide into the equivalent of a shouting match, and two things that keep it grounded and productive are, once again, knowledge and tradition. An open society always contains elements that drift toward extremes, and advocacy groups tend to interpret local and temporary circumstances as grave signs of ideological danger. Knowledge and tradition restrain the campaigns they mount, measuring their strategies by the curtailing examples of American history and civics and literature. They tie the arguments of the moment to founding principles and ideas, and hold them up against the best expressions of them through time. The example of Martin Luther King's dignified and unwavering nonviolence chastises social protest whenever it descends into vitriol and intolerance. The reluctant public service of George Washington, who filled the presidency for his country and not for private reward, embarrasses greedy politicians who use government as a stepping-stone to wealth. The bristling independence of the New York Intellectuals warns subsequent thinkers to beware fashionable ideas and the blandishments of popularity. Such object lessons ensure that skirmishes stay civil and evidence-based, and they censure a culture warrior who crosses lines of basic rights, freedoms, and respect. They breed sharper disputants, sending veterans of them into high positions in media, politics, and education better seasoned in ideological debate and with superior role models.

The presence of tradition and knowledge also keeps the process from sliding into relativism and power plays. In praising the overall effect of culture wars, we shouldn't level all the outcomes or focus only on safeguarding fair procedures. Some norms are better than others, some doctrines should remain in effect, some theories are true and others false, and sometimes the wrong side wins the war. Sometimes, indeed, worthy traditions fall prey to the war, and essential knowledge gets buried as battles approach. Here we arrive at the national implications of the Dumbest Generation. The benighted mental condition of American youth today results from many causes, but one of them is precisely a particular culture-war outcome, the war over the status of youth fought four decades ago. From roughly 1955 to 1975, youth movements waged culture warfare on television and in recording studios, outside national conventions and inside university administration buildings, and the mentors who should have fought back surrendered. This was a novel army, a front never seen before, with adults facing an adolescent horde declaring the entire arsenal of the Establishment illegitimate.

Two generations on, we see the effects of the sovereignty of youth, and one of them bears upon culture wars to come. Put bluntly, few members of the rising cohort are ready to enlist in them properly outfitted with liberal learning and good archetypes. An able culture warrior passes long hours in libraries and in public debate. He knows the great arguments, and he applies them smoothly to the day's issues. He acknowledges his better opponents, but never shies away from a skirmish. He mixes the arcane thesis with the engaging illustration, his rhetoric consistent with the loftiest sources but accessible to educated laypersons. It is the rare under-30-year-old who comes close to qualifying, even as a novice. They don't read enough books and study enough artworks, or care enough to do so. They don't ponder enough ideas or have the vocabulary to discuss them. They derive no lessons from history and revere few heroes outside pop culture and from before 1990.

For those few who are disposed to intellectual sport, they embark

automatically disadvantaged by their social habitat. However serious
their ambition and disciplined their reading, the would-be young intellectuals of today lack a vital component that earlier intellectuals
enjoyed from their teens through college and that they credited for
their later successes. It is: a youthworld of ideas and arguments, an
intellectual forensic in the social settings of the young. The New
York Intellectuals are a case in point. A 1998 documentary by Joseph
Dorman titled *Arguing the World* profiles four of them—Daniel Bell,
Nathan Glazer, Irving Howe, and Irving Kristol—and each one credits a major part of his formation to the fiery polemical climate of
City College in New York City in the 1930s and 1940s. Like all the
other brainy but poor kids in the city, Bell and others attended City
College purely for the education it provided—not for any direct
privileges, contacts, or money it might bring. They wanted learning
and colloquy, and their motives found ample room in the extraordinary habitat of the campus, the lead coming not from the teachers,
but from the students. "Most of the teachers were dodos," Bell recalls
on camera, "and we educated ourselves." Kristol agrees, stating in an
essay many years earlier, "The education I got was pretty good, even
if most of it was acquired outside the classroom" (Kristol). The cafeteria, not the seminar, was the debating place, and students divided
themselves up into different alcoves, one for jocks, ROTC, Catholics,
Zionists, African Americans, and the pro-Stalinist Left in Alcove 2
and the anti-Stalinist Left in Alcove 1. Bell, Howe, Kristol, Glazer,
and many others who ended up making distinguished academic careers sidled into Alcove 1 each day for a sandwich and Coke and the
latest pieces by Sidney Hook and Clement Greenberg. In Alcove 2,
Kristol remembers only two men, both prominent scientists later on,
one of them the convicted and executed spy Julius Rosenberg. Over
lunch Alcove 1 taunted and berated Alcove 2, and the Stalinists tried
not to reply, for they were under orders from the Party not to engage
Trotskyists at any time—which shows just how much intellectual

engagements mattered. The Trotskyists jockeyed with one another, too, running to class and returning an hour later to finish the argument. The experience, Kristol says, "put me in touch with people and ideas that prompted me to read and think and argue with a furious energy." One commentator in the film, Morris Dickstein, calls City College back then "a school for political disputation," and Howe marvels over the "atmosphere of perfervid, overly heated, overly excited intellectuality." Books and ideas counted most, and citations from Marx, Lenin, and Trotsky filled the air. Students passed around copies of *Partisan Review* and short stories by James Joyce and Thomas Mann.

This was boot camp for culture warriors. Alcove 1 trained future intellectuals in political radicalism and intellectual rigor, standards of erudition and aesthetic taste. It fostered adversarial postures and loaded rhetoric, but it also demanded genuine reflection and study, and particularly a sense of fallibility. The students may have been hotheaded sophomores, but they turned their fierce analysis upon the worldly questions of the day and upon themselves. In *Arguing the World*, Kristol remembers the

> internal self-examination . . . trying to figure out our own
> radicalism, and particularly that absolutely overwhelming
> question that haunted us, namely, Was there something in
> Marxism and Leninism that led to Stalinism?

In 1939, no ideological question mattered more, especially after the Hitler–Stalin pact. The answer might turn these young intellectuals upside down. Self-examination could lead to the apprehension that everything they thought was wrong, wrong about the world and wrong about themselves all the way down to their radical self-image. But they didn't care about self-esteem, nor did they aim to shore up a party line or preserve their heroes from accountability. To enter

Alcove 1 and hold your own, you had to read daily newspapers and nineteenth-century books, polish your speech and test your convictions, and embrace an intellectual attitude throughout. Ideas had consequences—that was the faith. The truth must be found, and however young, poor, and powerless these individuals were, they felt directly implicated in the doings of politicians 6,000 miles away and in the writings of thinkers six decades before.

Twenty years later, a New Left came along and prosecuted a culture war that began the steady deterioration of intellectual life among young Americans. We should remember, though, that many of them, for a time at least, thought the same way about books and ideas even as they attacked the institutions that purveyed them. "We devoured books and articles both polemical and technical," Todd Gitlin writes in his memoir *The Sixties: Years of Hope, Days of Rage*. Tracts by Jean-Paul Sartre and C. Wright Mills circulated among them. Tom Hayden wrote his master's thesis on Mill's work and criticized the outlook of two graduates of Alcove 1, Daniel Bell and Seymour Martin Lipset, for the themes they developed in the 1950s. In his own memoir, *Radical Son: A Generational Odyssey*, ex–Berkeley radical David Horowitz recalls that the Bay of Pigs fiasco sent him not into the streets but to the library "to get a copy of *Imperialism: The Last Stage of Capitalism* and read it for the first time." Gitlin, a former president of Students for a Democratic Society (SDS), goes so far as to remember his first colleagues in the movement as "steeped in a most traditional American individualism, especially the utopian edge of it expressed in the mid-nineteenth-century middle-class transcendentalism of Emerson and Whitman." When they met to hash out the famous Port Huron Statement, they debated old cruxes such as the perfectibility of man and the dangers of utopian thinking, not to mention communism, anti-communism, and anti-anti-communism.

The quality of their knowledge and reasoning didn't equal that of the New York Intellectuals, and the bookishness of what Gitlin terms "the SDS Old Guard" gave way quickly to various street theaters, the

Sexual Revolution, and the Weathermen. For the originators, though, a background in Leftist tradition from Marx to Frantz Fanon enhanced their standing, and the more they could expound the intellectual foundations of capitalism, colonialism, racism, and inequality, the better they could formulate an oppositional agenda. The reason it didn't last stems not from a conscious decision to become anti-intellectual, but from a particular corollary to their opposition. It was their conviction of having an unusual place in history, namely, a sense of their generation's singularity, its specialness. It comes across in the first section of the Port Huron Statement, entitled "Agenda for a Generation," and the young-old division continues throughout the document, setting a theme for the entire movement. "Our work is guided by the sense that we may be the last generation in the experiment with living," it declares. "But we are a minority—the vast majority of our people regard the temporary equilibriums of our society and world as eternally-functional parts." Complacency rules the 30-and-up crowd, the Statement asserts, while urgent concern motivates the youth. It acknowledges that young Americans "are used to moral leadership being exercised and moral dimensions being clarified by our elders," but for this cohort of students, "not even the liberal and socialist preachments of the past seem adequate to the forms of the present." No more "in loco parentis theory" for them, for they believed that their Leftist forebears, too, botched the radical project.

You see the impasse. The leaders of the Movement denounced the legacy of their elders, books and ideas as well as mores and institutions, in hasty broadsides, but at least they knew them well. They went to college, read the texts, idolized revolutionaries, and concocted an informed rejection of tradition. But their engagement with the past couldn't survive their self-affirming posture. They distinguished themselves from every other generation so dramatically, and chastised precursor intellectuals with such pious gall, that the entire relationship of past and present, revolutionary action and ideological tradition, broke down. They admired many thinkers, Mills, Marcuse, etc., but only temporarily, and as the Movement grew the reading of "Repressive Tolerance" and *The Power Elite* brought less credit than emulating men and women of revolutionary action, styles of radical will. To join Alcove 1, you had to have studied *Literature and Revolution* (Trotsky), and to prevail at Port Huron it helped to know your radical sociologists. But while the writing of the Port Huron Statement required book learning, the reception of it didn't. To compose phrases about "the dominant conceptions of man in the twentieth century: that he is a thing to be manipulated, and that he is inherently incapable of directing his own affairs," you needed some familiarity with social theory. But to read those phrases, especially when they were followed by flat rulings such as "We oppose the depersonalization that reduces human beings to the status of things," social theory was unnecessary. The successors of Old Guard SDS would draw an easy lesson: why bother to learn things and read books that are obsolete and irrelevant? A predictable descent commenced. The sixties generation's leaders didn't anticipate how their claim of exceptionalism would affect the next generation, and the next, but the sequence was entirely logical. Informed rejection of the past became uninformed rejection of the past, and then complete and unworried ignorance of it.

DO INTELLECTUAL POCKETS exist today similar to Alcove 1 or to Port Huron? I don't know of any. Sometimes people mention the College Republicans on different campuses, young conservatives who do read *The Weekly Standard* and *The Conservative Mind: From Burke to Eliot* and track the acts of Congress. They reside in an environment largely hostile to their outlook, which makes them thick-skinned and intensifies their get-togethers. They are more intellectual than their peers to the left, more experienced in polemic, and they grasp the battling ideas and policies at play in the culture wars. Feeling outnumbered and surrounded, they hone the defense of ideas and question assumptions and read books more than do their opposites. But I've observed that they often lack one thing essential to an exacting forensic. They operate too much in agreement with one another, uniting too consistently against a common foe, liberals and leftists on campus. They break down the inconsistencies of the campus Left, but they don't ponder inconsistencies within their own camps, such as the conflict between the consumerism fostered by market freedoms and the restraints exacted by religious instruction. The tendency is natural, but it's too partisan, and it deprives the College Republicans of the benefit of, precisely, "internal self-examination." It also encourages them to neglect the best traditions of their adversaries, the progressive canon from the Enlightenment forward. They end up responding only to popular, momentary expressions of progressivism on television and in newspapers, not the best books and essays from the last 100 years. So, when I talk with members of the College Republicans and I notice the premature polarization, I urge them to read John Dewey's *Democracy and Education* and the opening chapters in Marx's *Capital* on "commodity fetishism." But I don't know how many comply.

There are some equally engaged student groups on the other side, too, one of recent note being an updated SDS. About 2,000 novice left-wingers make up the membership, with more than 100 chapters opening across the country. An article by Christopher Phelps in *The Nation* profiles it as an energetic and "inclusive, multi-issue student group seeking social transformation." Like their 1960s precursor, SDS-ers of the present aim for "participatory democracy," a kind of local socialism that maximizes the will of citizens in public matters. They are proudly multicultural and fiercely anti–Iraq War. At the University of Alabama, Phelps reports, "SDS recently staged a 'die-in' to dramatize the war. Three Michigan chapters are investigating their universities' financial ties to the military industry." The activist echoes are clear, but one thing distinguishes this SDS from the old

one. In all the quotations from the leaders and remarks on their protests, not to mention the many letters *The Nation* printed subse-
quently, hardly any traces of theories, ideas, arguments, books, or
thinkers emerge. Everything is topical. They never ascend to reflec-
tive declarations such as "Doubt has replaced hopefulness—and men
act out a defeatism that is labeled realistic," as the Port Huron Statement does. "While SDSers are extraordinarily skillful at dissecting
race, gender, class and sexuality in their personal lives," Phelps writes,
"they show less aptitude, as yet, for economic research and political
analysis." Nothing about Foucault or feminists or Critical Race Theory, or more distant influences from radical tradition. They don't
even have much to say about the old SDS, except that the new one
allows more opportunities for minorities and women. One should
add, too, that the dissection of race, gender, class, and sexuality
they've mastered could not be more conventional, as one class assignment after another asks it of students from middle school on-
ward. In their remarks one can't find anything more complicated
than what a standard freshman orientation instills. In fact, the social
attitudes and political leanings the new SDS-ers espouse don't differ
from those of their 50-year-old humanities professors at all. They
only add to the outlook the energy and antics of youth.

However committed and intelligent these right- and left-wing
students are, the social settings they frequent simply do not provide
healthy breeding grounds for tomorrow's intellectuals. It's admirable
for them to organize and convene, to devise civic and political agen-
das, to turn off the television and join a campaign. But in "activating,"
so to speak, before doing their homework, reading Karl Marx *and*
Friedrich Hayek, T. S. Eliot *and* Jack Kerouac, they over-attach to
trends and circumstances that come and go, and neglect the enduring ideas and conflicts. They will argue vociferously over the War on
Terror, or racism in the United States, or religion and the public
square, but their points tend to be situational, that is, assertions about

what is happening and what should be happening. They don't invoke what Machiavelli said about the exercise of power, or cite the Federalist Papers on factionalism, or approve what Du Bois wrote about the color line. Their attention goes to the here and now.

These associations do not fulfill the conditions that produce thoughtful intellectuals. Intellectuals must address the pressing matters, but they must also stand apart, living and breathing a corpus of texts, ideas, and events that are independent of current affairs. They skip from the day's headlines to the most recondite writings, connecting public happenings to Great Books as, for instance, Francis Fukuyama in *The End of History* interpreted the fall of the Soviet Union through Hegel's dialectic of desire. Intellectuals occupy a middle ground between philosophical thought and popular discourse, between knowledge professionals and interested laypersons. They are positive mediators, reining in propensities on both sides. On one hand, by hauling academic inquiry into public forums, they keep knowledge from evolving into excess specialization and technical expertise, from withdrawing into the university and think tank as a useful technology or policy instrument. On the other hand, by remaining faithful to academic rigor and intellectual forebears, they keep knowledge from decaying into vulgar and cynical uses in the public sphere. They correct the esoteric professor as much as the imprudent politician. In a prosperous open society, the institutions of learning lean toward insulation and professionalism, while popular discourse drops to the least common denominator of mass culture. Intellectuals draw both back from the extremes, synthesizing them into the best democratic communication, an intelligent analysis of ideas and facts accessible to vast audiences.

A healthy society needs a pipeline of intellectuals, and not just the famous ones. An abiding atmosphere of reflection and forensic should touch many more than the gifted and politically disposed students. Democracy thrives on a knowledgeable citizenry, not just an elite team of thinkers and theorists, and the broader knowledge extends among the populace the more intellectuals it will train. Democracy needs a kind of minor-league system in youth circles to create both major-league sages 20 years later and a critical mass of less accomplished but still learned individuals. Noteworthy intellectual groupings such as liberal anti-communists in the forties, Beats in the fifties, and neoconservatives in the seventies steered the United States in certain ideological directions. History will remember them. But in every decade labors an army of lesser intellectuals—teachers, journalists, curators, librarians, bookstore managers, diplomats, pundits, amateur historians and collectors, etc., whose work rises or falls on the liberal arts knowledge they bring to it. They don't electrify the world with breakthrough notions. They create neighborhood reading programs for kids, teach eighth-graders about abolition, run county historical societies, cover city council meetings, and host author events. Few of them achieve fame, but they sustain the base forensic that keeps intellectual activity alive across the institutions that train generations to come.

Apart from ideological differences and variations in prestige, greater and lesser intellectuals on the Right and the Left, speaking on C-SPAN or in rural classrooms, focusing on ancient wars or on the Depression, blogging on Romantic music or on postmodern novels . . . all may unite on one premise: knowledge of history, civics, art, and philosophy promotes personal welfare and national welfare. Intellectuals may quarrel over everything else, but at bottom they believe in the public and private value of liberal education. Columbia professor John Erskine called it "the moral obligation to be intelligent" 90 years ago, and every worker in the knowledge fields agrees. In the heat of intellectual battle, though, they rarely descend to that level of principle and concord. They usually concentrate on friends and enemies within the intellectual class, where that conviction goes without saying, and in formulating rejoinders for the marketplace of ideas, they forget that the marketplace itself must be sustained by something else against the forces of anti-intellectualism and anti-knowledge. Intellectuals can and should debate the best and worst books and ideas and personages, and they will scramble to affect policies in formation, but what upholds the entire activity resides beyond their circles. It grows on top of public sentiment, a widespread conviction that knowledge is as fundamental as individual freedoms. For intellectual discourse, high art, historical awareness, and liberal arts curricula to flourish, support must come from outside intellectual clusters. Laypersons, especially the young ones, must get the message: if you ignore the traditions that ground and ennoble our society, you are an incomplete person and a negligent citizen.

This knowledge principle forms part of the democratic faith, and it survives only as long as a fair portion of the American people embraces it, not just intellectuals and experts. The production of spirited citizens requires more than meditations by academics and strategies by activists, and it transpires not only in classrooms and among advocacy groups. Learning and disputation, books and ideas, must infiltrate leisure time, too, and they should spread well beyond the cerebral cliques. This is why leisure trends among the general population are so important. They log the status of the knowledge principle, and when they focus on under-30-year-olds, they not only reveal today's fashions among the kids but also tomorrow's prospects for civic well-being.

As of 2008, the intellectual future of the United States looks dim. Not the economic future, or the technological, medical, or media future, but the future of civic understanding and liberal education. The social pressures and leisure preferences of young Americans, for all their silliness and brevity, help set the heading of the American mind, and the direction is downward. The seventies joke about college students after late-sixties militance had waned still holds.

"What do you think of student ignorance and apathy?" the interviewer asks the sophomore.

"I dunno and I don' care"—

It isn't funny anymore. The Dumbest Generation cares little for history books, civic principles, foreign affairs, comparative religions, and serious media and art, and it knows less. Careening through their formative years, they don't catch the knowledge bug, and *tradition* might as well be a foreign word. Other things monopolize their attention—the allure of screens, peer absorption, career goals. They are latter-day Rip Van Winkles, sleeping through the movements of culture and events of history, preferring the company of peers to great books and powerful ideas and momentous happenings. From their ranks will emerge few minds knowledgeable and interested enough to study, explain, and dispute the place and meaning of our nation. Adolescence is always going to be more or less anti-intellectual, of course, and learning has ever struggled against immaturity, but the battle has never proven so uphill. Youth culture and youth society, fabulously autonomized by digital technology, swamp the intellectual pockets holding on against waves of pop culture and teen mores, and the Boomer mentors have lowered the bulwarks to surmountable heights. Among the Millennials, intellectual life can't compete with social life, and if social life has no intellectual content, traditions wither and die. Books can't hold their own with screen images, and without help, high art always loses to low amusements.

The ramifications for the United States are grave. We need a steady stream of rising men and women to replenish the institutions, to become strong military leaders and wise political leaders, dedicated journalists and demanding teachers, judges and muckrakers, scholars and critics and artists. We have the best schools to train them, but social and private environments have eroded. Some of the kids study hard for class, but what else do they learn when they're young? How do they spend the free hours of adolescence? They don't talk with their friends about books, and they don't read them when they're alone. Teachers try to impart knowledge, but students today remember only that which suits their careers or advantages their social lives. For the preparation of powerful officials, wise intellectuals, and responsible citizens, formal schooling and workplace training are not enough. Social life and leisure time play essential roles in the maturing process, and if the knowledge principle disappears, if books, artworks, historical facts, and civic debates—in a word, an intellectual forensic—vacate the scene, then the knowledge young people acquire later on never penetrates to their hearts. The forensic retreats into ever smaller cells, where nerds and bookworms nurture their loves cut off from the world.

Democracy doesn't prosper that way. If tradition survives only in the classroom, limping along in watered-down lessons, if knowledge doesn't animate the young when they're with each other and by themselves, it won't inform their thought and behavior when they're old. The latest social and leisure dispositions of the young are killing the culture, and when they turn 40 years old and realize what they failed to learn in their younger days, it will be too late.

The research compiled in the previous chapters piles gloomy fact on gloomy fact, and it's time to take it seriously. Fewer books are checked out of public libraries and more videos. More kids go to the mall and fewer to the museum. Lunchroom conversations never drift into ideology, but Web photos pass nonstop from handheld to handheld. If parents and teachers and reporters don't see it now, they're blind.

If they don't respond, they're unconscionable. It's time for over-30-year-olds of all kinds to speak out, not just social conservatives who fret over Internet pornography, or political Leftists who want to rouse the youth vote, or traditionalist educators who demand higher standards in the curriculum. Adults everywhere need to align against youth ignorance and apathy, and not fear the "old fogy" tag and recoil from the smirks of the young. The moral poles need to reverse, with the young no longer setting the pace for right conduct and cool thinking. Let's tell the truth. The Dumbest Generation will cease being dumb only when it regards adolescence as an inferior realm of petty strivings and adulthood as a realm of civic, historical, and cultural awareness that puts them in touch with the perennial ideas and struggles. The youth of America occupy a point in history like every other generation did and will, and their time will end. But the effects of their habits will outlast them, and if things do not change they will be remembered as the fortunate ones who were unworthy of the privileges they inherited. They may even be recalled as the generation that lost that great American heritage, forever.

BIBLIOGRAPHY

Achieve, Inc. *Rising to the Challenge: Are High School Graduates Prepared for College and Work?* (2005).

Ad Council. *Engaging the Next Generation: How Nonprofits Can Reach Young Adults* (2003).

Alliance for Excellent Education. *Paying Double: Inadequate High Schools and Community College Remediation* (2006).

American College Testing (ACT). National Data Release, "Average National ACT Score Unchanged in 2005; Students Graduate from High School Ready or Not" (17 Aug 2005).

———. *National Curriculum Survey* (2007).

———. *Rigor at Risk: Reaffirming Quality in the High School Curriculum* (2007).

American Council of Trustees and Alumni. *Losing America's Memory: Historical Illiteracy in the 21st Century* (2000).

American Political Science Association, Task Force on Civic Education in the 21st Century. "Expanded Articulation Statement: A Call for Reactions and Contributions," *PS: Political Science and Politics* 31 (Sep 1998): 636–37.

Andrukonis, David. "We're Not Illiterate, We're Just E-Literate," *USA Today*, Generation Next blog (22 Aug 2006).

AOL Red Page (www.teens.aol.com/).

Armour, Stephanie. "Generation Y: They've arrived at work with a new attitude," *USA Today* (6 Nov 2005).

Arnold, Matthew. Preface to *Poems* (1853).

Benavot, Aaron. *Instructional Time and Curricular Emphases: U.S. State Policies in Comparative Perspective* (Fordham Foundation, 2007).

Bennett, Sarah, and Nancy Kalish. *The Case Against Homework: How Homework Is Hurting Our Children and What We Can Do About It* (2006).

Bennett, Stephen Earl, and Linda L. M. Bennett. "Book Reading and Democratic Citizenship Revisited" (unpublished paper, 2006).

Bierman, Noah, and Breanne Gilpatrick. "Many still struggling to graduate," *Miami Herald* (22 Apr 2007).

Bomer, Randy. "President's Update: Rational Policy for Adolescent Literacy," *The Council Chronicle* (March 2005).

Book Industry Study Group. *Book Industry Trends 2006* (2006).

Bradbury, Ray. *Fahrenheit 451* (1953).

Brookings Institution, Brown Center. *Report on American Education,* "Part II: Do Students Have Too Much Homework?" (2003).

————. *How Well Are Students Learning?* (2006).

Brooks, David. "The Organization Kid," *Atlantic Monthly* (April 2001).

Bureau of Labor Statistics. *The American Time Use Survey* (www.bls.gov/tus/).

————. *Consumer Expenditure Survey* (www.bls.gov/cex/).

Bush, George W. Letter on American Competitiveness Initiative, 2 Feb 2006 (www.whitehouse.gov/stateoftheunion/2006/aci/).

Business Roundtable. *Tapping America's Potential: The Education for Innovation Initiative* (2005).

Carlson, Scott. "The Net Generation in the Classroom," *Chronicle of Higher Education* (7 Oct 2005).

Carnegie Corporation. *Reading Next: A Vision for Action and Research in Middle and High School Literacy* (2004).

Census Bureau, United States. *The Statistical Abstract of the United States* (www.census.gov/compendia/statab/).

Center for Information & Research on Civic Learning & Engagement. *The Civic and Political Health of the Nation: National Civic Engagement Survey* (www.civicyouth.org/research/products/youth_index.htm).

Centers for Disease Control. "Youth Risk Behavior Surveillance—United States, 2005," *Morbidity and Mortality Weekly Report* (9 June 2006).

Chronicle of Higher Education. "What Professors and Teachers Think: A Perception Gap over Students' Preparation" (10 Mar 2006).

———. "How the New Generation of Well-Wired Multitaskers Is Changing Campus Culture" (5 Jan 2007).

Clemson University. "Computer/Laptop Frequently Asked Questions" (www.ces.clemson.edu/stdts/ps/laptop/laptop_faq.html).

Clink, Henry C., and Harry Arthur Hopf. *People and Books: A Study of Reading and Book-Buying Habits* (1946).

College Board. *The Neglected 'R': The Need for a Writing Revolution* (2003).

———. *Writing: A Ticket to Work . . . Or a Ticket Out: A Survey of Business Leaders* (2004).

Conference Board et al. *Are They Really Ready to Work?* (2006).

Conkey, Christopher. "Libraries Beckon, But Stacks of Books Aren't Part of the Pitch," *Wall Street Journal* (26 Oct 2006).

Corporation for Public Broadcasting. *Connected to the Future: A Report on Children's Internet Use* (2002).

Cunningham, A. E., and Stanovich, K. E. "What reading does for the mind," *American Educator* (1998).

Deluzuriaga, Tania. "Fifth-graders Using Computers, Not Paper, for Classroom Work," *Miami Herald* (18 Nov 2006).

Department of Education, United States. *What Democracy Means to Ninth-Graders: U.S. Results from the International IEA Civic Education Study* (2001).

————. *NAEP 2004 Trends in Academic Progress: Three Decades of Performance in Reading and Mathematics* (2005).

————. *The Nation's Report Card: Mathematics 2005* (2005).

————. *The Nation's Report Card: Reading 2005* (2005).

————. *A Profile of the American High School Senior in 2004: A First Look* (2005).

————. *Digest of Education Statistics, 2005* (2006).

————. *The Nation's Report Card: Science 2005* (2006).

————. *The Nation's Report Card: Civics 2006* (2007).

————. *The Nation's Report Card: History 2006* (2007).

Dorman, Joseph. *Arguing the World* (film documentary, 1998).

Douglass, Frederick. *Narrative of the Life of Frederick Douglass* (1845).

Downes, Stephen. "Educational Blogging," *EDUCAUSE* Review 39 (Sep–Oct 2004).

Draut, Tamara, and Javier Silva. "Generation Broke: The Growth of Debt Among Young Americans" (2004 briefing paper) (www.demos-usa.org/pubs/Generation_Broke.pdf).

Du Bois, W. E. B. *The Souls of Black Folk* (1903).

Educational Testing Service (ETS). *2006 ICT Literacy Assessment.*

EDUCAUSE. *ECAR Study of Undergraduate Students and Information Technology* (2006).

Eisner, Jane. "Like, Vote?" *Philadelphia Inquirer* (19 Sept 2004).

Epstein, Joseph. "The Perpetual Adolescent," *The Weekly Standard* (15 Mar 2004).

Federation of American Scientists. *Summit on Educational Games: Harnessing the Power of Video Games for Learning* (2006).

Fanton, Jonathan. "Do Video Games Help Kids Learn?" Panel remarks at Newberry Library (8 Feb 2007).

———. "With Prodigious Leaps, Children Move to the Technological Forefront," *Philadelphia Inquirer* (26 June 2007).

Finn, Chester E. "Our Schools and Our Future" (1991) (www.american experiment.org/publications/1991/19911108finn.php).

Flynn, James R. "Massive IQ Gains in 14 Nations: What IQ Tests Really Measure," *Psychological Bulletin* (March 1987).

Forrester Research. *Get Ready: The Millennials Are Coming* (2005).

Foundation for Individual Rights in Education. *University and College Students Survey Results* (2003).

Fuchs, Thomas, and Ludger Woessman. "Computers and Student Learning: Bivariate and Multivariate Evidence on the Availability and Use of Computers at Home and at School," CESifo Working Paper #1321 (2004).

Gardner, Howard. "The Study of the Humanities," *Daedalus* (Summer 2002): 22–25.

Gates, Bill. "How to Keep America Competitive," *Washington Post* (25 Feb 07).

Gee, James. *What Video Games Have to Teach Us About Learning and Literacy* (2003).

"Generation Y: Today's teens—the biggest bulge since the boomers—may force marketers to toss their old tricks," *BusinessWeek* (15 Feb 1999).

Gewertz, Catherine. "Young people typically plug in to new technology far more often on their own time than in school," *Education Week* (29 Mar 2007).

Gitlin, Todd. *The Sixties: Years of Hope, Days of Rage* (1987).

———. *Media Unlimited: How the Torrent of Images and Sounds Overwhelms Our Lives* (2002).

Gladwell, Malcolm. "Brain Candy," *The New Yorker* (16 May 2005).

Glassman, James. "Good News! The Kids Are Alright!" *Techcentralstation. com* (16 July 2004).

Goolsbee, Austan, and Jonathan Guryan. "World Wide Wonder? Measuring the (Non-)Impact of Internet Subsidies to Public Schools," *Education Next* (Winter, 2006): 61–65.

Grafton, Anthony. "Big Book on Campus," *New York Review of Books* (23 Sept 2004).

Gravois, John. "Colleges Fail to Teach American History and 'Civic Literacy,' Report Says," *Chronicle of Higher Education* (6 Oct 2006).

Grossman, Lev. "Grow Up? Not So Fast," *Time* (16 Jan 2005).

———. "*Time*'s Person of the Year: You," *Time* (13 Dec 2006).

Hall, Jacquelyn Dowd. "Don't Know Much about History," *OAH Newsletter* (Feb 2004).

Hargittai, Esther. "What Do College Students Do Online?" 14 June 2006 (www.esztersblog.com/2006/06/14/what-do-college-students-do-online/).

Harris Interactive. "Generation Y Earns $211 Billion and Spends $172 Billion Annually" (press release, 3 Sept 2003).

———. "Video Game Addiction: Is It Real?" (2 Apr 2007).

Harvard University, Institute of Politics. *The 11th Biannual Youth Survey on Politics and Public Service* (2006).

Heath, Shirley Brice, and Laura Smyth. *ArtShow: Youth and Community Development* (resource guidebook and accompanying documentary video, 1999).

Horatio Alger Association. *The State of Our Nation's Youth* (www.horatio alger.com/pubmat/surpro.cfm).

Horowitz, David. *Radical Son: A Generational Odyssey* (1998).

Hu, Winnie. "Seeing No Progress, Some Schools Drop Laptops," *New York Times* (4 May 2007).

Hymowitz, Kay. "It's Morning After in America," *City Journal* (Spring 2004).

Indiana University Center for Postsecondary Research. *National Survey of Student Engagement* (www.nsse.iub.edu/index.cfm).

Indiana University School of Education. *High School Survey of Student Engagement* (www.ceep.indiana.edu/hssse/).

Institute for Social Research, University of Michigan. *Changing Times of American Youth, 1981–2003* (2004).

Intercollegiate Studies Institute, National Civic Literacy Board. *The Coming Crisis in Citizenship: Higher Education's Failure to Teach America's History and Institutions* (2006).

Irving, Washington. *The Sketch Book of Geoffrey Crayon* (1819).

Jenkins, Henry, et al. "Confronting the Challenges of Participatory Culture: Media Education for the 21st Century" (white paper, 2006).

Johnson, Jeffrey G., Patricia Cohen, Stephanie Kasen, and Judith S. Brook. "Extensive Television Viewing and the Development of Attention and Learning Difficulties During Adolescence," *Archives of Pediatric & Adolescent Medicine* 161 (May 2007): 480–86.

Johnson, Kirk. "Do Computers in the Classroom Boost Academic Achievement?" (www.heritage.org/Research/Education/CDA00-08cfm)

Johnson, Steven. *Everything Bad Is Good for You: How Today's Popular Culture Is Making Us Smarter* (2005).

———. "Pop Quiz: Why Are IQ Test Scores Rising Around the Globe?" *Wired* magazine (May 2005).

Joy, William. Remarks at Aspen Institute Festival of Ideas panel "Technology and Community: Is the Definition of Society Changing?" (2006).

Kaiser Family Foundation. *Zero-to-Six: Electronic Media in the Lives of Infants, Toddlers, and Preschoolers* (2003).

———. *Generation M: Media in the Lives of 8–18-Year-Olds* (2005).

———. *The Media Family: Electronic Media and the Lives of Infants, Toddlers, Preschoolers, and their Parents* (2006).

Katz, Jon. "Birth of a Digital Nation," *Wired* (Apr 1997).

Kessler, Andy. "Network Solutions," *Wall Street Journal* (24 Mar 2007).

John S. and James L. Knight Foundation. *The Future of the First Amendment* (2004).

Kohn, Alfie. *What Does It Mean to Be Well-Educated? And Other Essays on Standards, Grading, and Other Follies* (2004).

———. *The Homework Myth: Why Our Kids Get Too Much of a Bad Thing* (2006).

Kralovec, Etta, and John Buell. *The End of Homework: How Homework Disrupts Families, Overburdens Children, and Limits Learning* (2000).

Kristol, Irving. "Memoirs of a Trotskyist," in *Neoconservatism: The Autobiography of An Idea* (1995).

Leu, Donald. "Our Children's Future: Changing the Focus of Literacy and Literacy Instruction," *The Reading Teacher* (Feb 2000).

MacArthur Foundation. Launch for Digital Media and Learning project (www.digitallearning.macfound.org/site/c.enJLKQNlFiG/b.2269135/k.8822/About_the_Launch.htm).

MacFarquhar, Larissa. "Who Cares If Johnny Can't Read?" *Slate* (17 Apr 1997).

McCluskey, Neal. "Ambition and Ability Don't Meet," *School Reform News* (1 Dec 2005).

McGrath, Charles. "Stranger Than Fiction: What Johnny Won't Read," *New York Times* (11 Jul 2004).

Mangu-Ward, Katherine. "Wikipedia and Beyond: Jimmy Wales' sprawling vision," *Reason* magazine (Jun 2007).

Medill School of Journalism, Northwestern University. "Y Vote 2000: Politics of a New Generation" (2000).

Mill, John Stuart. *On Liberty* (1859).

———. *Autobiography of John Stuart Mill* (1873).

Mindich, David. *Tuned Out: Why Americans Under 40 Don't Follow the News* (2005).

Morin, Richard. "What Every Student Should Know," *Washington Post* (17 Apr 2000).

National Associations of Elementary and of Secondary School Principals. "We Can't Leave Our Students Behind in the Digital Revolution" (13 Dec 2006) (www.naesp.org/ContentLoad.do?contentId=2114).

National Association of Manufacturers. *The Skills Gap 2001 Survey* (2001).

———. *2005 Skills Gap Report: A Survey of the American Manufacturing Workforce* (2005).

National Center for Education Evaluation and Regional Assistance. *Effectiveness of Reading and Mathematics Software Products: Findings from the First Student Cohort* (2007).

National Center for Education Statistics. *National Assessment of Adult Literacy* (www.nces.ed.gov/NAAL/index.asp?file=AboutNAAL/WhatIs NAAL.asp&PageId=2).

———. *Public Libraries in the United States: Fiscal Year 2001* (2003).

National Conference of State Legislatures. *Citizenship: A Challenge for All Generations* (2003).

National Constitution Center. "Press Release: New Survey Shows Wide Gap Between Teens' Knowledge of Constitution and Knowledge of Pop Culture" (2 Sep 1998).

National Endowment for the Arts. *Reading at Risk: A Survey of Literary Reading in America* (2004).

———. *2002 Survey of Public Participation in the Arts* (2004).

National Geographic Society. "Survey of Geographic Literacy" (www .nationalgeographic.com/roper2006/).

National Governors Association. "Rate Your Future" Survey (2005).

National School Boards Association, "Creating and Connecting: Research and Guidelines on Online Social—and Educational—Networking" (July 2007).

Neisser, Ulric. "Rising Scores on Intelligence Tests," *American Scientist* (Sep–Oct 1997).

Nellie Mae. *Undergraduate Students and Credit Cards: An Analysis of Usage Rates and Trends* (2002).

NetDay, Project Tomorrow. *Our Voices, Our Future: Student and Teacher Views on Science, Technology & Education* (2006).

Nielsen, Jakob (www.useit.com/alertbox/). "Be Succinct: How to Write for the Web" (1997).

————. "How Users Read on the Web" (1997).

————. "Eyetracking Study of Web Readers" (2000).

————. "Avoid PDF for On-Screen Reading" (2001).

————. "End of Web Design" (2001).

————. "First Rule of Usability? Don't Listen to Users" (2001).

————. "Kids' Corner: Website Usability for Children" (2002).

————. "Top Ten Guidelines for Homepage Usability" (2002).

————. "PDF: Unfit for Human Consumption" (2003).

————. "Usability 101" (2003).

————. "The Need for Web Design Standards" (2004).

————. "Accessibility Is Not Enough" (2005).

————. "Low Literacy Users" (2005).

————. "Teenagers on the Web" (2005).

————. "Top Ten Web Design Mistakes of 2005" (2005).

————. "Email Newsletters: Surviving Inbox Congestion" (2006).

————. "F-Shaped Pattern for Reading Web Content" (2006).

————. "Use Old Words When Writing for Findability" (2006).

Nielsen//NetRatings. "Social Networking Sites Grow 47 Percent, Year over Year, Reaching 45 Percent of Web Users" (11 May 2006).

————. "YouTube U.S. Web Traffic Grows 75 Percent Week to Week" (21 Jul 2006).

————. "User-Generated Content Drives Half of U.S. Top 10 Fastest Growing Web Brands" (10 Aug 2006).

————. "U.S. Teens Graduate from Choosing IM Buddy Icons to Creating Elaborate Social Networking Profiles" (11 Oct 2006).

Noel-Levitz, Inc. *National Freshman Attitudes Report* (2007).

Nussbaum, Emily. "My So-Called Blog," *New York Times Magazine* (11 Jan 2004).

Online News Association. Conference Panel of Teens, 2006 (www.journalist .org/2006conference/archives/000630.php).

Oppenheimer, Todd. *The Flickering Mind: The False Promise of Technology in the Classroom* (2003).

O'Reilly, Tim. "What Is Web 2.0?" (www.oreillynet.com, 30 Sep 2005).

Organization for Economic Co-operation and Development. *Programme for International Student Assessment* (www.pisa.oecd.org/pages/0,2987,en_3225 2351_32235731_1_1_1_1_1,00.html).

Pease, Donald. *Visionary Compacts: American Renaissance Writings in Cultural Context* (1987).

Pew Research Center. *Teenage Life Online* (2001).

———. "Data Memo, Re: College Students and the Web" (Sep 2002).

———. *Online Papers Modestly Boost Newspaper Readership* (2006).

———. *How Young People View Their Lives, Futures, and Politics: A Portrait of "Generation Next"* (2007).

———. *Public Knowledge of Current Affairs Little Changed by News and Information Revolutions, What Americans Know: 1989–2007* (2007).

———. *Social Networking and Teens: An Overview* (2007).

———. *Teens, Privacy & Online Social Networks* (2007).

Phelps, Christopher. "The New SDS," *The Nation* (2 Apr 2007).

Poirier, Richard. "The War Against the Young," *The Atlantic Monthly* (Oct 1968).

Poniewozik, James. "Joseph in the Technicolor Dream Factory," *Time* (17 August 2000).

Postman, Neil. *Amusing Ourselves to Death* (1985).

"Put That Book Down!" *Los Angeles Times* (14 May 2005).

Reich, Charles. *The Greening of America* (1970).

Richardson, Will. "Blog Revolution: Expanding classroom horizons with Web logs" (www.techlearning.com/shared/printableArticle.php?articleID= 171203059).

———. *Blogs, Wikis, Podcasts, and Other Powerful Web Tools for Classrooms* (2006).

Ricketts, Camille. "Dialing into the Youth Market: Cellphone Services and Products Become Increasingly Tailored to Teenage Users," *Wall Street Journal* (3 Aug 2006).

Robbins, Alexandra. *The Overachievers: The Secret Lives of Driven Kids* (2006).

Roth, Philip. *The Human Stain* (2000).

Schultz, Katherine. "The Small World of Classroom Boredom," *Education Week* (21 Jun 2006).

Scotland Inspectorate for Education, Scotland. *Improving Scottish Education: ICT in Learning and Teaching* (2007).

Sharma, Amol. "What's New in Wireless?" *Wall Street Journal* (26 March 2007).

Somin, Ilya. "When Ignorance Isn't Bliss: How Political Ignorance Threatens Democracy," Cato Insitute Policy Analysis no. 525 (2004).

Strauss, Valerie. "Odds Stacked Against Pleasure Reading," *Washington Post* (24 May 2005).

Strauss, William, and Neil Howe. *Millennials Rising: The Next Great Generation* (2000).

Students for a Democratic Society. *Port Huron Statement* (1962).

Sutherland-Smith, Wendy. "Weaving the Literacy Web: Changes in Reading from Page to Screen," *The Reading Teacher* (Apr 2002).

Texas Center for Educational Research. *Evaluation of the Texas Technology Immersion Pilot: First-Year Results* (2006).

Thacker, Paul D. "Are College Students Techno Idiots?" *InsideHigherEd.com* (15 Nov 2006).

TIMSS National Research Center. *Third International Mathematics and Science Study* (www.ustimss.msu.edu/).

Trotter, Andrew. "Federal Study Finds No Edge for Students Using Technology-Based Reading and Math Products," *Education Week* (4 Apr 2007).

Turtel, Joel. "Let's Google and Yahoo Our Kids' Education," *NewsWithViews.com* (24 Jun 2006).

Twenge, Jean M., et al. *Egos Inflating over Time: A Test of Two Generational Theories of Narcissism Using Cross-Temporal Meta-Analysis* (2007).

Twist, Jo. "The Year of the Digital Citizen," BBC News (2 Jan 2006).

UCLA Higher Education Research Institute. *The American Freshman* (www
.gseis.ucla.edu/heri/cirpoverview.php).

————. *Your First College Year* (www.gseis.ucla.edu/heri/yfcy/).

"Writer, Read Thyself," *Atlantic Monthly* (October 2004).

Zaslow, Jeff. "Plugged In, but Tuned Out: Getting Kids to Connect to the
Non-Virtual World," *Wall Street Journal* (6 Oct 2005).

Zimmerman, Frederick J., et al. "Television and DVD/Video Viewing in
Children Younger Than 2 Years," *Archives of Pediatrics & Adolescent Medicine*
161 (May 2007): 473–79.

INDEX

ABOUT THE AUTHOR

Mark Bauerlein is a professor of English at Emory University and has worked as a Director of Research and Analysis at the National Endowment for the Arts, where he oversaw studies about culture and American life, including the much-discussed *Reading at Risk: A Survey of Literary Reading in America*. His writing has appeared in *The Wall Street Journal*, *The Washington Post*, the *San Francisco Chronicle*, *The Weekly Standard*, *Reason* magazine, *The Chronicle of Higher Education*, and many other publications, as well as in scholarly periodicals such as *Partisan Review*, *The Yale Review*, *Wilson Quarterly*, and *PMLA*.